THE PRE-FORECLOSURE REAL ESTATE HANDBOOK:

Insider Secrets to Locating and Purchasing Pre-Foreclosed Properties in Any Market

By Frankie Orlando

THE PRE-FORECLOSURE REAL ESTATE HANDBOOK: Insider Secrets to Locating and Purchasing Pre-Foreclosed Properties in Any Market

Copyright © 2006 by Atlantic Publishing Group, Inc.
1210 SW 23rd Place • Ocala, Florida 34474 • 800-814-1132 • 352-622-5836–Fax
Web site: www.atlantic-pub.com • E-mail: sales@atlantic-pub.com
SAN Number: 268-1250

ISBN-13: 978-0-910627-66-5   ISBN-10: 0-910627-66-5

Library of Congress Cataloging-in-Publication Data

Orlando, Frankie (Akemi Frances), 1966-
 The pre-foreclosure real estate handbook : insider secrets to locating and purchasing pre-foreclosed properties in any market / Frankie Orlando.
     p. cm.
 Includes bibliographical references and index.
 ISBN-13: 978-0-910627-66-5 (alk. paper)
 ISBN-10: 0-910627-66-5
 1. Real estate investment--United States. 2. Foreclosure--United States.
 I. Title.

 HD255.O75 2006
 332.63'24--dc22
                    2006013812

ART DIRECTION, FRONT COVER & INTERIOR DESIGN: Lisa Peterson, Michael Meister • info@6sense.net
EDITOR: Jackie Ness • jackie_ness@charter.net
EDITOR: Rising Ambitions Media Group • risingambitions@yahoo.com
GLOSSARY COMPILED BY: Christina Mohammed

Printed in the United States

Contents

CHAPTER 6: HOW TO CONTACT HOMEOWNERS OF PRE-FORECLOSURE REAL ESTATE PROPERTIES 113

CHAPTER 7: EVALUATING PRE-FORECLOSURE PROPERTIES FOR VALUE 149

CHAPTER 8: DO THE MATH   185

CHAPTER 9: SWIMMING THROUGH PRE-FORECLOSURE NEGOTIATIONS   197

CHAPTER 10: COMING UP WITH THE MONEY 211

CHAPTER 11: "SUBJECT TO" DEAL 223

CHAPTER 12: SHORT PAYOFF SALE 233

CHAPTER 13: SELLING REAL ESTATE WITH LESS TIME AND EFFORT   243

CHAPTER 14: WHAT DO YOU NEED TO GET STARTED?   255

Chapter 15: How to Build Wealth Through Real Estate Pre-Foreclosures 263

Bibliography 269

Glossary 279

Index 341

Author Biography 346

FOREWORD

When I left the University of Miami with my MBA in Finance and MS in Information Systems, I knew I was going to use those degrees to create my own business. Like many college students, I did not know how those degrees would factor into a business I had not even started.

After a class at Miami in real estate law, though, I knew I wanted to be in the real estate business. Coming out of college in South Florida, I realized that jumping right into a booming real estate market was economically out of the question. Even before graduation, I began visiting real estate chat rooms on the Internet and speaking online to property investors, lenders, etc. It was the logical place for a person with an Information Systems degree to start and it turned out to be the springboard for me to create my business.

Through my research, I found that investors around the country were craving more timely and accurate information on pre-foreclosure properties. These people wanted to be part of a hot market, like the one in Wayne County, Michigan, near Detroit. There are literally thousands of foreclosures each month in Wayne County, which means there are thousands of opportunities to turn a profit while helping a homeowner out of a very stressful situation. With the proper education and accurate, timely, and organized information, the real estate riches were just a step away.

Problem was, these investors realized they were wasting countless hours of their day looking through court records to find the foreclosure information when they could use that time to approach the homeowners. After all, how can one person be expected to sift through thousands of foreclosures in the Detroit metro area? Or they were using low-cost "national" firms that sold outdated information to hundreds of thousands of people. The light bulb went off in my head! The booming, yet unusually slow, foreclosure business actually needed somebody like me— somebody who knew how to get information to people quickly and in a very organized fashion.

I then turned on the switch to my computer and created Default Research, Inc. I realized that, luckily for me, in about 2002, the Internet became a very important tool for providing foreclosure data. At first, the market was littered with companies that figured out that they could take outdated information from title companies (usually for free) and sell it to an investor for $50 per month. Seems unfair, right? These businesses sold "leads" to investors that were stagnant. Frankly, the "leads" were not stagnant, but dead. Many of the homeowners had already been contacted at least 100 times before the investor, who paid $50 for this "lead," had even been able to contact the homeowner in distress.

Frustration began to set in for these investors and many people resorted to going to the courthouse on their own and gathering the information. Now, depending on the size of your business or your courthouse, this may actually be feasible to do. But it is not efficient in any case! People were spending at least six hours a day in the courthouse. Then, once they had collected their own foreclosure documents, most of them still did not even have the property address. What these researchers/hopeful investors had was a legal description and then that had to be compared with the property assessor's site to simply find out the address of the home.

Now that that day is shot, finally, the investor has an address of a homeowner in distress. By this time, they still have to get to the property before other investors to lend their services. This does not leave much time for marketing—I sincerely believe one of the key to pre-foreclosure investing is marketing. Because you will be the first to approach a homeowner in distress with your quality, on-time leads, you might actually be the first to tell them their house is being foreclosed on. Therefore, the homeowner has to trust you and that can be established through marketing. Show these homeowners what benefit you have to offer them and why they should work with you. You never want them to think you are just another "vulture" trying to snatch their home away from them in their time of despair.

As the first to approach the homeowner, you can tell them that their time of despair will include hundreds of pieces of mail concerning their house, phone calls, and people knocking on their doors. The investors that can be trusted are the ones that make the deals that help the homeowners and also provide some return to the investor. Why waste your time and money following leads that have already made deals or cured their defaults.

This is where Default Research comes into play. Default Research offers the nations most up-to-date pre-foreclosure leads — my company's efficiency turns into profit for the client. With Default Research's leads, you have the opportunity to be the first to approach homeowners, because our leads arrive two to three weeks ahead of the competition. Default Research gathers the information directly from the courthouse, and you can be assured the information provided by my company is quality, fresh leads.

So fresh that we had one client in Wayne County take a whole Saturday helping people in distress. A very profitable Saturday I might also add. This client took three leads from Default Research and completed shorts sales on all of those leads. If you don't know what a short sale is, you can look in this comprehensive book — basically, it is a negotiation between the lender and the investor to avoid or mitigate foreclosure of the property. In the end, the property owner gets to walk away from the loan, avoid foreclosure, and the investor also gets to turn a small profit. In fact, he was able to make between four and five thousand dollars on each sale. Not a bad day's work. Plus, he was able to help three people move forward and to have bright futures despite their past property problems.

Remember, though, it's not just about being the first person to approach the homeowner or marketing your company. As with any project or endeavor, education is an integral part of any business. Pre-foreclosure investing is no different. With the vast amount of knowledge available in this book, it will provide you with the tools to success. With a thorough understanding about the foreclosure process, financing, and making contact with homeowners in distress, you will be able to succeed in pre-foreclosure investing.

To close, what I have been able to do is make the job for any investor or person looking to get into the pre-foreclosure business easier. What I wanted to do was take the information provided by foreclosure research companies and deliver leads in a timely and organized fashion. Whether you use Default Research or one of our competitors, be the first to approach a homeowner and be trustworthy. Then, you will be able to help people and be successful yourself. Good luck!

Serdar Bankaci started his real estate research company, Default Research, Inc., two years ago in Greensburg, PA. The growing company provides the most timely pre-foreclosure information to its clients offered anywhere in the country. Bankaci is also having an effect locally in his hometown. Since its creation almost two years ago, Bankaci has expanded from covering one state to seven, and more than doubled the amount of counties from eight to 30.

Education:
BSBA American University 2002 — Major in Finance
MBA University of Miami, FL 2004 — Major in Finance
MS Information Systems, University of Miami, FL 2004

Company contact information

Default Research, Inc.

P.O. Box 663

Mt. Pleasant, PA 15666

www.defaultresearch.com

support@defaultresearch.com

(888) 211-8396 – voice

(412) 291-1971 – fax

1

INTRODUCTION

Welcome to the world of pre-foreclosure investing. You may have heard successful investors and others talk about the wealth-building opportunities that they found by investing in foreclosures. Well, you, too, can build your wealth by investing in properties that are facing foreclosure, and here is your chance to learn everything you need to know to be successful in this field.

WHY REAL ESTATE INVESTING?

Real estate property is one of those things that are in limited supply. The planet is not growing new land, and we do not have any colonies on Mars yet. As the earth becomes more crowded and people's quality of life continues to improve, the one thing that we will always need — real estate — is in limited supply.

According to an article (**www.realtor.org/rmomag.NSF/pages /bizincomeexpensesurveyaug01**) published on *Realtor® Online Magazine*, Realtors (real estate agents who are members of the National Association of Realtors) earned an average annual income of $69,910 in 2001. If we interpolate that data to say that based on their 6 percent fee minus expenses (20 percent), they may have sold as much as $1,456,458 in real estate that year. How did we arrive at $1,456,458? We took $69,910 and divided by .80 (80 percent) to calculate their income before costs; $69,910 is 80 percent of $87,387.50. $87,387.50 is 6 percent (the average Realtor's commission on sales) of $1,456,458 in real estate property. If a real estate investor sold as much property at a 15 percent profit rate, they could net themselves $218,468.70 annually in income! At $180,000 a house, one would only need to invest in eight houses a year to generate that income.

What This Book Will Cover

The purpose of this book is to serve as a well-rounded introduction to the world of pre-foreclosure investing, and it is aimed toward the absolute beginner who has never before dabbled in real estate. We cover everything a new investor needs to know to begin his or her own personal journey toward building wealth in this market.

We provide background information on foreclosures and talk about how to find properties facing foreclosure, how to market services, and how to contact homeowners facing foreclosures. We will discuss how to evaluate properties for purchase, how to come up with an offer price that makes sense, how to swim through negotiations with all interested parties, and how to come up with the money.

We talk in detail about two hotly debated topics in pre-foreclosures: the "subject to" deal and the short payoff sale. We conclude this book with advice on how to sell the property once you buy it, what you need to get started, and how to look at the big picture of what you are doing.

TRENDS IN FORECLOSURES

If everybody else is getting on the bandwagon, you may worry if there are going to be enough pre-foreclosure properties for you to invest in. The Mortgage Bankers Association of America (**http://mbaa.org/**) releases a National Delinquency Survey every quarter that reports how many homeowners are delinquent in their mortgage loan payments and how many will actually go to foreclosure. The most recent survey (**http://mbaa.org/news/2005 /pr1214.html**) — which was based on data collected for the 2005 third quarter and released December 14, 2005 — reported that 4.44 percent of all mortgage loans were delinquent and that the percentage of houses in the foreclosure process was .097 percent. If we look at the number of mortgage loans written in 2005, we can interpolate these percentages into the numbers. Plunkett Research (**www.plunkettresearch.com/Industries /BankingMortgagesCredit/BankingMortgagesCreditStatistics /tabid/233/Default.aspx**) reported that $10.5 trillion of outstanding mortgages existed in 2005. They also reported that the median house price was $208,400. Using that information, we can deduce that, on average, there could be 503,838,772 current mortgages existing in 2005. During the 2005 third quarter, perhaps as many as 22,370,441 mortgages were delinquent and up to 4,887,236 properties actually went into foreclosure. That's a lot of real estate property to occupy your time and energy!

WHY ARE SO MANY HOUSES IN FORECLOSURE?

With all the hype about investing in homes that are facing foreclosure, you might wonder why so many houses continue to go into foreclosure these days. The reason is that circumstances have caused problems with homeowners' finances. They were once able to make their mortgage loan payments, but now they cannot. The following reasons often lead to foreclosure:

- The homeowners may be facing legal problems that are tying up their finances or savings.

- The houses may have physical problems that the current homeowners cannot or do not want to remedy (that is, it would cost them more to fix the house than what the house is worth, or maybe they do not have that kind of money).

- The homeowners may be facing tax problems that are overburdening their finances.

- The homeowners were renting the property out at too low a rate to cover their mortgages and expenses.

- The homeowners had too much debt to begin with before they purchased the house.

- The homeowners or somebody close to them has health problems, which either prevents them from making enough money to pay their mortgage or requires them to spend their money on medical treatments.

- The economy — a downturn in economic conditions can have a trickle-down effect on everybody's finances.

- The homeowners have lost their jobs.

- The homeowners overextended themselves with other expensive purchases (boats, cars, private school tuition, vacations, etc.).

- Predatory lending practices may have provided the

homeowners with an opportunity to buy "more house" than they really could afford. In other words, their debt load may have been too heavy for most banks to ethically agree to the mortgage.

- The homeowners may have had stiff mortgage payments due to falling prey to sub-prime mortgage rates.

- The house may have been purchased with a government-backed loan program that has less stringent qualification standards than normal mortgage applications.

- The homeowners may have been forced to move due to job relocation and have been unsuccessful with attempts to sell the house.

- The homeowners may be going through a divorce and cannot agree on how to handle the property.

- With "no money down" deals, high loan-to-value ratios are becoming commonplace. At the first sign of financial problems, many people do not have any reason to stay in the house.

With all of these possibilities, it is easy to see how common it is for houses to go into foreclosure. The trick for you will be to find these properties before they actually become foreclosures. If you understand why a house is being foreclosed, you will gain a better chance of developing an effective rapport with the homeowner—you can better speak the homeowner's language. Understanding what can go wrong helps you from over-generalizing homeowners as you try to build a relationship with them.

Why Invest in Foreclosure Properties?

Properties in foreclosure offer the following benefits to real estate investors:

- Motivated sellers

- Motivated lenders

- Lower purchase prices

- Lower down payments

Is Pre-Foreclosure Real Estate Investing for You?

For somebody just starting out, pre-foreclosure real estate investing could mean lots of opportunity and moneymaking potential. At the same time, it requires that investors be on their toes and careful in their decision making. It also takes a lot of time — real estate investments are illiquid, meaning that you cannot get your money back quickly. The fastest turnaround time that an investor could probably get the money out would be in a matter of weeks and more likely a couple of months.

Besides having to devote a considerable amount of time, you also will encounter a lot of unhappy people. Therefore, you must come across as reasonably sympathetic while still walking the line between what you want and what the homeowners want. With all the interaction you must have with the owners and lenders, you must be a people person with good communication and negotiation skills.

Having said that, investing in pre-foreclosures is known to require a lot of "sweat equity" in finding properties, working the deals, getting the properties ready for market, and selling them. By understanding the foreclosure process — and by taking advantage of a situation that you did not create and one in which the homeowner cannot remedy — you can build a wealthy future for yourself by investing in real estate.

2

Understanding Foreclosures

In order to effectively act on information about a house facing foreclosure, you must understand exactly what foreclosure means. This chapter discusses the general process for buying houses today, what a foreclosure really is, how state statutes make a difference, and how government agencies like Freddie Mac, Fannie Mae, HUD, the FHA, the Department of Veterans Affairs (DVA), and the SBA all fit in.

Buying Houses Today

When most people buy a home, they do not have enough money to buy the property outright the way they would buy a new outfit or dinner. Most people obtain a loan from a lender and then use the borrowed money to buy their home.

Most people talk about "getting their mortgage" from the lender. The mortgage is not the loan money that the homeowner gets from the lender—a person gets a loan from the bank to buy the house, and the mortgage is the agreement between that person and the lender. This agreement states that if the homeowner does not pay the lender back within a set time period and in a timely fashion, the bank gets the property that was paid for with the loan money.

The property that is purchased with the lent money is the equity that the homeowner uses to secure the loan. If the homeowner does not make the mortgage payments, the lender has the right to take the home and sell it to get its loan money back. This is the part of the mortgage agreement that should interest you, because it is, in effect, the foreclosure component of the mortgage. The bank establishes a first lien on the property with the mortgage or deed of trust. A lien means the homeowner has pledged the equity of the property to secure the loan. This is a voluntary lien to which the homeowner agreed.

Liens are covered in the section Common Types of Liens in Chapter 7: Evaluating Pre-Foreclosure Properties for Value. The mortgage is essentially a lien placed upon the property itself should the homeowner default on the loan payments.

In the United States, we have two common types of agreements between homeowners and lenders to set up property liens for the purposes of borrowing enough money to buy a house: the mortgage and the deed of trust. Which agreement type that is used to secure a home loan depends on state laws — state use is about 50-50 (half of the states use mortgages and half use deeds of trust). State laws dictate just about everything to do with a foreclosure; no federal laws regulate foreclosure (except for some affecting HUD foreclosures).

When a state follows "title theory," a mortgage is used to convey property ownership to the homeowner. When a state follows "lien theory," a "deed of trust" is used to convey property ownership to the homeowner after the loan has been paid in full.

With the mortgage, the property is the homeowner's until he or she defaults on the payments. With the deed of trust, a third party holds the deed to the property; the "homeowner" does not receive ownership until he or she has paid off the mortgage. We emphasize this distinction because whether the loan was secured by a mortgage agreement or a deed of trust agreement can have a big impact on how the property can be foreclosed.

With a loan and mortgage relationship, there is the borrower, the homeowner who needs the money to buy the house, and a lender — usually a bank — who provides the money as a loan that is secured by the property. Other terms for the homeowner in this case may be "borrower" or "mortgagee." (We will usually refer to this person as the homeowner.) The lender is also known as the "mortgagor," and it is usually a public institute like a bank, but it can also be an individual who likes to back real estate mortgages. (Progressing along in the book, we will usually refer to this entity as the bank since, in most cases, you will be dealing with banks during the foreclosure process.)

With a deed of trust, the agreement is no longer just between the homeowner and the lender. Now we have a third party, a trustee, who holds the title to the property until the homeowner fulfills his or her loan obligation. Trustees are usually neutral parties (not associated with the homeowner or the lender) and are typically lawyers or title insurance companies.

So with house buying, we are looking at two agreements: the loan agreement and the lien (set up either through a mortgage or a deed of trust). Both documents should interest you as a potential investor.

Usually when one buys a house, the person has to put some money down as part of the purchase — typically between 10 and

20 percent. There are also "no money down" deals, which are quite popular. With the mortgage home loan, besides the loan amount, a couple other numbers are important: the interest rate and the mortgage lengths. Back in the early 1980s, interest rates were commonly in the double digits, ranging between 12 and 15 percent. Current interest rates for mortgages are much lower — around 6 percent for most mortgages.

Typical mortgage loan lengths depend on the type of mortgage agreement but usually range between 15 and 30 years (with 30 years being much more common). Many new mortgage loan agreements are based on shorter time periods. Although these mortgage loan agreements are not really intended for the homeowner to pay off the loan in these short time periods, they are still very popular. Traditional mortgage loan agreements involve a basic agreement whereby the lender lends the money to the homeowner and sets up a monthly payment schedule for the homeowner to pay back the original loan plus compounded interest. Most mortgage loans can then involve payments of two to three times over the original loan amount after accounting for all the interest.

A **conventional mortgage loan program** is the same as a fixed-rate plan. With the fixed-rate plan, the mortgage payments' interest rate is the same throughout the life of the mortgage. Fifteen and 30 years are the most common lengths for this type of mortgage plan. The conventional mortgage loan program is attractive to home buyers who plan to stay in their house for a long period. While this loan program may not give an outstandingly low interest rate, people like it because it also locks in the interest rate for the life of the mortgage. Homeowners can always refinance down the road if interest rates drop a couple of points (or enough to make paying closing costs worth it when everything is said and done). Conservative homeowners prefer this mortgage type. Unless you are dealing with a couple facing divorce, you probably will not see as many traditional mortgages with the properties you find facing foreclosures. Homeowners facing foreclosure usually go for the less conservative and more speculative mortgage loan programs.

Another popular loan program is the **adjustable rate mortgage program (ARM)**. With the ARM, the mortgage is still over a 15- or 30-year period, but the interest rate is determined over a specified time period (either every year; every three years; or every five, seven, or ten years). The interest rate will usually follow a pre-selected index, and it may go up, down, or both, depending on the state of the economy. The ARM usually includes a low introductory interest rate for a period, after which the interest rate is then updated based on the index rate. People who might go for this type of loan may include home buyers who do not plan to be in the house much longer than the introductory period or people who feel interest rates will drop further but do not want the hassle or costs of a refinance.

A new ARM variation is the **hybrid ARM,** which works like a fixed-rate mortgage for a set time period and then flips over to an ARM for the second part of the mortgage. Hybrid ARMs are also called delayed adjustment ARMs. A common breakdown for a hybrid ARM is 7/1, meaning that for the first seven years, the mortgage payments use a fixed interest rate. After the seven-year period, the interest rate is then adjusted once a year, every year following.

Other types of mortgage loan agreements between homeowners and lenders include:

- **Jumbo programs** are 15- or 30-year programs for larger mortgage amounts than what Fannie Mae and Freddie Mac will cover ($417,000 in 2005 for a single-family home). These loans will usually have higher interest rates than those in a conventional mortgage program.

- **Balloon programs** (also called partial amortization programs). In a balloon program, the name is based on the length of the first part of the loan. Typical balloon programs are 5/25 or 7/23 programs (the first number being the period the homeowner pays the lower interest rate and the second period being the time the loan is converted to a traditional mortgage loan). With a balloon program, for the first part of the loan, homeowners pay a lower mortgage payment than what they would have to pay for a 30-year program. They are not paying the fully amortized interest that typically comes with a 30-year program. Their principal amounts are set up as if they were part of a 30-year plan. After the introductory period is over, homeowners are responsible for coming up with the balance of the loan. In most cases, the homeowners simply refinance. Balloon programs are popular with homeowners who do not plan to be in their house for longer than the introductory period. Balloon programs are also popular with people who had bad credit when they bought their house. They were able to qualify for the balloon program at a not-so-good rate with the idea that they would use the time during the introductory period to rebuild their credit so they could refinance at a better rate when the mortgage came due at the second part of the program.

- **Interest-only programs** can be set up with either a

fixed interest rate or an adjustable interest rate. With an interest-only program, the homeowner only pays back the interest on the loan for the first part of the loan (typically 10 years in a 30-year fixed-rate loan). After the first ten years, the homeowner will begin to make larger payments to begin tackling the actual loan principal.

The majority of mortgages written today stem from mortgage documents that were drawn up and approved by the Federal Housing Administration (**www.hud.gov/offices/hsg/fhahistory .cfm**). In any mortgage agreement, there is language that specifies that the homeowner will pay the debt, keep the house insured, and will not demolish it without notifying the lender. Upon default of the loan payments, the entire principal becomes due. The lender consents to a receiver in case of a foreclosure (the receiver would either be an agent of the court or a trustee).

The mortgage or deed of trust is not a promissory or IOU. It is the security instrument that lenders use to make sure the borrower will pay back the amount that the bank lent them (the home buyer signs this agreement in a promissory note).

If the bank did not have the legal right to request the entire principal as due, it could end up in court continuously suing deadbeat borrowers for overdue mortgage payments. If it looks like the borrower is not capable of paying back the entire amount, the bank has the right to accelerate the time when the total amount becomes due. The bank then gets to foreclose on the property within a set time period rather than having to go to court to get its belated payments from the homeowner.

What Is a Foreclosure?

How many of you remember some old black-and-white movie that shows a poor farm owner losing everything on his property because the bank was foreclosing it? Real estate legal proceedings have since evolved so that now foreclosures fairly well protect homeowners from unscrupulous lenders and lenders from deadbeat homeowners. At one time, many state laws stipulated that borrowers who were in default of their loans had to forfeit all rights to their properties. Now most states give the borrower an "equity of redemption," a time period in which the homeowner has an opportunity to resolve impeding foreclosure, either by paying off the debt or even selling the property before it forecloses. So when we talk about a house being in foreclosure, we are really talking about the "equity of redemption" period when the lender must legally provide time for the homeowner to make things right with the bank. So what current foreclosures really do is close the "equity of redemption" period so the mortgage backer can sell the house and get its equity back. A few states have strict foreclosures (for example, Connecticut and Vermont), but most states do not allow banks to outright take possession of the property when homeowners are late with their payments.

Legally speaking, a foreclosure is the legal proceeding by which the party who loaned money that was secured by a deed of trust or mortgage can now force the sale of the property. After a property is foreclosed, the lender can have the house auctioned to redeem its equity in the property.

Legal proceedings revolve around two documents: the loan agreement and the deed of trust or mortgage. The bank uses these documents to stake its claim on the equity of the house should the homeowner not make good on his or her promise to pay back the money borrowed to purchase the property.

When the homeowner starts missing loan payments, most banks will begin to notice. Stories exist about HUD homes being six months in default of payment before any legal action is taken. Usually by the third missed loan payment, the bank will initiate the foreclosure process. The homeowner should have received several notices of delinquent payments from the bank before actually receiving a formal notice of foreclosure.

After the bank has decided that it will not get its money from the homeowner, the bank chooses to act on the part of the mortgage agreement that states its right to accelerate the amount due. So instead of having to wait monthly to sue the homeowner for late payments the way a landlord would with tenants, the bank can ask that the total amount be due by a certain date allowable by law. If the homeowner cannot come up with the money, the bank will foreclose on the property and auction it.

Generally, what happens at the beginning of the foreclosure process is the bank makes public notices of its intent to sell the property. The bank may also work with the homeowner in an attempt to remedy the situation so that the homeowner keeps the house and the bank receives its money. This is the period we refer to as the pre-foreclosure period — the homeowner is in default of the mortgage, official notice has been made, and now the bank must wait a specific time period (state dependent) before it can auction off the property.

After the house is successfully foreclosed (in the bank's eyes and legally, it is ready for auction), the property will go up for auction. If the house is sold during the auction, the bank will hopefully get back most of the money it loaned the homeowner as part of the mortgage. If the house is not sold at auction, it becomes a lender-owner property (REO) — usually owned by HUD, DVA, Fannie Mae, and Freddie Mac. A big question that often comes up is, "Why sell?" In other words, why should the lender sell the house at all? Why don't the banks keep the houses as investments? Banks and other lending institutions are not in the business of owning real estate. They do not want to manage properties. They want to deal with money. This is why properties are auctioned after the foreclosure period.

We talked earlier about how there is no federal standard for the lien document. Most states will use either a mortgage or a deed of trust for the banks to set up a lien on a property in order to approve a loan. How a property will be foreclosed depends mostly on whether the property was secured by a mortgage or by a deed of trust.

Judicial Versus Non-Judicial Foreclosures

What the foreclosure process is like will depend on whether the property is in a state with judicial or non-judicial foreclosures. Foreclosures are highly individualized at the state level. While judicial foreclosures are generally similar in different states, the details in terms of timelines can vary greatly based on state statutes.

Remember how we emphasized the difference in the security vehicles that banks could use to secure the homeowner's promissory note? Depending on state law, lenders could use either a mortgage or a deed of trust. If a state dictates the use of a mortgage, then any foreclosure will probably follow a judicial process. If a state dictates the use of a deed of trust, then any foreclosure will probably follow a non-judicial process.

Regardless of which process is used, whether judicial or non-judicial, either one does not reduce the chances that a house will be foreclosed. However, the type of process used does make a difference to you as an investor — you must understand the process in order to use your time wisely.

Foreclosure law is set and upheld at the state level, so it can be unique in each state. Usually there is a correlation between the type of security instrument used to secure the home loan (mortgage versus deed of trust) and the type of foreclosure. When states use mortgages as a lien against the property or when lenders want to put the property in foreclosure, they will need to go through the court system. For this reason, they will follow a judicial foreclosure system. In this case, if the homeowner defaults on the payments, the lender must go to court to justify its claim on the property. The property sale will be under court sanction; hence the name "Sheriff's Sale."

When states use deeds of trust, the lender is usually seen as the true owner of the property, at least until the loan is paid off (since the homeowner does not hold the deed to the property). Most deeds of trust will have a "power of sale" clause whereby the homeowner gives preemptive approval to the lender to sell the property in case of a default on the loan payment. So, if the homeowner fails to keep up the payments, the lender has the right to foreclose the property without having to go to court to establish its right to do so. This is a non-judicial foreclosure, so the lender can sell the property without court sanction. This is also called the "Trustee's Sale".

What does all this mean to the real estate investor? Non-judicial foreclosures are typically a lot quicker than judicial foreclosures from beginning to end because they do not involve the court system. If your state uses the non-judicial process, you will need to be on your toes to stay ahead of the lender's schedule.

One positive aspect about states using the non-judicial foreclosure process is that they typically do not stipulate a redemption period for homeowners. This works for investors, in general, because they do not have to worry about a homeowner coming back within the redemption period and buying the house back at the price it was auctioned for. The redemption period only applies if the house is foreclosed. So if you buy the property before the foreclosure, the redemption period will not apply. The redemption period is not a good deal for investors because while they might get their money back in this case, they will not be compensated for the time and energy they invested in purchasing the house or for any improvements or repairs made to the property.

Judicial Foreclosure Process

In a judicial process, the lender must file a lawsuit against the borrower in order to effect a foreclosure. This process will take longer than a non-judicial process since the courts monitor the process closely. No matter if the process were judicial or non-judicial, the steps still result in the auctioning of the property.

The following steps occur during a judicial foreclosure process:

- The borrower is in default of the mortgage payments, usually 90 days behind.

- The lender files a Complaint of Foreclosure or Motion to Foreclose with a local court. The fancy legal term for this is *Lis Pendens*, and it is a "notice of pending action" telling the courts that the lender will file a lawsuit for the right to foreclose the property.

- The lender petitions the court to enter a Summary Judgment of Foreclosure.

- The court sends a Notice of Hearing to interested parties.

- The court holds the Foreclosure Hearing. Any interested party can attend; the defendant can prepare an answer to the lender's complaint to try to persuade the judge not to allow the foreclosure.

- The court provides a Final Judgment or the Summary Judgment.

- The court schedules a date and sends a Notice of Sale.

- The court hosts the property auction (Sheriff's Sale).

- The property is sold to the highest bidder at the auction.

- If nobody buys the property at auction, it becomes Real Estate Owned (REO) by the lender.

- If the mortgage agreement includes a redemption rights clause (almost all states mandate them when a judicial process is used) and the buyer chooses to exercise that right, the Sheriff will take hold of the deed or certificate until after the redemption period expires (could be a long time).

NON-JUDICIAL FORECLOSURE PROCESS

With a non-judicial foreclosure, a "power of sale" clause can be written into the deed of trust, in which case the borrower pre-authorizes the sale of the house to satisfy the promissory note should he or she default on the loan payments. Most home loans secured by a deed of trust will have the "power of sale" clause written into them. It is possible in some states for a mortgage to have a "power of sale" clause written into them as well (if the state supports it); in which case, any foreclosure would follow a judicial foreclosure process. If the mortgage or deed of trust has a "power of sale" clause stipulating exactly how the house is to be foreclosed, then the property trustee will follow that language. Otherwise, a non-judicial foreclosure follows the process dictated by state law.

Typically, the following steps occur in a non-judicial foreclosure:

- The borrower is in default of the mortgage payments, usually 90 days behind. The number of days of delinquency depends on state statutes.

- The lender files a Notice of Default (NOD) with the real estate property records as well as to anybody with an interest in the property (including the homeowners).

- The lender schedules the property sale and files a Notice of Sale.

- The trustee holds the auction and sells the property (the Public Auction or Trustee's Sale).

- The property is sold to the highest bidder.

- If the property is not sold at the auction, it becomes an REO to the lender.

- If the buyer exercises the redemption clause, the property will be held until the redemption period expires. Many states following a non-judicial process for foreclosure will not provide a redemption period, but each state is unique. Look up your state's exact laws regarding foreclosure and redemption. The redemption clause should greatly interest you as a real estate investor. We will look at this topic in detail shortly in the section titled How Can The Redemption Period Affect Investors?

OTHER FORECLOSURE PROCESSES

The majority of states have set up their foreclosure laws to follow either judicial or non-judicial processes. Since a couple of states specify other foreclosure processes, to be thorough, we will cover them here:

- **Strict foreclosure.** Strict foreclosure is what you think of when watching an old TV show and see a farmer losing his farm to the bank. With a strict foreclosure, when (and if) the property is sold, any extra money (over any liens owned) does not go back to the homeowner. Instead, the lender gets to keep the property and sell on its own schedule when (and if) it wants to. If a property has any equity in it at all, the lender will stand to gain a lot when acquiring the property through a strict foreclosure. Strict foreclosure is used primarily in Connecticut and Vermont. Even though no auction is pending, a pre-foreclosure period still exists before the lender takes ownership of the property. Homeowners in Connecticut and Vermont would, in theory, be more willing to deal with you since they stand to lose all equity with a strict foreclosure.

- **Executory.** The executory process occurs in Louisiana as a type of judicial process. Judicial processes in Louisiana can be "ordinary" (what other states use) or follow an executory process, which is very similar to a "power of sale" clause, whereby homeowners basically waive their rights to an "ordinary" judicial process. With the executory process in Louisiana, the homeowner has three days to come up with the money they owe after receiving a Notice of Default by the bank. If they do not, then the property is considered foreclosed and given back to the lender. With houses foreclosed via the executory process, no real pre-foreclosure period exists for you to work your magic. However, you can still make money investing in real estate in Louisiana as long as the executory process is not used.

- **Entry and possession.** The "entry and possession" process occurs in New England states such as Maine, Massachusetts, New Hampshire, and Rhode Island. Foreclosure by "entry and possession" is similar to strict foreclosure without an auction. After the specified time has past since the homeowner's last payment, the lender simply comes in and takes possession of the property (peacefully with witnesses).

Because there are different types of foreclosures in the United States, as a real estate investor, you need to learn more about foreclosure processes in your state and what the foreclosure process will be specifically for each investment property that interests you.

What Does Your State Do?

Each state has its own legal definition for foreclosure. To find your own state's legal definition, go online to obtain this information or to find out where you can request information directly. Make sure you access your state government's primary source regarding foreclosure statutes as opposed to a commercial Web site that may not have the most updated information. Many commercial sites are woefully incorrect; confirm any information you find with a primary source.

Some states such as Alabama, North Dakota, Michigan, Maryland, and Washington use more than one process (although, more than likely, it will be easy to determine which one is usually used to foreclose a house). The following table (current as of January 2006) summarizes the types of liens used (mortgage or deed of trust), the foreclosure process used, the general timeline for a property to get foreclosed in that state, and whether or not that state has a redemption period.

Table 1: States and Their Foreclosure Processes

STATE	MOST COMMON FORM OF SECURITY	PROCESS	TIMELINE IN MONTHS	REDEMPTION PERIOD?
Alabama	Mortgage	Non-Judicial* Judicial - rare	2-3	365 Days
Alaska	Deed of Trust	Non-Judicial* Judicial	4	365 Days for Judicial Foreclosures Only
Arizona	Deed of Trust	Non-Judicial* Judicial	3-4	None
Arkansas	Mortgage	Judicial* Non-Judicial	3	365 Days for Judicial Foreclosures Only
California	Deed of Trust	Non-Judicial* Judicial - rare	4	365 Days for Judicial Foreclosures Only
Colorado	Deed of Trust* Mortgage	Non-Judicial* Judicial	3-6	75 Days
Connecticut	Mortgage	Judicial Strict Foreclosure or Foreclosure by Sale	3-6	Court Decides
Delaware	Mortgage	Judicial	6-7	60 Days
District of Columbia	Deed of Trust	Non-Judicial	2-4	None
Florida	Mortgage	Judicial	5-7	None

STATE	MOST COMMON FORM OF SECURITY	PROCESS	TIMELINE IN MONTHS	REDEMPTION PERIOD?
Georgia	Deed of Trust* Mortgage	Non-Judicial* Judicial	1-3	None
Hawaii	Mortgage	Judicial* Non-Judicial	7	None
Idaho	Deed of Trust* Mortgage	Non-Judicial	5-9	365 Days
Illinois	Deed of Trust* Mortgage	Judicial	10	90 Days
Indiana	Mortgage	Judicial	9	None
Iowa	Mortgage* Deed of Trust	Judicial* Non-Judicial	6-7	20 Days
Kansas	Mortgage	Judicial	4	365 Days
Kentucky	Mortgage* Deed of Trust	Judicial	5-7	365 Days
Louisiana	Mortgage	Judicial Period (Executive Process and Ordinary)	6-8	None
Maine	Mortgage	Judicial Entry & Possession	8-10	90 Days
Maryland	Deed of Trust* Mortgage	Judicial	2-5	Court Decides
Massachusetts	Mortgage	Non-Judicial* Judicial	3-5	None
Michigan	Mortgage	Non-Judicial* Judicial	2-3	30-365 Days
Minnesota	Mortgage	Non-Judicial* Judicial	3-4	180-365 Days
Mississippi	Deed of Trust	Non-Judicial* Judicial	3-4	None
Missouri	Deed of Trust	Non-Judicial* Judicial	2-3	365 Days
Montana	Deed of Trust* Mortgage	Non-Judicial* Judicial	5-6	None
Nebraska	Mortgage* Deed of Trust	Judicial* Non-Judicial	5	None

STATE	MOST COMMON FORM OF SECURITY	PROCESS	TIMELINE IN MONTHS	REDEMPTION PERIOD?
Nevada	Deed of Trust	Non-Judicial* Judicial	4	None
New Hampshire	Mortgage	Non-Judicial* Judicial - rare	2-3	None
New Jersey	Mortgage	Judicial	10	10 Days
New Mexico	Mortgage	Judicial	5-6	30-270 Days
New York	Mortgage	Judicial* Non-Judicial	10-15	None
North Carolina	Deed of Trust	Non-Judicial* Judicial	4	None
North Dakota	Mortgage	Judicial	4-5	180-365 Days
Ohio	Mortgage	Judicial	7-8	None
Oklahoma	Mortgage* Deed of Trust	Judicial* Non-Judicial	6-7	None
Oregon	Deed of Trust* Mortgage	Non-Judicial* Judicial	5	180 Days
Pennsylvania	Mortgage	Judicial	9	None
Rhode Island	Mortgage	Non-Judicial* Judicial	3	None
South Carolina	Mortgage	Judicial	5-6	None
South Dakota	Mortgage	Judicial* Non-Judicial	5	30-365 Days
Tennessee	Deed of Trust* Mortgage	Non-Judicial* Judicial	2-3	730 Days
Texas	Deed of Trust* Mortgage	Non-Judicial* Judicial	3	None
Utah	Deed of Trust* Mortgage	Non-Judicial* Judicial	5	Court Decides
Vermont	Mortgage	Judicial* Strict Foreclosure Non-Judicial	4-10	180-365 Days (pre 1968 mortgages get 365 days and post 196 8 mortgages get 180 days)

STATE	MOST COMMON FORM OF SECURITY	PROCESS	TIMELINE IN MONTHS	REDEMPTION PERIOD?
Virginia	Deed of Trust	Non-Judicial* Judicial	2-4	None for Non-Judicial process; when judicial process occurs, has 240 Days
Washington	Deed of Trust* Mortgage	Non-Judicial* Judicial	5	None
West Virginia	Deed of Trust* Mortgage	Non-Judicial* Judicial	2-4	None
Wisconsin	Mortgage	Judicial* Non-Judicial	10	365 Days
Wyoming	Mortgage* Deed of Trust	Non-Judicial* Judicial	3	90-365 Days

* This form happens more often than other forms.

For the state you want to do business in, go directly to that state's statutes to understand exactly how the foreclosure process currently works there. This site, ForeclosureLink. com (**http://foreclosurelink.com/statelink_page.htm**) offers an interesting summary of state timelines for foreclosure, but you should verify how things work by contacting your local government. Do not take somebody else's word for how things work for each state, especially online, where information can be wrong and/or outdated.

If you want to learn more about foreclosure processes at the state level, check out the United States Foreclosure Network (USFN) (**www.usfn.org**). The site offers the *Foreclosure Desk Guide* that you can order for $38.

Ultimately, except for a few states, many of the states use both judicial and non-judicial processes, so research property by property, and watch the timeline for each property that interests you.

[44]

WHEN DO FORECLOSURE PROCEEDINGS START?

The mortgage loan payment is technically late on the fifteenth of any month for most lenders and mortgage loans. Between Day 45 and Day 60, the bank will "officially" alert the homeowner of the delinquency and will usually mention that foreclosure proceedings will be forthcoming. This is called a "Letter of Intent to Foreclose." Most mortgages and deeds of trust are written so that after the homeowner misses three loan payments, the bank can go ahead and initiate the foreclosure process. This is so the bank has some way to remedy receiving late payments or not receiving any payments at all. Otherwise, the bank would be forced to go to court to sue the homeowner in an attempt to get its money.

Usually by Day 90, the bank will begin legal proceedings to begin a foreclosure by filing a Complaint of Foreclosure with the local courthouse and by filing a *Lis Pendens* or Notice of Default (NOD). These documents are the public warning notice to anybody interested that the lender has begun the process to foreclose the property. This is when the clock starts ticking for the interested pre-foreclosure real estate investor — you!

On average, you will have a minimum of 90 days (plus publication time of another 20 or so days) to work your deal with the homeowner before a property is foreclosed. This is just an average. You can look at the average timeline for your state in Table 1: States and Their Foreclosure Process). This average is based on the number of days required for the *Lis Pendens* or the Notice of Default (NOD) to be posted before the property can be auctioned plus the number of days that are required to advertise the auction. If a state usually uses the judicial process, then the timeline will take longer than a non-judicial process as the foreclosure works its way through the court system. You can find out specifically what the time period is for your state by looking at the statutes.

How Can the Redemption Period Affect Investors?

As a real estate investor, you should know the redemption period for foreclosures in your state. Nowadays, most states do not allow strict foreclosures, so a homeowner is not going to come home from work one day and find his or her house foreclosed without prior notice. Current foreclosure law gives the homeowner sufficient time to try to rectify the situation to keep a house from actually going into foreclosure.

However, after a house has gone to foreclosure, the owner may still get the chance to "redeem" his or her property. Most states using mortgages and judicial foreclosures will have statutes giving the homeowner a chance to get the property back even after foreclosure and auction.

As long as you buy the property from the homeowner before the house is foreclosed, the redemption clause will not apply. So, in essence, the redemption clause would never affect you if you make all of your purchases in the pre-foreclosure period. However, should you find yourself tempted to buy a property at auction or after as an REO, make sure you know what the redemption period is in that state. Otherwise, you may find yourself in an unpleasant situation in which you have successfully purchased a property with the intent to resell for a profit only to find the homeowner knocking on your door. Homeowners can and will take back the house from you, leaving you in the hole for your time and energy plus any money you may have spent on the property. We will go into detail about the advantages of buying a property during the pre-foreclosure period as opposed to buying at auction, but we can tell you now that the redemption period is one of those reasons.

How Do Government Agencies Like Freddie Mac, Fannie Mae, HUD, the FHA, DVA, and SBA Fit In?

From a pre-foreclosure point of view, it doesn't matter too much who insured the mortgage in the first place because you will not be dealing with the insurers. As mentioned before, if the property does not sell at the auction, the property then becomes an REO to the lender/bank that managed the mortgage. However, if the mortgage was insured by a government agency, that insuring group will usually step in and buy the property.

Usually, when a person wants to buy a house, the lender requires a down payment (usually 15 to 20 percent of the total price of the house). Certain government agencies have programs through which they will insure the mortgage, thereby letting the prospective homeowner move into the house with no down payment (the Department of Veteran Affairs, for example) or as little as 3 percent down (the FHA, for example).

If you are interested in buying an REO property, you can check any one of these agencies' Web sites for listings of current REO properties:

- Freddie Mac (**www.freddiemac.com**)

- Fannie Mae (**www.fanniemae.com**)

- HUD (**www.hud.gov/offices/hsg/hsgabout.cfm**)

- FHA (**www.hud.gov/offices/hsg/hsgabout.cfm**)

- DVA (**www.va.gov**)

- SBA (**www.sba.gov**)

The scope of this book is not on property at auction or once it becomes an REO. We want to focus on the advantages to the real estate investor of picking up properties during the pre-foreclosure period, before they go to auction or become REOs. To put these benefits in perspective, we will explain the limitations of waiting to buy property at auction or as REOs.

As a real estate investor interested in pre-foreclosure properties, your ears should perk up if you learn that a property of interest has an FHA or VA loan. FHA and VA loans have a much better chance of being assumable without triggering any action on the bank's part than any other type of loan. Since 1986, the new home buyer still needs to qualify to assume an FHA-backed loan. According to FHA.com (**www.fha.com/prequalify.cfm**), new home buyers will probably qualify for an FHA loan if:

- They have at least two years of steady income.

- Their income has been increasing over the past two years.

- They do not have any more than two "30 days late" statements in their credit report over the past two years.

- They have not had any bankruptcies in the past two years and their credit has been solid since.

- They have not had any foreclosures in the past three years and their credit has been good since.

- The mortgage payment is no more than 30 percent of their gross income.

The investor who is purchasing property as an REO will want to become very knowledgeable about these government agencies. If you stick with investing in properties in their pre-foreclosure period, an important reason why you would care if a government agency such as FHA were backing the loan would be to determine if you could legally assume the loan.

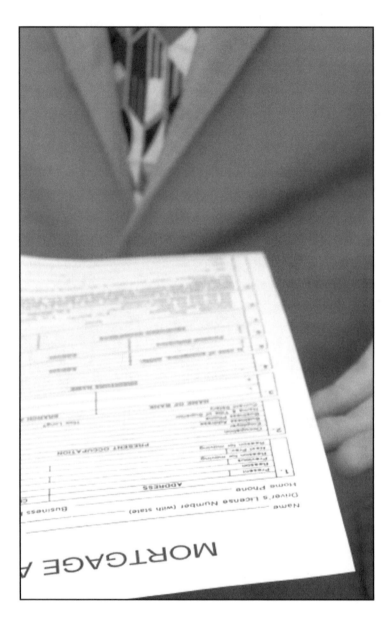

3

How Pre-Foreclosures Fit in the Picture

You may have heard of people buying houses at the foreclosure auction or, if the house was not successfully auctioned, from a government agency after the house has foreclosed. To successfully invest in pre-foreclosures, you must understand where in the foreclosure process you want to get involved.

Understanding the Foreclosure Process

Houses can actually be bought at any of the following foreclosure stages: pre-foreclosure, at auction, and after a house has been foreclosed and (if it was not successfully sold at auction) goes back to the lender. As previously mentioned, this book focuses on the pre-foreclosure period.

Defining Pre-Foreclosure

A house is in pre-foreclosure after the lender has made a public notice of its intent to foreclose the house but before the house is actually auctioned. Investors will normally have about three months to work a deal with the homeowner, from the time the homeowner receives the first foreclosure notice to when the property actually gets auctioned.

Problems with Buying at Auction

As you know, after the exemption period has expired and the homeowner has not paid the bank and stopped the foreclosure, the bank then auctions the property to recover the equity in its loan. Seems like all you ever hear about is buying properties at auctions once they become foreclosed. You may be wondering, what is wrong with waiting to buy the house at the auction?

Auctions are, well, auctions. Ever see how crazy people get at auctions? You know about the hypnotic pull of eBay, right? Imagine what bidding is like at a foreclosure auction.

Besides the generally frenzied mood at foreclosure auctions, the following occurrences could present problems for an investor:

- There is a possibility that you will be bidding against a team that has already decided how to price the properties.

- Even if other bidders are not working together, you are definitely up against more competition at an auction than you would be working one-on-one with the homeowner during the pre-foreclosure period.

- You cannot inspect the property before the auction.

- You must demonstrate the ability to bid in cash. (Most states require that bidders have a minimum amount of cash on hand for a deposit, usually at least 5 percent of the purchase price. Virginia, for example, requires a 10 percent deposit unless the deed of trust contains other language. Some sales may require up to 20 percent.)

- You may not have enough time to properly research the title before placing your bid.

- The property title may not be insurable.

- The property may not be insurable as is. This may not affect you if you plan to keep the property. However, if you plan to sell the property, chances are that most home buyers will need a mortgage loan to buy the property. You cannot get a mortgage without the property being insurable. This does not mean you should not touch such a property at auction, but it does mean you would be gambling with what you will have to do with the property in order to be able to sell it down the road.

- All sales are final.

- Properties are bought as is.

- Auction sales are not negotiable by law.

- Auction sales may have legal problems (that is, technical errors the homeowners can use to have the auction results postponed by court order until the foreclosure has been resolved legally).

- Some federal organizations such as the IRS can still redeem their liens on the property, even after a foreclosure.

- If the homeowners still reside in the property, you must deal with their eviction.

- If the property's mortgage has a redemption clause, you could lose the property to the original homeowner. (We have talked about the redemption clause before, but this is where you really want to watch it.) The redemption clause, when written into a mortgage document, gives the homeowner the right to get the property back if he or she pays what is owed to the lender within a specified period of time — after the house was foreclosed and auctioned! If you made repairs to the property after buying it at auction, watch out! Should the homeowner redeem the property, you will not be compensated for your repair costs.

At any rate, the lender will not make a profit if the property is purchased at the auction. Any money that is in excess of the original mortgage — plus fees and any legally upheld second liens — goes back to the homeowner. Foreclosure sales are different from strict foreclosures, in which case the house immediately becomes the lender's property instead of going to sale. In strict foreclosures, the lender can stand to make a profit from taking the property from the homeowner because it gets to keep any equity that may have been built up since the homeowner first bought the property.

Buying a property at auction can make sense if you did your research and wanted to buy the house but you were unable to work your magic with the homeowner before the house went to auction. Just make sure you do your math before you get crazy and commit yourself to a property not worth the sale price at an auction (Check out Chapter 8: Do the Math).

PROBLEMS WITH BUYING AFTER A HOUSE HAS FORECLOSED

While buying a foreclosed house might make great sense to somebody who is looking to move into it (since the person will likely get the house at fair market value), it does not make sense to buy a foreclosed house as an investment. Since the lender will sell the house at fair market value, it doesn't make sense for an investor to pay that much because it reduces the potential for profit when the investor turns around and sells the house.

The lender or bank does not want to own the property, which is now designated as Real Estate Owned (REO). However, the lender will not let the property go for a steal, which is why it will try to sell the property as close to fair market value as possible.

Besides not being a great financial deal, buying a property after foreclosure could also present the following problems:

- You have to have verifiable funds to buy the property.

- Because the house is vacant at this point, most of the utilities will be turned off, making it impossible for you to have the plumbing, heat, water, etc., inspected properly.

- If the lender accepted a "deed in lieu of foreclosure" from the homeowner, any secondary liens may still apply.

- You will need to handle eviction if the homeowners do not vacate the property on their own.

- If a redemption period is in effect, the homeowner may redeem the property.

WHY FOCUS ON PRE-FORECLOSURES?

As an investor, buying houses during the pre-foreclosure period works in your favor. Sellers are motivated. You can often invest with little money, especially compared to buying at an auction where you are required to put cash down for a deposit. You have more time to inspect the house, less competition from other buyers, and no need to worry about the homeowner's ability to redeem the property.

With pre-foreclosures, you focus on motivated sellers. They can include people going through divorce or job relocation. In today's real estate market, many people buy houses without any money down. So when they run into financial problems, they do not feel compelled to fight as hard to keep their house because they have built up equity. They just want to sell the house and be done with it.

When working deals with homeowners in the pre-foreclosure period, you often have more leeway with your investing power. Buying at auction requires more cash up front, and buying a property after it has become an REO is just like buying a regular house with the stringent credit checks and debt load assessment. But when you buy a house during the pre-foreclosure period, you have the freedom to try to work out a purchase deal that makes sense for you and the homeowner. You might even be able to swing something with the homeowner that lets you take the property without your having to formally get a new mortgage loan on your own.

Working pre-foreclosure deals puts the ball back in your court as opposed to bidding on a property during the auction. You have more time for due diligence in inspecting the property. You can also go home and work your math to find out what purchase price works for you. The utilities are still on, so you have the opportunity to do a real walk-through inspection, which is rarely possible if the property has become an REO and is abandoned.

When focusing on pre-foreclosures, you are beating out the competition from people waiting to buy at the foreclosure auction. It is no different than knowing a neighbor who has a time-share in the Bahamas and wants to sell it. By having an early rapport with your neighbor, you will get first dibs on the time-share and possibly a better price than what you would have to pay if you wait until after your neighbor advertises the time-share leaving you have to compete with other interested buyers. So instead of waiting for friends to tell you about their time-shares, you will discover leads through your earnest research and networking.

Buying properties in their pre-foreclosure period can save you time. You do not have to be dependent on somebody else's timetable to close your property deal. You can work as fast as you want to, not having to wait for dates to hit the way you would if you wanted to buy the property at auction.

As you know, when you buy a property during the pre-foreclosure stage, you will not have to worry about homeowners trying to redeem their properties during the redemption period, which can be anywhere from 10 days to two years (like in Tennessee). While most states' foreclosure statutes deal with how properties are handled as they go through the foreclosure process, a few states also have laws that protect homeowners from predatory foreclosure consultants who try to swindle property through fraud, deception, and unfair dealing. These state statutes usually mandate that home equity sales contracts must include a "notice of cancellation" or a "right of rescission," in which case homeowners can cancel their purchase agreements.

California is particularly reputable for its stance against foreclosure consultants who attempt to scam homeowners of their houses. In California, the homeowner has five business days to exercise the right of rescission; however, this may not be applicable if the property is a second home or an investment property.

Find out what your state laws dictate regarding mortgage foreclosure consulting and become familiar with those that protect homeowners from predatory practices. California, Missouri, and Minnesota currently have such laws in place. Maryland is trying to get similar laws passed.

How to Locate Pre-Foreclosure Properties

To successfully invest in pre-foreclosure properties, locating such properties is a core activity. Other important tasks include successfully evaluating properties and compelling homeowners to sell you their properties before they are foreclosed. You cannot, however, work your magic if you do not find the properties first.

You can find pre-foreclosure properties by viewing public foreclosure notices as well as other types of public notices, paying somebody else to find you property listings, networking, and doing your own marketing.

Public Records and Legal Notices

The great thing about working with foreclosures is that just about everything must be public knowledge. Even if your state uses non-judicial processing of foreclosures, the lender's actions must be made public knowledge. Becoming successful in pre-foreclosure investing does not require you to know special people to find out about special deals. Lenders are required to make public postings as well as file with the courts (in judicial foreclosures).

The first thing to look for is the *Lis Pendens* or the Notice of Default (NOD) as these two notices will give you the best head start to research and buy properties during the pre-foreclosure period. The second thing to look for is the auction notice. Hopefully, you will have come across the *Lis Pendens* or the NOD first. But if you somehow missed these notices, you still might have a chance if you find a property via the auction notice. Just realize that by the time the auction is announced to the public, you will not have that much time to work a deal with the homeowner — ten days to a month in most states.

It might make sense for you to hire a person or company to find these records for you and keep you posted on updates. Remember, however, that this third party is not doing anything that you could not do for yourself. If you are just starting out, it might make sense to save as much money as possible by doing most of the footwork yourself. However, if you have more money than time, certainly go ahead and use a service to find these listings for you. (We talk more about paying for property listings later in the section Paying for Property Listings.)

Lis Pendens/NOD

Find out how your state handles foreclosures and how public notices are released. Every state has its own process for this depending on whether the judicial or non-judicial process is used. The lender may have sent a few reminder or warning messages to the homeowner. However, filing the *Lis Pendens* or NOD is the first legal action the lender takes to foreclosure the property. With judicial processes, look for *Lis Pendens* notices. With non-judicial processes, look for Notices of Default.

Also be sure to find out whether or not your state requires public notices. If it does, all foreclosure notices will be documented with the County Recorder. You should also find out if your County Recorder offers access to an online database of public foreclosure notices. If it does, great, you are "in." If your county does not put the records online, you can still go in person to view them.

If your state does not require public notices, you will need to view local newspapers' legal sections. Call the local County Clerk to find the names of its approved "newspapers of record."

The *Lis Pendens* usually includes the following information:

- Lender

- Homeowner

- Other interested parties (this can give you a preview of other liens that may be on the property)

- Property information (this does not include financial information in terms of what the homeowner owes, just information identifying the real estate packet)

- Date posted

- Lender's lawyer

The best way to understand what you are looking for is to find a real *Lis Pendens* that is used in your local area; you can find one in a local newspaper of record. Make sure you understand every part of it. If there is something you do not understand, find out what it means.

NODs usually contain the following information:

- Homeowner

- Amount overdue

- Date posted

- Lender's lawyer

- Homeowner's lawyer

Auctions

As we said before, auction notices may not give you enough of a head start to do your homework before approaching the homeowner or lender about buying the property before foreclosure, but they may give you enough time to try a last-ditch effort to get the property before the auction.

Overall, checking the *Lis Pendens* and NOD is the best way to find out about a house facing foreclosure, as they are the first legal notices that the lender plans to foreclose on a property. However, you may still want to review auction notices just to make sure that no hot properties have slipped through your radar.

Other Sources for Pre-Foreclosure Properties

Consider tapping secondary sources for information on pre-foreclosure properties. You will find that many secondary sources will eventually cross-reference properties that you find in legal notices and public records. Depending on how comfortable you are with relying on your intuition, you may not want to wait for lenders to actually start the foreclosure process. You can jump the gate by working houses that are probably headed toward foreclosure but have not yet reached the pre-foreclosure period. Signs that a property may be heading toward foreclosure include divorce proceedings, bankruptcy proceedings, probate filings, and "for sale by owner" ads in the newspaper.

DIVORCE PROCEEDINGS

Divorce is one of the major reasons that houses become foreclosed. A property that was once affordable with a dual income or a shared interest in how the income was spent is no longer affordable during a separation or a divorce. Now, one of the spouses has to finance a second house or an apartment. Even if both spouses have enough money to finance separate living quarters, they may not agree on how their monies should be spent. As a consequence, the house they bought together often faces foreclosure because neither spouse can afford the property alone or cares to keep it (for whatever reason).

Depending on your comfort level, you may want to contact homeowners in the midst of divorce proceedings to see if they want to sell their house to you. While you will usually find motivated sellers, you must also be prepared to deal with people who are not at their best. They may be angry at each other and the world at large, or they may not be thinking with clear heads. Also be careful: if you start working with one of the spouses, make sure that's the one who has the legal right to sell the house. If it isn't, find out how likely the other spouse or any other parties of interest will be to sell you the property. Otherwise, you are just wasting your time working with somebody who cannot sell the house to you on his or her own.

Many investors find that houses in the midst of divorce proceedings are more trouble than they are worth because the investor must deal with all the drama and animosity as well. If you are the type of person who is not bothered by this, then by all means, try a couple and see where it takes you. If the idea of working with people going through messy divorces bothers you, keep in mind that many foreclosures are the result of impending divorce.

Bankruptcy Proceedings

Most real estate investors find dealing with people actively going through bankruptcy a real drain on their time. Bankruptcy usually forestalls foreclosure proceedings as the homeowner is trying desperately to keep the house. If you have another target property where the owners are not considering bankruptcy, spend most of your energy on that house because it will be easier and quicker to get.

In short, bankruptcy proceedings normally do not equal impending foreclosures; most people who are seeking to file bankruptcy are doing so as a last-ditch effort to protect their assets from liens on debts owed. Depending on the type of bankruptcy filed, there is a chance that the lender will force a foreclosure, in which case the homeowner may be interested in talking with you.

Homeowners can file for two types of bankruptcies: Chapter 7 or Chapter 13. The chapters refer to the specific types of bankruptcy regulations listed in Title 11 of the United States Code. To learn more about general U.S. bankruptcy law, check out this site hosted by Cornell Law School that lists current federal bankruptcy laws (**www4.law.cornell.edu/uscode/html/uscode11 /usc_sup_01_11.html**).

A Chapter 7 bankruptcy is also known as liquidation. With

Chapter 7, homeowners liquidate all of their assets to give to creditors, and, in turn, their debts are wiped clean. Interestingly enough, state law determines which of the homeowners' assets — if any — are protected. For example, Florida limits the amount of house equity the homeowner would lose in a Chapter 7 bankruptcy. Chapter 7 filings are usually more attractive to homeowners because they are enabled to clear their debts and have a better chance of keeping their homes.

With Chapter 13 bankruptcy filings, homeowners are not trying to get out of their debts but are actually trying to restructure the debts so they can pay them off without as much penalization. There may be no or very low interest rates on debts, and the homeowner usually has up to five years to pay them off. With Chapter 13 filings, homeowners will try to keep their homes as this type of bankruptcy also protects homeowners' equity in their homes.

When new bankruptcy laws came into effect on October 15, 2005, federal law made it harder for people to file for Chapter 7 bankruptcy. Therefore, people who don't qualify for Chapter 7 bankruptcy are forced to file Chapter 13. This is good news to you as the real estate investor. When homeowners file for Chapter 13 bankruptcy (which offers homeowners less protection from foreclosure than Chapter 7), lenders have more of a say in the matter. If the lender feels the homeowner will not make good on the debt restructuring in a Chapter 13 bankruptcy filing, the lender can ask for a "Relief from Stay" to get the bankruptcy dismissed. If the courts agree, then the foreclosure is back on schedule. If the foreclosure date has come and gone already, the courts or trustee will schedule a new auction date in a matter of weeks.

The homeowner can fight the "Relief from Stay" by filing for another bankruptcy. In this case, the lender can counteract by filing a "Relief from Stay with Prospective Relief," which asks the courts to go ahead with the Chapter 13 bankruptcy but to still let the lender auction the property. If the courts consent, the homeowner gets to go through with the bankruptcy to resolve other debts but will not get to keep the house.

The courts decide whether or not a person qualifies for a Chapter 7 bankruptcy by using a "means test" that determines whether the debts could be paid off—in which case the Chapter 7 is converted to a Chapter 13 bankruptcy—or if they should be dismissed entirely. If you are interested in bankruptcy proceedings, you should check out any number of bankruptcy Web sites, including the federal online database PACER (Public Access to Court Electronic Records) (**www.pacer.psc.uscourts .gov/index.html**). On the PACER site, you pay 80 cents per page retrieved. You can also use other Web sites that charge monthly membership fees for access to bankruptcy filings, including:

- BankruptcyAction.com (**www.bankruptcyaction.com**)

- BankruptcyData.com (**www.bankruptcydata.com**)

- American Bankruptcy Institute (**www.abiworld.org**)

You may decide that you don't want to actively pursue properties whose owners are going through bankruptcy. However, if you really like a particular property or think the owners may not be successful in their attempt to file for bankruptcy, you may want to keep tabs on their filings. Especially if the homeowners cannot qualify for a Chapter 7 and are left with no other choice but to file for a Chapter 13; remember that the lender has the legal right to have the property foreclosed no matter what happens with the homeowners' bankruptcy filing. So keep tabs on the property if you think there's a good opportunity for making a profit—if only you can convince the homeowners to sell the property to you.

To learn more about bankruptcy in general, here are some great Web sites:

- Nolo (**www.nolo.com/resource.cfm/catid /462a9501-9b21-4e09-a08c5a7b8af51a79/213/161**)

- Cornell's Wex site (**www.law.cornell.edu/wex /index.php/Bankruptcy**)

- American Bankruptcy Institute (**www.abiworld.org**)

The bottom line with bankruptcy filings and foreclosures is this: At the end of the day, a homeowner who is actively seeking bankruptcy will be a much harder "sell" for you than a homeowner who is facing foreclosure and for whom bankruptcy is not a viable or possible solution.

Probate Filings

With a probate filing, the house's homeowner has passed away and the house is in probate. This means that when a person dies, a probate court must verify that the homeowner's will is valid, inventory the estate, and make sure that all taxes and fees are paid in full and that the estate is distributed according to the will.

Possibly, the person who has inherited the house and its mortgage payments will not be able to afford them and, therefore, will be looking to sell the house. This is mostly a matter of timing. Even if a house has a good amount of built-up equity in it, the people who were willed the property may not be in the right position in their lives to take on the mortgage payment. In this case, they may be very motivated to sell the property before an inevitable foreclosure occurs.

Be careful how you deal with family members at this time as you do not want to come across as insensitive or as "ambulance chasers" — to borrow a term usually used for lawyers. A sensitive, reasonable approach would be to draft a short letter to the family with a clear message and your contact information. If they are interested, they will let you know. Do not pressure the family any more than this.

Newspaper Advertisements

We already talked about public notices in newspapers. Now, consider "owner" advertisements in newspapers. Homeowners may place ads to either rent their homes or to sell them (via "for sale by owner" ads, or FSBO, pronounced "fizz-bo"). Homeowners who try to sell their property on their own may be down on their luck and do not want to lose any money in Realtor's fees. Many times, these homeowners are more open to creative financing solutions — like selling their property to you. You can find FSBO listings in many small neighborhood newspapers.

Newspapers can also be a great source of other types of leads. Consider checking out the obituaries. However, do not contact a family directly after spotting an obituary. Similarly to a probate situation, you could simply send out a well-crafted letter expressing your desire to purchase the house should they plan to sell it.

Paying for Property Listings

In this section, we will talk about the different services you could use to help you dig up pre-foreclosure properties: public auction Web sites, public *Lis Pendens*/NODs Web sites, and hired "bird dogs." In this case, we will focus on the time-versus-money balance since you are not paying anybody to find information that you could not find yourself.

Using a Public Foreclosure Service

With a public foreclosure service, you are not paying somebody to dig up information that is not readily accessible to the public, like with a private investigation service. Some public foreclosure services want you to believe they are finding information you cannot get on your own. Do not believe the hype.

Of course, you are excited and want to jump in headfirst. But do not spend money to earn money when you have not yet earned any money. So instead of paying money to a public auction site before you have flipped your first property, flip your first property and then use the proceeds to help you become more efficient in your business. Everybody enjoys setting up a new business. The problem is that people often find themselves laying out all these "necessary" business costs only to find they are not that good at what they need to do in order to recover their investments.

Of course, if you would rather pay for listings, by all means, go ahead. But if you are literally just starting out, you may want to save your hard-earned cash until you can really afford to pay for services like this. This will also give you more time to research various sites to determine which ones you like the best.

One more caveat about using public auction and *Lis Pendens* sites: Before you go hog-wild and sign up for as many services as you can afford, remember that you will make more money closing deals on properties that offer the most return on your investment. Solidly working ten foreclosure properties is better than scanning hundreds that are too far away and a drain on your time. So instead of signing up for a statewide foreclosure list, you might be better off spending your time focusing on properties right in your own county. You do not want to fall victim to "analysis paralysis" where all you do is scan sites for interesting properties. You want to spend enough time finding properties that look good when you crunch the numbers but then spend the rest of your time actually working those properties.

Given that you are more likely to follow up on properties close to you, it makes sense to look into public auction and *Lis Pendens* sites servicing your state. Many of these sites offer a free trial period, after which you can sign up and pay either a monthly fee or an annual subscription. You may find some sites that are advertised online as "auction sites" but upon inspection find that they also offer *Lis Pendens* listings.

Find out how the information will be available to you. While using a site to browse listings is fine, you will also want a site that offers downloading options for the contact lists so you can use them for your direct mail campaign without having to type the information. Just make sure you can download the information in a format that works for you.

While it makes sense to focus on your geographical area, you may come across a nationwide site offering good coverage in your area as well as competitive prices on a national scale. Make sure you can search or filter through the listings so you do not waste time browsing through listings that are not relevant to your area.

The following public auction sites provide great nationwide coverage:

- ForeclosureNet.net (**www.foreclosurenet.net**)

- Foreclosure.com™ (**www.foreclosure.com**)

- Foreclosures.com (**www.foreclosures.com**)

- RealtyTrac® (**www.realtytrac.com**)

- Reozone (**www.reozone.com/index.php**)

Test a couple of these sites at the same time. Look at how thorough the listings are and how often they are updated as well as how information can be downloaded. These sites can give you a good sense of what a nationwide site can offer in comparison to one that offers only regional listings.

USING BIRD DOGS

So far, we have talked mostly about listings, advertisements, postings, etc. — information about foreclosures that is open to the public. But in the real estate business, many successful investors use bird dogs to help them get a leg up on the competition.

The concept of the bird dog goes back to hunting lingo for a dog that is trained to help hunters find and capture birds. In the real estate business, bird dogs help investors "run down" properties that are in all likelihood in or facing foreclosure proceedings. A good bird dog is your "person on the street" — one who, as a part of the job, spends a lot of time on the road driving around residential areas.

Finding a good bird dog is not too hard. Drivers for companies such as FedEx®, UPS™, and pizza parlors — anybody whose job it is to drive around neighborhoods all day will make a good bird dog. Even postal workers, police officers, contractors, utility workers, and home nurses all have good "insider" knowledge that could work for you.

All you are asking them to do is look for properties that have suddenly become distressed. This could be a house where the grass is no longer cut or the lawn is no longer being cleared of debris. It could also be a house whose owner is no longer there or is, for whatever reason, unable to maintain the property.

Depending on the quality of your sources, you will want to consider either paying them outright for each lead or waiting to give them a cut when — and if — you successfully close on a property. Either way works. How you work the payout just depends on the quality of the leads you are getting and how the bird dog wants to get paid. Figure out how much money you could spend for each lead as opposed to one payment for each house you successfully buy and sell. Try to shift the balance so that the bird dog gets a bigger payout when they accept one payment for each house sold. If this does not net you quality houses with good profit gains, you do not have to continue the service. In general, expect to pay bird dogs between $500 and $1,000 for tips on deals you actually close.

You can announce that you are looking for a bird dog in the newspaper and online. You can also bring up the opportunity with drivers that you encounter on a daily basis (a delivery person, local mechanic, etc.). Qualify the properties your bird dogs are giving you. You may want to occasionally have somebody else watch the same area to make sure your bird dog is doing a good job. Emphasize that you want exclusive listings — this means that sharing your listings with other "employers" is not acceptable.

When you're just starting out, you may want to spend your spare time looking for distressed properties yourself. This will not only save money but also will give you a firsthand impression of the property in terms of figuring out a sale price that will net you a sweet profit.

Using bird dogs makes real sense once you get the ball rolling and you are spending all your time flipping properties. Before you get to this point, you can probably do a little footwork yourself.

NETWORKING

We have already explained that successful real estate investing is not contingent on who you know. Certainly, being on friendly terms with local banks and the County Recorder can only make your work easier. Most—if not all—foreclosure proceedings involve public notices, so this is one business where anybody not afraid of a little research can access the same information as a seasoned real estate investor.

But just like in any business, the more you network and spread your circle of connections, the easier it will be for you to do business. It also doesn't hurt to get chummy with the title or abstract company that writes up NODs in your local area. See if you can work out a deal in which the company gives you listings of the NODs they write up in exchange for you using their services when you close on properties you bought using their information.

Other people to network with include divorce attorneys as well as probate, bankruptcy, and foreclosure specialists. Lawyers are not supposed to divulge confidential information; however, they may think of you first when clients tell them they want to sell their properties quickly to avoid foreclosure. Make sure you "scratch their backs" too by using their services when you need them.

Remember your networks during the holidays with a card or a small gift. Do not be fake about this stuff; people can tell when you are not being sincere with your friendship. But if you keep people in your network in mind by using them when you can, they will remember you and recommend you to homeowners who are looking to sell their properties quickly. So build up valuable "partnerships" with people who can help you organically. A real network of interested parties will help you find the most motivated sellers with properties that will work for you.

Marketing Your Services

You may have thought about marketing your properties once you buy them, but do not forget to get the word out from the beginning that you are interested in buying pre-foreclosure properties. Help motivated homeowners reach you. While you may find it rewarding to dig up pre-foreclosure properties before your competition does, imagine how sweet it would be if you had homeowners who are facing foreclosures seeking you out because of your own marketing?

With effective marketing, you can really differentiate yourself from your competition. So let people know what you want. Get the word out. You want to buy pre-foreclosure houses! This helps you when you qualify properties to work on because you have raised the bar from "distressed homeowners facing foreclosure" to "motivated homeowners who want to sell their property." Which group will give you the higher rate of return in terms of your time investment and the chance that you will close on a house? Definitely motivated homeowners who want to sell their properties!

Focus on guerrilla marketing tools — they are easy, effective, and, most important of all, cheap to use. Hey, we would all like to rent a hot-air balloon or a plane to carry our message to the public. Even if you have the means for that, you will always want to look into using the following tools: newspaper advertisements, online advertisements, business cards, magnetic car signs, e-mail signatures, bandit signs, door hangers, co-op mailing campaigns, flyers, local cable TV ads, and even a Web site. (These topics are covered in detail in Chapter 5: Effective Marketing: Getting Homeowners and Home Buyers to Come to You.)

With any marketing campaign, keeping track of costs (in terms of money and time) helps you to evaluate the best marketing tools. We will discuss this in detail after going over the various marketing tools you have at your disposal. We will also discuss how a direct mail campaign can help you effectively attract interested homeowners. Since this is a more directed approach (we are not marketing to the general public but are targeting people who we know are facing foreclosures), this is covered separately in Chapter 6: How to Contact Homeowners of Pre-Foreclosure Real Estate Properties.

CASE STUDY

Default Research, Inc.
P.O. Box 663, Mt. Pleasant, PA 15666
www.defaultresearch.com
support@defaultresearch.com
(888) 211-8396 – voice
(412) 291-1971 – fax

Serdar Bankaci – President and CEO
Josh Chernikoff – Vice President of Communications

Like many things in life, I stumbled upon the idea for my pre-foreclosure information business. I started out to form a real estate consulting business, but through my research, I noticed many people posting inquiries about how to find the most up-to-date pre-foreclosure listings. All these investors were going to the courthouse to get their own up-to-date listings – I decided to take care of that step for them.

When searching for houses going into foreclosure, you can't just "stumble" onto that information. To find them, you could go to the courthouse and search through the listings. This generally is not a good approach, because instead of focusing your time on contacting homeowners, you will be spending your entire day digging through listings in the courthouse. A listing service is the best way to get pre-foreclosure listings. However, you must be careful about what service you use. If you join a national company that charges $30 – $50 a month for the entire United States, then you will probably be at the back of the pack when approaching homeowners. You want to ensure that you use a quality service that provides up-to-date information. These will generally run for about $50 – $100 per county.

The need for the most up-to-date information is crucial! Getting the leads two to three weeks ahead of the competition with a quality service can mean the difference for two people – the person in default and the person trying to help them. By getting the leads early, you are able to be the first, and maybe only, to assist the person in foreclosure distress. Timely leads are also the key tool for turning a profit.

Default Research's customers have seen success rates 10 to 20 times that of the competition. With Default Research you will know that you will be one of the first people to approach the homeowner.

5

EFFECTIVE MARKETING: GETTING HOMEOWNERS AND HOME BUYERS TO COME TO YOU

While you could spend a lot of time digging up houses about to foreclose, another way to use your time wisely is to build effective marketing campaigns that will have motivated homeowners contacting you. In this chapter, we will discuss how you can effectively use the following marketing tools: newspaper advertisements, online advertisements, business cards, magnetic car signs, e-mail signatures, bandit signs, door hangers, co-op mailing campaigns, flyers, local cable TV ads, and Web sites.

When designing some of your marketing campaigns, you should target both motivated homeowners who want to sell a property as well as people who would buy that same property from you. Unless it is financially feasible, do not design your copy so that it only attracts one group of potential clients. If you are strapped for cash or just starting out, it is more economical to design ads that attract all interested parties.

Advertise in Newspapers

Advertising in newspapers is one of those classic means of attracting interested parties. Even in this day and age of the Internet, people still like to open up a newspaper over a hot cup of coffee and read it. Newspaper advertisements are traditional, open to the public, targeted to specific geographical areas, and cheap.

When writing your newspaper advertisements, try to write them from the homeowner's point of view. Keep your ads short and sweet, and do not give your homeowner any reason not to call you. In advertising, copywriters use the AIDA formula:

- **"A"** stands for Attention Getting. Start out with an attention-getting line.

- **"I"** stands for Interest Building. Show you know where readers are coming from and what interests them.

- **"D"** stands for Desire Building. Show the reader how you can help. Make your service or product desirable to the reader.

- **"A"** stands for Call for Action. This is where you ask for the order (figuratively speaking).

Let us talk a little more about that tricky "Call to Action" part of the AIDA formula. Never end a communication with a prospective client without explicitly asking them to call you, buy something, or look at something. Tell them what to do. While this might seem pushy at first, the truth is that when it comes to advertising, people like to be told what to do. Otherwise, they will just sit there and say, "What am I supposed to do next?" So make sure you always end your communications with a concrete call to action — to contact you!

With really short advertisements, you may not have the opportunity to break everything down into the four distinct sections of the AIDA formula. So just make sure you start out with an attention-grabbing line and end with information on how to contact you.

The following sample advertisement aims to grab the reader's attention with the fact that Bob will buy your house and pay for it in cash! This ad is sure to grab the reader's attention if he or she is facing financial difficulties. However, make sure you only use this type of wording if you are actually able to pay cash for a house.

Figure 1: Sample Advertisement for Newspaper

> ## We BUY Houses! CASH!
> Stop Foreclosure. Take Care of Your Debt.
> Call Bob at XXX-XXX-XXXX

This next advertisement should stop any homeowners facing foreclosure right in their tracks.

Figure 2: Sample Advertisement for Newspaper

> ## FACING FORECLOSURE?
> Save Your Equity and Your Credit!
> Call Bob at XXX-XXX-XXXX

With the next advertisement, we chose to write copy that attracts both homeowners looking to sell their properties and prospective home buyers. The only problem with this advertisement is that we do not explicitly mention foreclosure. After you flip a couple of properties, you should have enough money to maintain both "Buy" and "Sell" advertisements at the same time. Of course, you should track your marketing efforts to see if you get good returns for posting separate advertisements. If you do not, go back to the combined-use ad.

Figure 3: Sample Advertisement for Both Buying and Selling

> **Smith County Real Estate**
> **BUY and SELL Properties!**
> Call Bob at XXX-XXX-XXXX

If you noticed, the language in these advertisements does not promise anything to the reader. You want to be careful about using wording like "I can help," because, in truth, while you are helping homeowners (and yourself), a good share of them obviously have financial problems. In this desperate state, they will easily look to you as some sort of hero (or a nice sucker) in this situation. So make sure you are upfront and let them know that this is a business for you and that you are involved because you want to buy their property, not to help them "fight" foreclosure and keep their house.

It is perfectly fine, however, for you to offer advice to homeowners who are trying to fight foreclosure. In fact, you may find it ethically the right thing to do when you think you have information that can help them. However, do not get too involved or emotionally invested. First of all, nobody is paying you to care. If you do not get your first property successfully and flip it at a profit, you are wasting your time. Second of all, you must stay detached enough so you do not lose your perspective in the situation and cut down your profit. Finally, you must be sure to let the homeowners know how much—or how little—you are trying to help them. They might get angry with you at the end and turn on you, accusing you of predatory behavior and even making legal problems for you. A number of states (notably California) have statutes protecting homeowners from foreclosure consultants who operate scams or engage in other unethical practices. So do not ever let your behavior reach a point where it may be questioned later on.)

When you are just starting out, you can stick with placing classified ads instead of banner ads. Four or five lines of copy might run you $25 to $100 for a week's run. Be sure to look into small free newspapers as well as larger newspapers. The benefit to advertising in smaller free newspapers is that they may target a specific geographical area, and this makes sense for you since what you are buying and selling ties to a specific plot of land!

ADVERTISE ONLINE

According to an article on Internet Retailer (**www.internetretailer .com/dailyNews.asp?id=15847**), Jupiter Research predicts that revenues for online advertising will grow to $18.9 billion by 2010, more than double the $9.3 billion spent in 2004. There is a reason why online advertising is so hot: It works! While placing ads in newspapers never hurts, using targeted online advertising can also attract many motivated homeowners.

You can place advertisements in newspapers' online editions that look just like they would in the print versions. However, there are so many more ways to use the Internet to market your wants and services. When the Internet first started up, the only way you could advertise online was to buy space on a prominent Web site. Now, Internet marketing tools include search engine ads like those on Google, site-targeted ads, directory listings, Yellow Page listings, and free list servers.

Consider using search engine advertising services like Google AdWords (**https://adwords.google.com/select/**). Services such as this offer the following advantages that you will not get with a newspaper:

- You can have your ads displayed based on targeted keywords.

- You can pay "per click" if you want your ad to appear in keyword-targeted searches, or you can pay "per view" or "per impression" for site-targeted views. This helps you get better bang for your buck.

- You decide how much you want to pay for your advertising. Besides the size of your ad, you can also determine how high you want it to rank compared to other ads and how often you want it to be displayed. Online advertising affords you much more flexibility with how much you want to spend and how you want to spend it.

If you have ever used Google, then you must have noticed those small advertisements that appear above and to the right of your search results with the heading "Sponsored Links."

Figure 4: Google AdWords Screenshot

To use Google AdWords, you will need to set up an account with Google. After you have registered, using Google AdWords is fairly straightforward. You pay a one-time activation fee of $5. After that, how much you spend on your ads depends on where and how much you want your ads to be displayed. You do not have to pay to display your advertisement for an entire week or even an entire day.

With keyword-search ads on Google, your ad comes up on the right-hand side. In this instance, you only pay "per click" — that is, only when somebody clicks on the ad and is linked to your Web site. You decide how much you want to pay, anywhere from $0.01 to $100 CPC ("cost per click").

The price difference determines where your advertisement will show up in comparison to other ads. If somebody else pays more for the same keywords, then his or her advertisement will come up before yours in a Google search listing. You can also decide what your daily budget will be in terms of how many times you want your advertisement to get clicked on. For example, you may find that you max out your budget by midday; in this case, you do not want your advertisement displayed so that it gets clicked on after you have reached your daily budget.

For site-targeted ads, you pay "per impression." An impression means "a viewing." You only pay every time somebody sees your advertisement. You can start with a rate as low as $0.25 CPM ("cost per thousand" impressions). (Do not make the mistake of thinking the M in CPM stands for million! It stands for the Roman numeral M, or 1,000.) To figure out how much this will cost you, take the number of impressions and multiply by the CPM rate. You might sign up for 1,000 impressions a week, which would end up costing you $250 a week. Again, just as with the keyword-search ads, you decide how many impressions you want to display in a day or a week based on your marketing budget.

When using site-targeting advertisements with Google AdWords, advertisers actually get to pick the sites where they want their ads to appear. The only limitation is that this only applies to sites that are part of the Google Network. Google has more information on site-targeting advertising at its Help Center (**https://adwords.google.com/support/bin/topic.py?topic=342**).

This is an example of a Google ad placed on a targeted site. In this case, you would pay per impression as opposed to per click with keyword-search ads.

Figure 5: Google Site Targeted Screenshot

AdBrite (**www.adbrite.com**) is another popular service offering site-targeting advertising. With AdBrite, the advertiser can buy ads on a flat rate or on a CPC basis. If buying ads on a CPC basis, you will need to pay a one-time sign-up fee of $4.95. AdBrite sells both text and banner ads. With the flat rate, the advertiser usually gets a choice of placing their advertisement for a day, a seven-day period, or a whole month. Based on the site's statistics, buying the advertisement on a flat rate is usually cheaper than buying per click.

When constructing search engine ads, follow a format close to your newspaper advertisements. Instead of putting contact information within the ad, use the extra copy to convince the reader to click on through to your site. The point of the ad is to lure the reader to your Web page. With the following Google ad copy, look at how effective the domain name can convince the reader that you buy and sell real estate property.

Figure 6: Sample Google AdWords Advertisement

> Stop Foreclosure. Take Care of Your Debt.
> We BUY Houses! CASH!
> BobSmithBuysHouses.com

With this next advertisement, we reinforce the geographical area in which we want to focus our work. We also picked a domain name that emphasizes the area in which we want to buy houses.

Figure 7: Sample Google AdWords Advertisement

> Stop Florida Foreclosure.
> We BUY Houses! CASH!
> NoFloridaForeclosures.com

The big rub about using online search ads is that you must have a compelling Web site for users to look at once they click through. Marketing online using keyword-search ads does not make sense if you do not have a Web site to point people to should you peak their interest.

We will talk more about setting up shop online with your own Web site, but for now, let's focus on what you would need to effectively use keyword-search ads. You can decide whether to have a shallow landing page or a huge site (one with tons of informative pages). You might want to try both and see which one gives you a higher conversion rate. The conversion rate is based on how many people move from just visiting your site to actually contacting you, and it is what Webmasters watch to measure a site's effectiveness. So in essence, your conversion rate will tell you how successful your site is in "converting" site visitors to clients.

Once you get up and running, you should collect statistics on your Web site and compare your conversion rates to real estate benchmarks. You may already be familiar with conversion rates in terms of direct mailings or telemarketing. People also collect information on conversion rates for Web sites, and the rates differ based on the industry and what specific services or products you are selling online.

With the shallow landing page, all you have is basically one page with benefits and contact information. All the site visitor can do is contact you, either by e-mail or phone. The logic behind a shallow site is that you use the landing page to excite the visitor about contacting you, and at the same time, you do not provide links outside of that page. This helps funnel the traffic so that all the visitor can do is either close your site or click on a link to contact you.

With a larger site, instead of having just a single page, you provide many pages of information. While you are offering much more information, you are diluting the chances that the visitor will actually contact you. However, a benefit of a content-rich site is that it can showcase your knowledge and experience with dealing with pre-foreclosures. The idea behind a large site is that the user will be so impressed with your ability that they will feel compelled to contact you. Another benefit is that the more content your site has, the better your search engine results will be.

It makes sense to start out with a shallow landing page so you at least have something people will be directed to when they click on your ad. Include testimonials, statistics, or other types of information that compel a visitor to contact you. It may be hard for people to contact a complete stranger about their intimate financial problems, so include a small picture of yourself on the site plus a short bio. Keep out any pictures of your Jaguar, your vacation home, or anything else that could alienate you from prospective clients. As you build your business, you can revisit your contact Web site and expand it if you have the time or money. You may still want to keep parallel sites and monitor their conversion rates to see which site brings in more qualified leads.

Within your Web site, you may want to consider including a brief form that visitors can use to communicate information to you. Design the form so that it collects information that will help you qualify your leads and prioritize them based on which ones you can flip for the best profit. Do not make the form so long that it would be a drag to people; they will not take the time to fill it in. But if you offer a couple of drop-downs, radio buttons, or check boxes, you might be able to quickly prioritize your leads so you follow the hottest ones first. You might ask whether or not the person is facing foreclosure and, if so, if the person has just received the first foreclosure notice or if the property is already scheduled for an auction. You might also ask why the property is getting foreclosed (for example, financial problems, relocation, divorce, lost job, etc.) and see what answers you get.

If you are using Google AdWords, one great benefit is that you know your ad will really connect to the right demographics. Imagine a homeowner who is facing foreclosure, desperately searching the Internet trying to find out how to get out of hot water. What could seem more like an answer to his or her prayers than one of your advertisements? Suppose the homeowner follows the ad to your site, where you explain what you can do for the person and how this will help evade foreclosure. Sounds good, doesn't it?

You will need to watch your marketing return on investment (ROI) as far as comparing keyword-search ads to site-targeted impressions to determine which ones net you the most money. On the one hand, the keyword-search ads can quickly attract people before they go to other sites. On the other hand, people who like to research will more than likely find your ads more credible if they are on well-researched sites about foreclosures or real estate in general.

While both of these forms of advertisements can do a lot to lure traffic to your site, there are also other forms of online advertising, many of which may not cost as much. Another approach is to buy advertising in online directories. A directory works differently from a search engine. Directory listings are usually qualified by staff members who visit various sites, consider them worthy of inclusion, and then categorize them into the right section of the directory. Directories are posted by Web owners on their own sites; in this case, the validity of the directory can be questionable. But while search engines use pretty sophisticated algorithms to return the "best" sites in keyword searches, at the end of the day, the search results have not been qualified by the human eye.

Look into the following online directories:

- Open Directory (**http://dmoz.org**) is great because you do not have to pay to have your site added. You will need more than a landing page to get included in this directory, however. The neat thing about Open Directory is that once you get in, not only will your site be added to a number of partner sites, but it will also get picked up in a number of the top search engines.

- Yahoo.com (**www.yahoo.com**) is well known as a search engine, but they also have a directory.

- LookSmart (**www.looksmart.com**) is another site offering a directory listing.

Figure 8: Yahoo Directory Screenshot

With these directories, you do not have to pay for the views or clicks, but you usually will need to pay once to have your site added and probably again annually to remain in the directory. For example, Yahoo.com charges $299 to review your site and include it in its directory. If you find you are getting qualified leads through your listing, you will want to pay the $299 annually to keep your site included.

Better than these general online directories are online Yellow Page listings. This is because, again, we are working with the demographic of homeowners who are frantically looking for somebody to help them. Online Yellow Page listings work just like paper versions. Most online Yellow Pages will offer you a basic listing for free, but you will need to pay extra for anything fancy or beyond the basic listing.

Look into Yellow Page listings such as Yahoo Yellow Pages (**http://yp.yahoo.com**) or Verizon SuperPages (**www.superpages.com**). If you want sponsored listing privileges (that is, your contact information gets listed above the regular alphabetical listing), be prepared to pay for it! In Yahoo Yellow Pages, you do not have to pay to be included in the basic directory. However, rates for upper-tier listings range from $25 to $60 a month. Yahoo Yellow Pages gets its listings from InfoUSA. To get your business added to InfoUSA, send an e-mail to **update@infousa.com**. For Verizon SuperPages, you can also get a free listing, but sponsored listings will cost more.

Figure 9: Yahoo Yellow Pages Screenshot

Stick with free listings until you start making money. Wait to pay for upgraded listings after you flip your first couple of properties and you have time to see whether or not your Yellow Pages directory listing is helpful.

Finally, Craig's List (**www.craigslist.org**) is a great site that serves as a "classified bulletin board" divided into general metropolitan areas — and it usually will not cost one penny. Although Craig's List is incorporated, it works generally as a non-profit and only charges for job postings in the San Francisco area and soon the Washington D.C. area — this is enough to cover costs and pocket a little extra. Postings on Craig's List only stay on for seven days, so you will need to remember to keep your postings current. But this is a great site to advertise for free and target your general area.

Business Cards

Business cards are not just for people walking around in suits! You want to make it easy for people to contact you, so hand your business cards to everybody you come into contact with. You can get a cheap starter set for a good price at any local office supply store, or you could even print them yourself at home.

You can buy a box of blank inkjet business cards for about $20 (200 – 250 a box) or even a set of blank magnetic business cards for about $10 (box of 30) from Staples.com or OfficeDepot.com. Consider passing out your business cards at places where a lot of people will see them — cafeterias, employee lunchrooms, etc.

If you are comparing prices in terms of printing them yourself or paying somebody else to print them, do not discount the cost of ink. Plus, if you can find a professional set of cards for the same

price, go for the professional set. They will always look better —
the cards won't have smeared ink or perforations on the edges.

You can buy a starter set of professionally produced business
cards for less than $10 from any of the following sites:

- Overnightprints (**www.overnightprints.com**)

- Vistaprints (**www.vistaprints.com**)

Keep your business cards simple and to the point; keep them
neutral and not as compelling as your advertisements. If
somebody is facing foreclosure, they may not want to see
everything when they look at your business card. You also want
your business cards to be designed in a way that you can use
for both homeowners looking to sell their properties and people
looking to buy properties from you.

With the following sample card, we spell out that Bob Smith
deals with properties facing foreclosure.

Figure 10: Sample Business Card

With the next two business card designs, we do not blatantly
say that Bob Smith focuses on pre-foreclosures. They work well
because these same cards can be used for both homeowners and
home buyers.

Figure 11: Sample Business Card

Bob Smith
Real Estate Investor

---

bsmith@abcrealty.com
XXX-XXX-XXXX
P.O. Box 123
Any Town, State, Zip Code

Figure 12: Sample Business Card

Bob Smith
Real Estate – BUY and SELL

---

bsmith@abcrealty.com
XXX-XXX-XXXX
P.O. Box 123
Any Town, State, Zip Code

The point of the business card is to make it very easy for interested homeowners to contact you. With your business cards — and your business in general — you may want to consider logging "doing business as" so you can put a business name on the card without actually incorporating. This is not the same thing as incorporating your business. You still do business as a self-employed investor, but logging "doing business as" allows you to use a catchy name to actually run your business. Many people work as self-employed without incorporating; in this case, all they need to do is contact their local government to log a "doing business as" to record their business name. Unlike trademarks, "doing business as" is usually limited to the county level. So somebody two counties away could be doing business as "Sure Thing Real Estate," and you could too. However, you should make sure that the name of your business does not conflict with any trademarks or copyrights at the national level. You want to spend a little time researching your business name to make sure you do not run into problems later.

To do business using a name other than yours will usually require licensing within your state, even if you keep your business a sole proprietorship. Most states refer to this as "doing business as" or as a trade name. Check the state you live in to find out how to get your trade name registered. Trade names must be unique within each state per type of business. New Jersey, for example, has an online form you can fill out to request a check, make a reservation, or register a trade name at the Business Entity Name Availability Check and Reservation — Registration Service site (**https://www.state.nj.us/njbgs/njbgsnar.htm**).

Besides actually licensing the trade name within your state, you may also want to consider obtaining trademark protection. Trademarks are "distinctive symbols, pictures, or words" that help to brand a product. Trademarks are protected by the Lanham Act (Chapter 22 of Title 15) (**www.law.cornell.edu/uscode/html/uscode15/usc_sup_01_15_10_22.html**) and can only be provided by the U.S. Patent and Trademark Office (**www.uspto.gov**). Filing is available online. Fees run $325 per class of goods or services. For more information on the Trademark Electronic Application System (TEAS), check out the TEAS index page (**www.uspto.gov/teas/index.html**). When applying for a trademark, the trade name can be accompanied by the symbol ™. Once the trademark has been successfully registered, the owner can use the symbol ®, which means "registered trademark."

With the next business card, you can see how much better "doing business as" can be in terms of branding your services. We also coupled the domain name with the "doing business as" name to double the impact. Your domain name does not have to match your business name, but if you are just starting out, give it some thought.

Figure 13: Sample Business Card

```
┌─────────────────────────────────────────────┐
│  Bob Smith                                    │
│  ABCReal Estate – BUY and SELL                │
│  ABCRealEstate.com                            │
│  ─────────────────────────────────────────    │
│  bsmith@abcrealty.com                         │
│  XXX-XXX-XXXX                                  │
│  P.O. Box 123                                 │
│  Any Town, State, Zip Code                    │
└─────────────────────────────────────────────┘
```

In order for your business cards to work, you must get them out of your hands and into the hands of people who can make a difference. Always carry some cards with you—in your wallet or purse, jacket, and your car. Practice handing them out casually, as if you are just making it easy for people to contact you. Even leave them with people who say they are not interested. Just hand it to them and say, "Well, in case you change your mind, maybe you wouldn't mind giving me a call."

Visit your circle of networks and routinely pass out a handful of your cards for them to forward to people they come across who might benefit from talking with you. Also include a card in any correspondence you send out; it makes it easier for an interested party to contact you later.

Car Signs

Ever notice how it is practically impossible to the ignore writing on cars at stoplights? You simply cannot keep yourself from reading the signs if they are in front of you. While you could look into getting your advertisement painted on your car, also consider getting magnetic signs, which can serve as a constantly moving billboard to everybody else on the street and in parking lots. If you can get family members to put them on their cars as well, by all means, do so. The more "free" advertising you can get, the better.

Note: Make sure you take the signs off before you visit a property in person. Most people are embarrassed about facing foreclosure and do not want you telling the whole neighborhood about it! You might want to stick a reminder on your visor. Do not wait to take the signs off after you pull up to the property; by then, the damage has already been done. If the homeowner sees that you did not pull off the signs until after you pulled up to the property, they will be annoyed with you. For this reason alone, using magnetic signs might be a better idea than actually having your car painted!

When designing your magnets, keep in mind that you want to use them for attracting sellers as well as making it easy for home buyers to contact you. So use a design similar to the one for your business card, keeping it simple and making sure your phone number is printed in as large a font as possible. You may want to code it so that people will have an easier time remembering your phone number on the fly (for example, XXX-XXX-XXXX, "I LOVE HOMES").

You can pick up a set of car magnets for about $20 to $40 a pair. Not a bad price for mobile advertising! Just wait to pick up a pair until you have flipped your first property. You can buy them from any local sign company, or you can try one of these online sources:

- MagneticSignsOnTime (**www.magneticsignsontime .com**)

- Speedy Signs (**www.speedysigns.com/signs /magnetic.asp**)

- Accent Signs and Graphics (**http://store.yahoo.com /accentgraphics/magneticsigns.html**)

- AA Instant Sign (**www.aainstantsign.com/magnetic.htm**)

E-Mail Signatures

You know what an e-mail signature is, right? It is the catchy title/ contact information you supply at the end of each e-mail. Make sure you send out all of your e-mails with your new title as a Foreclosure Specialist and a catchy phrase or sentence like "I buy all houses" or "I buy/sell homes." Also make sure you include your cell phone and your Web site address (if you have one). This is one of those guerilla methods of marketing yourself that costs you nothing.

Set up your e-mail software to automatically attach your new signature to all of your outgoing e-mails. In Microsoft Outlook 2003, to set up an automatic e-mail signature, click on Tools on the toolbar. From there, choose Options. On the Options screen, click on the Mail Format tab. On that tab, click on the Signatures button to create a new signature.

Figure 14: Microsoft Outlook Option Tab

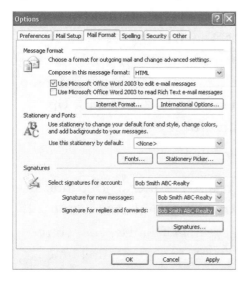

On the Signatures tab, you have the options of editing, removing, or creating a new signature. In the example below, the basic e-signature describes what you do and provides a number of different ways the e-mail recipient can contact you.

Figure 15: Microsoft Outlook Signature Edit Screen

How many leads will you get with your e-mail signature? Not hundreds, but you never know. Your new e-mail signature is free, and it cannot hurt. Word-of-mouth is a great way to market your services and also stands as a low-key reminder to your contacts about what you do.

BANDIT SIGNS

Bandit signs are extremely popular with entrepreneurs just starting out investing in real estate. Most cities, however, have ordinances against them. That is why we call them "bandit signs" and not "legal signs."

Bandit signs are those plastic signs you see posted on telephone poles and stop signs (any kind of post) that people tend to notice at red lights and other traffic stops. You may also see them on their own metal or wooden stakes stuck into the ground right next to stop signs and along road medians. You might have seen some advertising "How to Lose Weight in 7 Days," "Trash Pick-Up," "Yard Services," and even, "We Buy Houses!" You might have even seen postings for car washes, garage sales, and lost pets.

Are bandit signs effective? Yes. Cheap? Yes. Illegal? Depends on a city's ordinances. In Austin, Texas, for example, these types of signs have been illegal for over 20 years! Of course, you won't be charged if you did not know (that is, you were a first time violator), but if you are a repeat offender, watch out!

Just because you have seen bandit signs for political campaigns, that does not mean your signs are legal too. Many cities have special exceptions for signs they think benefit their inhabitants. So do not get a false sense of security just because you have seen them along your streets.

The beauty of bandit signs is that they cost close to nothing to produce and posting them is free. You do not have to pay anyone for space; in most instances, the only problem is that they are illegal to post. If you are not sure, find out what your city/county ordinance is for bandit signs before you get them printed. If your county allows billboards, it may be more lenient about bandit signs. (Speaking of billboards, you can use them to reach thousands of people each day. A very compelling message on billboards heading away from a busy city is "You could be home now!" with the idea that you have a house you could sell to the driver that would shorten his or her commute. Just wait to buy a billboard ad until after you have successfully flipped your first couple of properties.)

With your bandit sign design, keep it simple. "Avoid Foreclosure. I'll buy your house and you get the equity! Call XXX-XXX-XXXX" is a good example. Just in case you misunderstand the local ordinances, you may want to use a temporary cell phone number that you do not plan to keep around for too long. But do not do this as a way to get around city ordinances — it's better to obey ordinances and be safe instead of sorry.

Better yet, focus on distributing flyers in public buildings, many of which have bulletin boards where you can legally post flyers. Not only will you not have to worry about city ordinances, your flyers will usually be better protected against the elements. You also will not have to worry about vigilante sign removers — people who drive around, take offense at bandit signs, stop their cars, pull over, and take down your signs!

One more thing while we are talking about illegal means of advertising: no mailbox stuffing. You can send out postcards or letters using stamps, but you have to pay for the postage! Many people do not realize that mailbox stuffing is illegal. It is not as if you are trying to pass your postings as if they were mailed or get your postings distributed fraudulently through the U.S. mail. But, apparently, the U.S. Postal Service is rather possessive of its mailboxes. So no mailbox stuffing, or face the wrath of the U.S. Postal Service.

DOOR HANGERS

As far as we know, door hangers are legal (unlike bandit signs and mailbox stuffing). While these work well when you are selling pizzas, we are not that hot about using them when working with foreclosures. You know why? The majority of people are not facing foreclosure. Putting these hangers on people's doors might seem presumptuous or as morbid yet gleeful anticipation.

You can get door hangers printed for $.05 to $.50 apiece, depending on the paper quality, the number of colors used, and the quantity ordered at one time. You also need to factor in the cost of distributing the door hangers. Until you make enough money to cover all of your costs, do not pay somebody else to do what you can do. So go ahead and hang them yourself the first couple of times.

Some foreclosure "gurus" swear by the use of door hangers. But you may find better use of time working your direct mail campaign. Nevertheless, if you have the time and energy, by all means, get ahead of your competition by distributing your door hangers in neighborhoods with properties you would be interested in flipping.

If a property has signs posted against soliciting, honor them. If you still want to contact the owners, you might have a better chance with a hand-addressed letter.

Co-op Mailing Campaigns

Co-op mailing campaigns are different from direct mail campaigns (which we will discuss in detail in Chapter 6: How to Contact Homeowners of Pre-Foreclosure Real Estate Properties). With direct mail campaigns, you are going to target homeowners who you know are facing foreclosure. With the co-op mailing campaign, you are targeting an entire neighborhood or zip code. You have seen this type of mail before; they include a pack of coupons or sales literature from a group of businesses (hence, the "co-op" part of the campaign).

Co-op mailing campaigns can work, but if you have to choose between a co-op mailing campaign and a direct mail campaign for the same amount of money or time, the direct mail campaign wins hands down each time. This is because you are starting with an extremely qualified lead bank (a list of homeowners facing foreclosure), and this audience is much more apt to take notice than a complete neighborhood.

Co-op campaigns are very popular in the business world, especially when retailers partner with branded manufacturers to advertise. In this case, a manufacturer will provide a discount or split the costs of advertising with their distributors. An example of this would be in the floral industry where Teleflora and FTD routinely advertise in the local newspapers. When they do this, they offer local florists a chance to get in on the action at a discounted rate (since they are picking up some of the tab). That kind of co-op would not make sense for you as a real estate investor; you are not going to find some national mortgage insurer or national real estate association that is going to go half with you on your next mailing campaign. You can, however, find a number of other businesses that are willing to share distribution and mailing costs with you to get your shared messages out to the public. Either join a group of businesses and send out mail together or use a service that distributes your literature along with coupons and flyers from other businesses. This type of co-op mailing campaign will save you money on envelopes and postage.

Deciding when to start a co-op mailing campaign is tricky business. On the one hand, you are paying extra for somebody else to distribute your literature, and they will want to make a profit for themselves. On the other hand, you may find it much cheaper to use a service when you consider the postage costs. When you do use a co-op mailing campaign, you need to consider your "partners." Find out what other sales literature is going out with your advertisement. Does it make sense for you to send out your sales literature with this batch? Will you have any competition from other real estate investors?

With the co-op mailing campaign, you will need to carefully consider what your advertisement will say. Remember, you are targeting homeowners facing foreclosure, so these are people who will take whatever money they can get from you. You do not really want to offer them a "discount" on your purchase price, and you also have to be careful about making promises since you do not know anything about the property in question. You could offer a free consultation, a quick 24-hour turnaround with possible numbers, or even a free report showing them how much money they would get from you and how fast it could happen. Do not pay extra for more copy—keep it to the 1/3-page size. This is another area where you want to exclusively target potential home sellers. Trying to target both home sellers and home buyers would send mixed messages and probably scare away either camp.

Flyers

We have already covered bandit signs and how, in most places, they are illegal. Here, we will cover a slightly different variation of the public notice: the flyer. Print flyers on bright-colored paper and post them wherever you legally can. Make sure you keep your message short and simple, and include your contact information. You may want to put the contact info on detachable tabs that people can tear off and keep. In the following example, we show a flyer with detachable tabs that is short and to the point.

Figure 16: Flyer Example

FACING FORECLOSURE? WE BUY HOUSES. 100% CASH. CALL BOB SMITH XXX-XXX-XXXX				
Bob Smith **Real Estate – BUY and SELL** bsmith@abcrealty.com XXX-XXX-XXXX P.O. Box 123, Any Town, State, Zip Code	**Bob Smith** **Real Estate – BUY and SELL** bsmith@abcrealty.com XXX-XXX-XXXX P.O. Box 123, Any Town, State, Zip Code	**Bob Smith** **Real Estate – BUY and SELL** bsmith@abcrealty.com XXX-XXX-XXXX P.O. Box 123, Any Town, State, Zip Code	**Bob Smith** **Real Estate – BUY and SELL** bsmith@abcrealty.com XXX-XXX-XXXX P.O. Box 123, Any Town, State, Zip Code	**Bob Smith** **Real Estate – BUY and SELL** bsmith@abcrealty.com XXX-XXX-XXXX P.O. Box 123, Any Town, State, Zip Code

Make sure you get in the habit of updating your flyers on a routine basis. You do not want to go through the trouble of distributing your flyers once only to leave them there, wilted-looking without any more tabs to be pulled off. Check every couple of weeks to see when you need to re-post your flyers.

Copies cost $0.06 per sheet at Kinko's (**www.kinkos.com**). You can also get copies at Staples (**www.staples.com**) and Office Depot (**www.officedepot.com**). Please do not go out and buy yourself a copier before you flip your first property. Even after that, make sure you do the math and work out which route is cheaper — going to Kinko's or buying your own copier (taking into account paper and ink costs as well as maintenance). Since we are not talking about distributing these door to door, you may decide to post your flyers yourself.

Local Cable TV Ads

Since we have talked so much about cheap advertising, you may be wondering, "Why are we now talking about TV ads?" Well, we are not talking about the Super Bowl here! You can get some quick spots on local cable stations for as little as $15 to $25 a spot for late-night spots and maybe $100 for airing during more regular times.

Of course, do not start out with TV advertising to reach potential clients. Once you start making some money, then you may want to tap into this market. TV spots work the same way as online search engine ads in terms of demographics. They speak to the demographic of homeowners who are facing foreclosure and do not know what to do. These homeowners are up late, worried, and cannot sleep. What does the homeowner end up doing? They turn on the TV for some easy distraction.

Contact your local cable station. The people there should be able to provide some numbers so you can figure out if or when you want to start airing your own ads. Remember to keep them simple. You do not need to hire a bunch of actors and have a whole script worked out. Just use the TV spot like a virtual billboard—display a simple advertisement with a voice-over and your contact information.

Use the Internet

Setting up a Web site online is a favorite marketing tool. On your site, advertise what you do and what you want with pre-foreclosure properties. To help popularize your site with the search engines, have keyword articles written as part of your site and post them elsewhere on the Web with links back to your site.

Lurk on forums and post, post, post to get the word out about your site. This will organically build up your Web site so that during search engine results, your site will come up. Make sure you sprinkle your geographical location in the text liberally; you do not want to attract people from halfway across the nation.

Offer to send site visitors more information if they sign up with an e-mail address, which you can use to establish an e-mail campaign to encourage them to contact you for more information on how to resolve their foreclosure problems. This way, you can stay in contact over the next six or seven weeks while they muddle their way through their foreclosure process. They may have a change of heart and decide to contact you.

Information about how to improve your search engine rankings is outside the scope of this book. However, many books have been written about this, so you will not have any problem finding more information. Overall, the two key things to do is go heavy on relevant keywords and have a lot of content on your site. The more content you have, the more relevant your site will appear to search engines. The same thing applies with the keywords in your site. Make sure your site is full of keywords that are relevant to the areas you want to invest in (either by state or county); this will help your site come up when a person types in matching search terms.

Web sites are wonderful because they can work for you 24/7 while you work your deals, research properties, or get caught up on much-needed sleep. After you lay out the investment to get the site up and running and with very little effort on your part, your site will continue to market your services into the future.

Start out small with no more than a landing page. This is because you want to spend less time building out the site and more time focusing on your core tasks of finding and buying pre-foreclosure properties.

As you gain experience and (hopefully) more money, you can spend more time working on your Web site. If you are not experienced in this area, you can get help, but make sure you do not spend more than you need to. Along that note, search online to find cheap but reliable hosting solutions. They may include:

- 1&1 (**http://order.1and1.com**), which offers hosting from $2.99 per month to $19.99 per month before they start going into big-time hosting.

- GoDaddy (**www.godaddy.com**), which offers hosting from $3.95 per month to $19.95 per month. Clients get 10 percent discounts if they sign up for a year and 20 percent discounts on the monthly fee if they sign up for two years.

- BlueHost (**www.bluehost.com**), which offers hosting at $6.95 per month with no strings attached.

A bunch of free hosting solutions are available. However, you need to be careful not to violate the "Acceptable Use Policy" as you try to make money with your site (not via e-commerce but by getting good leads). So make sure you read the fine print. Also, many free Web sites do not look professional if you have to include references to the host or the host's other businesses.

Monitoring Your Marketing Campaign

It is important to track your marketing efforts to make sure you are getting the best bang for your buck. How do you do this? You distinguish the results. Use a separate voice mail or extension just for messages so potential sellers can record how they discovered you; or, you can just ask them, "How did you hear about me and my services?" Also track your time when comparing marketing efforts. You can either qualify your time on a "cost per hour" basis or monitor how time-intensive your marketing efforts are. The point is to qualitatively measure your marketing efforts, with consideration to your money and your time.

Keep a record of how many sellers are contacting you per marketing effort (for example, 25 calls a week from flyers, 2 calls a week from your TV advertisement, etc.) so you can see what your cost per seller is for each type of marketing campaign. But do not stop here; take it further and record which sellers actually become moneymakers to you in terms of deals you successfully close. This may help you determine which marketing effort brings in the best sellers.

Qualifying your homeowners is a necessary task to assess your marketing efforts. For example, if your flyers net you twice as many calls as your TV ads but you end up closing more of your TV ad leads (with the assumption here that, for whatever reason, those leads are better qualified), spend your money on the TV ads.

Periodically review your marketing campaign to determine how you should best spend your money and efforts. Do not think you should spend more money on efforts to get more responses on them. Use the 80-20 rule: Spend your efforts on the top, easy 80 percent of sellers you obtain. Do not spend money, for example, on door-to-door flyers if you find your targeted postcards net you ten times the money in terms of successfully closed deals. If somebody else wants to spend all of their money bringing in the reluctant 20 percent, fine, let them; you focus on the easy 80 percent.

Make sure you include all of your marketing costs, including online memberships for *Lis Pendens*/NOD lists, Google AdWords ads, and e-mail campaigns. You will soon get a clear picture of the best way to concentrate your marketing efforts. The worst thing you can do is shoot in the dark by not measuring the effectiveness of each marketing effort. You may find you are spending money on marketing efforts that are not returning good leads for you to spend your time and energy on.

Tracking your marketing does not have to be confusing or complicated. You can decide what you want to track in terms of your return on your efforts. Do not feel compelled to spend more time tracking data you feel is helpful. Also, you do not have to keep track of this every month. You may want to revisit your marketing efforts from time to time or especially when you have a gut feeling that one of your marketing efforts is not working the way it should. This spreadsheet example could help you track your marketing efforts.

Figure 17: Marketing Spreadsheet

MARKETING TOOL	FLYERS	BANDIT SIGNS	GOOGLE ADS	YAHOO ADS	NEWS AD	DIRECT MAIL
Jan-06						
Cost						
Calls						
Qualified Calls						
Good Properties						
Feb-06						
Cost						
Calls						
Qualified Calls						
Good Properties						

Another thing to consider: If something is not working for you,

you may just need a little help with your copy writing. Before you abandon a tool, try wording your advertisement differently and even consider getting professional copywriting help if your own tactics do not seem to be working that well.

Once you start up on your marketing, you will not believe how easy it is to get the word out to people that you are interested in buying homes facing foreclosure. The less money you spend on marketing, in effect, the more money you make for yourself. But do not spend all your time digging up foreclosures. Market yourself and let interested, motivated homeowners come to you!

How to Contact Homeowners of Pre-Foreclosure Real Estate Properties

We have talked about how to use unqualified campaigns in an attempt to dig up homeowners who are facing foreclosure. In this chapter, we focus on how to contact homeowners of properties we know are in the pre-foreclosure period. So in essence, we are shifting the focus from unqualified leads to qualified leads (homeowners who are motivated sellers).

While you focus on communicating with homeowners, you should also use the same list of leads to start researching their properties (as explained in our next chapter, Chapter 7: Evaluating Pre-Foreclosure Properties for Value). The two processes go hand in hand. You cannot effectively press forward in your communications with the homeowner if you do not do your homework on the property (to find out how much is owed on the property and how much you think you can sell the property for). You will not have the time to give each property individual attention. So evaluate the properties, and then prioritize them in terms of which ones you should focus on first.

Getting Organized

Before we get started with our actual work of contacting individual homeowners, we need to talk about getting organized. At this point in the game, you should be thinking of the next stage: homeowners actually contacting you, interested in hearing what you have to say. So now we are moving from the macro level of a list of properties to a micro level of evaluating each property on its own. It wastes your money to set up a folder for every property's homeowner you initiate communications with. However, you may want to keep a running list of all such properties that you can refer to when you do hear back from a homeowner.

Once you start hearing back from homeowners, you should begin some sort of filing system to help you stay organized. For each property, document your communications with the homeowner; write down your notes from conversations you have with any interested party involved with the selling of that property. Without getting too far ahead of ourselves, we will want one place where you keep track of your evaluation research (covered in the next chapter) for each property as well as any negotiations you start with the homeowners plus any title research.

How you do this depends on your resources and how you like to work. Are you a computer person? Do you like to write things down in a notebook? Does a loose-leaf binder make more sense to you? It does not matter how you do it, just as long as you stay organized. You want to make each homeowner you work with feel special in his or her own way. You do not need to memorize their birthday or their kids' names, but you do need to keep their numbers and facts straight. Even though you may be working your way through hundreds of foreclosure leads, you never want to make the homeowners feel like just another number. Treating a homeowner like that is a sure way to kill any special rapport you may have developed.

You are also going to be too busy to risk losing or misplacing information you have taken the time to track down for a property. If you have done the comps on the property, you need a place to keep it. A method that makes sense would be to use a folder for each property once you start to collect papers for it plus a general notebook where you jot down your day–to-day proceedings. This might be an area you develop over time, figuring out what type of organizational system works best for you. The point is, do not begin contacting homeowners without anticipating hearing back from them. So be organized and ready to keep track of what you start getting back for each property. Otherwise, you will not be effective or efficient at flipping pre-foreclosure properties at a profit.

WHY WOULD A PRE-FORECLOSURE HOMEOWNER WANT TO TALK TO YOU?

Up to this point, we have just been talking about houses. Finding houses that are about to foreclose. Finding houses that look distressed. Lists of houses. Lists of public notices. These all are inanimate objects — objects of our desire, but we cannot just take them. What do we need to do next? We have to deal with the homeowners! Maybe the idea of interacting with homeowners is making you a little nervous. You are asking yourself, "Why would a homeowner facing foreclosure want to talk to me?" They are angry at the world, frustrated with their financial situation, and possibly frightened of what the future will bring. Facing foreclosure is not a pleasant experience for anybody.

Consider some of the reasons people like to say why homeowners appreciate hearing from somebody who wants to snatch their house from the jaws of foreclosure. These reasons are not usually as valid as you would like after you think through them:

1) They have equity built up in the house that they do not want to lose.

Be careful about this reason. The truth is that, in many states, when the lender forecloses and auctions the property, any equity built up in the property minus liens owed goes back to the homeowner. So if a house has equity built up in it and not a lot of secondary liens on the property, there is a good chance the homeowner will get the equity back.

A few states, notably Vermont and Maine, allow strict foreclosures. With strict foreclosures, the lender is not required to auction the property and return excess equity. The lender takes possession of the property and owns it outright. The homeowner loses any equity that was in the house.

If a foreclosed property has a number of secondary liens, the lien holders will get their part of the house equity before the homeowner will. However, if you agree to buy the house from the homeowner and take on the secondary liens at a reduced amount that makes purchasing the property worth your while, the homeowners may come out ahead because they will get back some of the equity. This is a little trickier, because if the lien holders agree to reduce the lien amount in order to let you buy the property, they are banking on the fact that the house auction will not produce enough money for them to get back what is owed to them—they do not believe enough equity exists in the house.

Now you could have a homeowner who is facing foreclosure and has been unsuccessful in selling the house on his or her own in the short time they have before auction. If there is any equity in the house after the mortgage loan and secondary liens are paid, the homeowner will receive it after the auction. You could be dealing with homeowners who, while facing financial problems along with not being able to pay the house payments, may be interested in getting whatever equity they can get back from the house in a sale as soon as possible. In other words, they have already resigned themselves to losing the house. Now, they are just waiting for the bank to auction the house so they can get back a little bit of equity. If you could give them their equity now instead of three months down the line, they might be interested in hearing what you have to say.

2) They are concerned about their credit report and would rather do anything than get a bad mark due to a foreclosure.

You need to be careful about this reason as well since most people facing foreclosure are probably already having credit problems. They may have already reached rock-bottom with their FICO score, so a foreclosure would not have anywhere to go on their credit report! If a homeowner did not put any money down and has little or no equity built up in the house, they may favor selling the property to you quickly before getting into any real credit problems. Also, if the homeowners, for whatever reason, cannot convince a judge to allow them to file for bankruptcy, they will see a harsher impact on their credit report and FICO score as a result of a foreclosure (as opposed to a bankruptcy).

Understand the ubiquitousness of the credit report and FICO score so you can talk the homeowners' language as pertinent to an impending foreclosure. The three main credit-reporting agencies are TransUnion (**www.transunion.com**), Experian (**www.experian.com**), and Equifax (**www.equifax.com**). Your credit report is your report card for how well you deal with credit, and lenders and credit card companies use it to determine your creditworthiness. Lenders use it to decide if they should enter into a mortgage agreement with somebody. Credit card companies use it to decide if they should open an account for someone and how much the balance should be. Your credit report contains the following information:

- Personal information

- Public judgments against you (unpaid child support, unpaid liens, bankruptcy, foreclosures, etc.)

- Credit information (credit cards opened, balances, payment history, etc.)

- Number of requests to review your credit history

People investigating your credit report do not usually go through the report line by line themselves; instead, they look at your FICO score. Each of the credit-reporting agencies produces its own version of the FICO score. FICO stands for Fair Isaacs & Co (**www.fairisaac.com/fairisaac**), which was the first group to develop the FICO score. Experian calls it a FICO score; you can learn more about the FICO score on Fair Isaacs & Co.'s site at **www.myFico.com**. At TransUnion, they call it the EMPIRICA score; and at Equifax, the BEACON score. All three scorecards are relatively the same, although a person's score may differ based on which credit-reporting agency and, hence, which algorithm is used to determine your score.

At Experian, the FICO score has a range of 300 to 850; the higher one's score is, the better, credit-wise. A person would be hard-pressed to find a decent mortgage with anything lower than a FICO score of 500. The FICO score is broken down the following way:

- 35 percent of the score is based on the person's past payment history.

- 30 percent of the score is based on the person's credit use.

- 15 percent of the score is based on the person's credit history.

- 10 percent of the score depends on what type of credit the person has used.

- 10 percent of the score depends on the number of inquiries into the person's credit report (this loosely translates into how much credit the person has tried to get lately).

In terms of negatively affecting a FICO score, the homeowner cannot get much worse than a foreclosure. Right up there would also include bankruptcies, car repossessions, involuntary liens against the property, charge-offs, and collections records. There is no debate on whether a foreclosure will negatively impact one's FICO score. The larger question is, Does the homeowner care? What if the homeowner has already had his or her car repossessed and credit cards are maxed out? Maybe the homeowner is dealing with a drug problem that prevents clear thinking; the person could have lost his or her job in a way that makes it very hard to get a new one in the same area. You could very well be dealing with a homeowner who has already damaged his or her FICO score or frankly does not care what happens to it at this point.

The only way you can work a bad FICO score in your favor is if you are dealing with a homeowner who is ignorant of the impact the foreclosure will have on the FICO score or the homeowner really anticipates a change in the fortune such that he or she could buy another house in the near future. A foreclosure will stay on the credit report for around seven years and, in that time, will affect the credit score. If you find a homeowner like this, you are in a sweet spot because you have found one homeowner who is "motivated to sell"!

Now that we have just attacked the two myths of why a homeowner would prefer dealing with you over going through with a foreclosure, consider two very real reasons why a homeowner would want to sell you his or her property:

1) The homeowner does not want to go through foreclosure.

This is a very real, valid reason. People do not like to go to court. They do not like looking like failures. They do not like being in the public eye. Even if it means they lose a little bit of the house equity, they may be more interested in selling their house to you now than having to live through the foreclosure of their house in three months.

2) Selling their house to you gives them a fast resolution to their foreclosure problem.

This is another real, valid reason why many people would prefer to work with a foreclosure specialist—they just want to get things over with. Once foreclosure proceedings begin, the homeowners may decide they do not want to fight the foreclosure. They cannot come up with the money to pay what they owe, and they do not see any change in the foreseeable future. To them (even if this is not the absolute truth in the matter), foreclosure seems inevitable. The homeowner cannot, however, just flip a switch and turn out the lights on everything. Well, they might be able to with a "deed in lieu of foreclosure," but not all lenders will accept this. (We cover the "deed in lieu of foreclosure" in detail later on in this chapter, but suffice it to say that sometimes the homeowner can basically hand the keys to the property [and the deed!] to the lender and walk away. In this case, the lender agrees to the title transfer in lieu of the foreclosure if it wants to save court costs and thinks it is not worth going to court and seeing the property all the way to auction.) So the same amount of time that lets you try to work as many pre-foreclosure deals as possible can also seem like slow torture to the homeowner facing inevitable foreclosure.

In this case, you can help the homeowner resolve the problem right now — not two to nine months down the road. By selling the house to you and handling all of the details with the house, the homeowner can, in effect, "walk away" from the problem. This subset of homeowners (the group feeling foreclosure is inevitable yet dreads waiting around for it to be finalized) is your sweet set: the motivated sellers we keep talking about. They may not have any equity in the house. Perhaps they have secondary liens. And maybe they do not have any money to make necessary improvements before trying to sell the house at a profit. They are not fighting the foreclosure; they just want to pack their bags and get out. If you smell a homeowner with this kind of attitude, do whatever you can to close the deal (if the numbers work for you). You will find that this group will give you the fastest ROI.

Remember:

- In most cases, you are dealing with motivated sellers.

- While you can group homeowners facing foreclosures into general categories, each homeowner is an individual person with his or her own history. Treat each person with respect and dignity. Do not assume you know everything about the situation or the homeowner.

Ways to Contact Homeowners Facing Foreclosure

In this section, we will discuss the various ways to contact homeowners facing foreclosure: direct contact, cold-calling by phone, direct mail campaign, and e-mail campaign. For each method, we will describe what it is and go over the pros and cons.

Direct Contact

The first way that comes to mind in terms of contacting a homeowner facing foreclosure is by direct contact. We are talking about driving over there, walking up the driveway or sidewalk, and starting a conversation with the homeowner.

There are several problems with this tactic. One, the homeowner may be hostile. Two, the person may be in denial about facing foreclosure. Three, even if the homeowner is accepting of the situation, this person doesn't know you from Jack. Most people would blanch at the thought of directly contacting a homeowner facing foreclosure.

If you consider yourself outgoing and feel comfortable talking with strangers, then you may want to head on out there. Just don't say you weren't warned. For your first couple of interactions, you should probably come up with a general script of what you are going to say. Introduce yourself quickly and explain that you buy houses. Mention that you saw this property listed in the newspaper and that you want to know if the homeowners are interested in selling. If the homeowner does not respond positively, try to leave a business card in case he or she has a change of heart. Do not be pushy; in any event, you need the homeowner's cooperation to buy the house before foreclosure. You will not win points by trying to embarrass or manipulate the homeowner.

Make sure you listen when the homeowner tells you to "shut up and get out of here." It's still that person's property (albeit possibly for not much longer). Before you get scared off of this method, consider that if you are confident you could carry off direct contact with the right tone and aplomb, then by all means, you should try doing this a couple of times and see where it gets you. You will eventually have to talk to the homeowner if you ever plan to get anywhere with the property. As easy as the direct mail campaign is, the truth is that nothing beats a face-to-face meeting to build rapport and get the ball rolling. If you want to make money investing in pre-foreclosures, you will need to not only talk to the homeowner but also convince him or her to sell the property to you at a price that makes sense for you.

COLD CALLING BY PHONE

Most people shudder when they hear the phrase "cold call." But keep the following thought in mind: An unqualified cold call is very different from a qualified cold call. With qualified cold calls, you are working with a list of houses you know are facing foreclosure, so you also know that the homeowners are not in a good spot. This is different from calling people randomly using the white pages or some other phone list. In this case, your leads have not been well qualified, and they probably would not give you the time of day.

The problem with making cold calls is that people are not going to discuss their personal financial information over the phone with a stranger. They do not know you and may feel like your call is an intrusion of privacy. Still, calling people directly can be a good thing if you are comfortable doing it.

When you make the call, introduce yourself and explain that you buy houses. Say you saw the property listed in the newspaper and that you want to know if the homeowners are interested in selling. If they are not, try to get your name in there again so they can contact you if they change their minds. Try to mention that you will send something their way to follow up on your phone call.

The good things about cold calling by phone over direct contact in person are that you can:

1) Go through a list of properties much faster by phone than by foot.

2) You can leave voice messages when the homeowner is not home or is not picking up the phone. This will give the homeowner a chance to mull over your services. Some people like to call in person but target times they suspect the homeowner will not be home (as in normal business hours) so they can leave a carefully scripted but natural-sounding message on the answering machine. It works for some people!

Leaving a phone message should never be your last attempt to contact a homeowner facing foreclosure. Always follow up your phone campaign with a personalized letter. Send something out that summarizes your phone conversation with the homeowner but also provides extra information.

Direct Mail Campaign

Out of all the ways you can contact the homeowner, this is one of the simplest and most effective processes once you understand how to manage your word processing software's form letter feature (for example, Mail Merge in Microsoft Word).

Why does the direct mail campaign work? First of all, you only need to exert a low effort to contact a group of well-qualified leads. With Mail Merge, for example, you can type one letter and print out hundreds that are personalized to each homeowner. Second of all, you can be persistent without being "in your face" annoying. Never send out just one letter to a residence. Set up a schedule and send out three to five letters (over a one- to two-month period) to each homeowner, introducing yourself and explaining what you want and what you can do. Finally, the best thing about direct mail campaigns is the response. People who contact you in return are well qualified. They are interested in what you have to say. You have found your "motivated sellers."

Using form letters for your direct mail campaign is so easy! You could go through and update the address in each of your letters manually, typing in the name of the homeowner and their address instead of trying to create a new letter each time. This would not take you as long as it would in the old days, when you had to actually type or write each letter itself or make copies, which can end up looking pretty tacky.

The point to using form letter features like Mail Merge is that for each of your listings of properties facing foreclosure, you will not be contacting the homeowners just once. Your goal will be to send each homeowner a set of letters (three to five). With this in mind, it makes sense for you to use a form letter feature on your word processor so you can automate putting the letters together.

To create a form letter, you "merge" two different documents: the body of the letter and a list of contacts. The word processor uses the two documents to produce separate letters for each contact from the list. Each letter is personalized, and you can use the same list to send subsequent letters.

Creating form letters with Mail Merge in Microsoft Word 2003 requires three documents: the data source, the main document, and the finished merged document. The data source is the list of addresses you use to fill in the form fields in the main document. This can be another Word document, an Excel spreadsheet, an Access database, or a Microsoft Outlook Contact list. You can use other data sources, but you will need to set them up within Word. Our example of a data source is a simple Excel spreadsheet that contains a contact list used to keep track of homeowners who are facing foreclosure. You can keep one Excel spreadsheet for all your contacts using a field to help you keep the dates straight, or you could have a number of separate Excel spreadsheets for each set of direct mail campaigns you send out. You can set up the Mail Merge to only merge the addresses you want to send out by checking the content in one of the other fields.

Figure 18: Excel Data Source

mail-merge-example

	A	B	C	D	E	F	G	H	I	J	K
1	Date Rec I	First Name	Last Name	Address1	Address2	City	State	Zip Code	Letter1	Letter2	Letter3
2	1/2/2006	John	Masters	380 Partridge Street	Fairfax	VA	22031	1/5/2006			
3	1/2/2006	Cheryl	Johnson	500 Sycamore Street	Fairfax	VA	22033	1/5/2006			
4	1/2/2006	J.J.	Edwards	123 Apple Avenue	Annandale	VA	22038	1/5/2006			
5	1/2/2006	David	Chen	3884 Brady Lane	Burke	VA	22045	1/5/2006			
6	1/2/2006	K.	Custer	4321 Indian Flame La	Burke	VA	22045	1/5/2006			
7											

H ◀ ▶ H \ Sheet1 ⟋ Sheet2 ⟋ Sheet3 ⟋

The main document contains the form fields that will be replaced with fields from your data source. Notice the toolbar included at the top of the screenshot. It is the Mail Merge toolbar; you will need to pull it up to merge the documents. Alternatively, you can click Tools, Letters and Mailings, then Mail Merge to access Word's Mail Merge features.

Within the main document, you specify where you want to replace the form fields with your data source by clicking on the "Insert Merge Fields" button on the toolbar. Word will go to the data source you selected and give you a listing of fields based on the headings in your data source. Double chevron tags indicate the merge fields. For example, the title is replaced with <<Title>>. Use the <<Skip Record If>> rule so you can select only the records you want to use to produce a form letter. You can also set up fields so Word will prompt you for additional information per record if you want to further personalize the letters.

Figure 19: Mail Merge Main Document

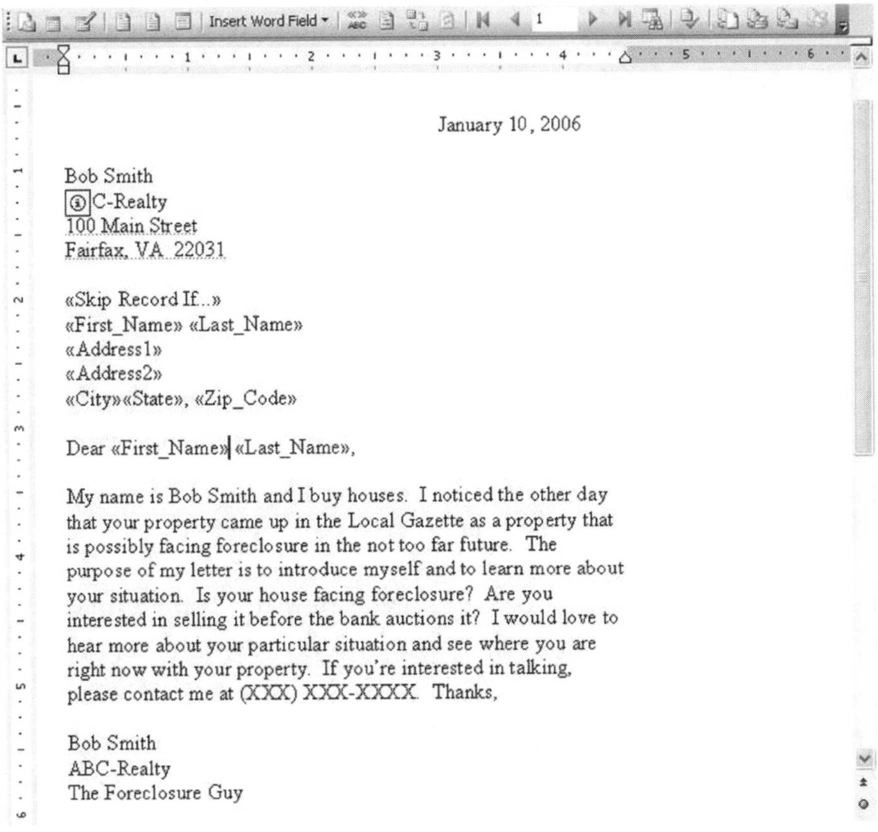

January 10, 2006

Bob Smith
ABC-Realty
100 Main Street
Fairfax, VA 22031

«Skip Record If...»
«First_Name» «Last_Name»
«Address1»
«Address2»
«City»«State», «Zip_Code»

Dear «First_Name» «Last_Name»,

My name is Bob Smith and I buy houses. I noticed the other day that your property came up in the Local Gazette as a property that is possibly facing foreclosure in the not too far future. The purpose of my letter is to introduce myself and to learn more about your situation. Is your house facing foreclosure? Are you interested in selling it before the bank auctions it? I would love to hear more about your particular situation and see where you are right now with your property. If you're interested in talking, please contact me at (XXX) XXX-XXXX. Thanks,

Bob Smith
ABC-Realty
The Foreclosure Guy

The finished merged document (there will be one long document with new pages for each contact record) will look just like your main document, but the merge fields will be filled in from data in your data source. You can choose to merge the data to your main document, to a new document, or directly to the printer. If you do not print directly to the printer, you will have another opportunity to fine-tweak the letters. The following example shows the first two pages of the merged document.

Figure 20: Finished Merged Document

When constructing your letters, follow the AIDA formula explained in the Advertise in Newspaper section. As a reminder, start with an attention-getting headline or introduction. Follow with a brief description of what the homeowner may be dealing with (that is, their problems). Follow this with an introduction of yourself and what you can do for the homeowner. End each letter with a direct request for the homeowner to contact you.

When writing the letters, make sure you do everything you can to make them look unique (as opposed to mass-produced or mass-marketed). Do not use one hundred copies with the same salutation, like "Dear Homeowner." If you do not go through the trouble of personalizing the letters, you are just wasting your time. It may seem like you are doing a lot to contact homeowners, but in the end, unless you personalize the letters, all you are doing is busywork.

Likewise, do not use labels on the envelopes. Hand-address the envelopes yourself (or pay somebody else to do it for you once you start making money flipping properties). It will be very tempting and easy to create labels using your form letter feature as opposed to writing the addresses by hand — after all, you have already gone through the trouble of creating your data source. But think about what will happen — and you know this to be true because you do it yourself. If you use labels to address your envelopes, you significantly reduce the chances that the homeowner will actually read the letter. If you consider your own behavior with mail you receive, you will think twice about using labels.

You can use your form letter features to send out e-mails as part of your e-mail campaign. Regardless of how you use the form letter features, maintain a schedule. Use a spreadsheet or even a notebook to record when you will send out your letters. To make the best use of your time, set aside an hour or so once a week to print out your letters. Also, instead of printing off a letter every day, go ahead and optimize your work time so that you reduce your set-up time.

E-MAIL CAMPAIGN

At first, an e-mail campaign might seem off-target; after all, you are dealing with a specific geographical location. You never know, however, how somebody might learn about your services. An e-mail campaign might be appropriate if somebody opted in on either your Web site or another site to which you pay to receive opt-in e-mail addresses; you would only want to buy a list of homeowners if they fit your criteria of being interested in avoiding foreclosure in your geographical area. In this case, an e-mail campaign is similar to your direct mail campaign except that instead of possessing their mailing addresses, all you have are e-mail addresses.

Why do e-mail campaigns work? E-mail campaigns require low effort; you can set them up with the Mail Merge feature. E-mail campaigns, just like your direct mail campaigns, focus on a set of interested people. You are not spamming people through the Internet; you are contacting people who have expressed an interest in fighting foreclosure. If what you send them is compelling enough, they should let you know.

Set up a schedule and send out a series of three to five e-mails to the homeowner introducing yourself and telling them what you can do to help. You will need to work off of an e-mail list of people in your geographical area so you can visit the properties in order to actually work the pre-foreclosure acquisition. Do not send out all the e-mails in one week; space your e-mails to go out every week or every other week.

When you construct your e-mails, do not forget to take into account recent anti-spam laws. Sending e-mails to your contacts must follow legal standards; while you can write what you want, you must always follow these guidelines:

- Always identify yourself.

- Do not use false or misleading subject lines.

- Tell the recipient how you got his or her e-mail address.

- Indicate your e-mails are advertisements.

- Include a valid mailing address for your business.

- Give the recipient an opt-out method — and make sure you honor this when people say they do not want to receive your correspondence.

If you have any more questions about what you can and cannot do legally via e-mail, head over to the FTC's Web site and read more about the CAN-SPAM LAW (**www.ftc.gov/bcp/conline /pubs/buspubs/canspam.htm**). Running afoul of this law could cost you up to $11,000 each violation!

Do not forget to use the AIDA formula to build your e-mail letters. You do not have to try to get everything across in just one e-mail. Take your time building up a relationship with your e-mail recipient; with each e-mail, share a little bit more. Share something personal — but not too personal — and maybe something in light of the weather or the season, if you can tie it in.

The tricky part about these e-mails is that you want to give just enough information to come across as helpful, but you do not want to give too much. In other words, you do not want to give so much helpful information that the recipients decide they know enough to fight the foreclosure on their own without you. One way you can do this is by talking around topics without actually walking the recipient through a process. For example, you might mention that there are ways to delay a foreclosure. That is enough information. Do not list the different ways to do it or provide any details further than that. You want the recipient to contact you for more information.

Keep asking the recipient to commit to your services. This might seem awkward to you at first. The recipient, however, understands you are "helping" them within a professional relationship. They already know there must be something in this for you, otherwise why would you persist in contacting them? So go ahead and spell out what you want them to do. To visit your Web site, contact you directly by phone, send you an e-mail; whichever way you want, make sure you ask the recipient to go ahead and contact you.

You might think an e-mail campaign sounds like a lot of bother. The truth is, you will find it about as time-consuming as your direct mail campaign. The good thing about it is once you have set up effective letters, your campaign is virtually free to do (since you do not have to pay anything to actually send your e-mails).

Finding Homeowners

The funny thing about homeowners whose homes are about to foreclose is that they oftentimes are not home! It can be hard to find people who are having financial difficulty. You may have the property address only to find that the homeowner is not living there anymore. While this might be a dead-end for most investors, with a little research, you might be able to break through this impasse and make first contact!

The following online search sites might help you:

- White Pages (**www.whitepages.com**) is a free service you can use.

- Anywho.com (**www.anywho.com**) is from AT&T's directory listings but only includes published listings.

- Yahoo (**http://people.yahoo.com**) has a good people search you can access for free.

- PrivateEye (**www.privateeye.com**) offers a service for a fee. You can access its people-finder search engine for $39.95 a month or $14.95 for a 24-hour period.

- KnowX.com (**www.knowx.com**) works two ways in terms of pricing. You can pay $2.95 per person search or you could subscribe monthly ($29.95 a month with no registration or activation fees). A day pass is $19.95, but for $10 more, you get a whole month in which you can try to find homeowners online.

- Intelius.com (**http://find.intelius.com/search-name .php?searchform=name**) does not offer a monthly subscription service. Instead, its reports are $7.95 per person search.

When you are first starting out and have not yet flipped your first property, forget about paying to find homeowners who are not living at the properties facing foreclosure. Simply update your records and, if you cannot find any updated addresses for them, move on. You can work with this type of homeowner later when you start making money.

Alternatively, you could try a public source for addresses that might dig up an absentee homeowner. Other sources for finding people no longer residing at the home but are listed on the property title might be:

- City and county business licenses

- City and county jail records

- City and county public library patron records

- County voter registration records

- Federal prison records

- Social Security Administration Death Index

- State bar association memberships

- State driving records

- State fishing records

- State hunting records

- State prison records

- State professional licenses

- State vital statistics records

You have many different ways to find absentee homeowners. While playing detective might pull up a few "missing" homeowners, make sure you keep your day full with your core activities. Save digging up missing people for your rainy days. As long as you have valid contact addresses for other homeowners, work those properties first.

Tips for Dealing with Homeowners

Dealing with homeowners is really the be-all and end-all to your success. Of course, you have to understand the foreclosure laws in your state and real estate investing in general. But really, to close on a house facing foreclosure, you must deal with the homeowner effectively. In this section, we will share some tips for how to deal with homeowners. After you are in the business for a while, you will develop your own sense for what to say or do when talking to homeowners facing foreclosure.

USE RESTRAINT AND CAUTION WHEN DEALING WITH HOMEOWNERS

You are dealing with stressed-out people who are at their low point financially. They will be crying on the phone with you, sometimes even begging you to help them. Or they may be angry with everybody and see you as a variation of the ambulance chaser.

Do not give homeowners facing foreclosure any money, not even a payday loan. Ever. Okay, if you want to make copies for them and it helps you close on the deal any sooner, go ahead. But limit your help to actions that will bring you one step closer to possessing the title to the property.

Do not get emotionally involved. This can be a hard constraint for new real estate investors to operate in. You may find yourself more comfortable dealing with homeowners if you take on a friendly stance. But being too friendly will backfire on you. You will find yourself drained emotionally and may suffer a lapse of judgment or even lose your "killer instinct" in doing what you need to do to close the deal. Lack of planning or poor judgment does not make the homeowner's emergency yours. Even if you did want to help them, you probably could not. Anything you do at this point would just be a drop in the bucket.

Remember your goals while you work pre-foreclosure properties. You are looking for a property with great potential for you to buy below market price and then turn around to sell at a profit. You can buy the property because you have a good credit rating and you have the cash or credit to invest in the property. You can help the homeowner by buying the property and taking it off of their hands, thereby preventing an inevitable foreclosure. This is the only way you can help the homeowner and still make this relationship work for you.

Do Not Stop After One Contact

Just because the homeowners do not agree to sell you the house the first time you contact them does not mean they will not come around. Their reality can change on a daily basis, so persistence pays off. Just do not become a nuisance. The homeowners will go through their own stages of acceptance as they go through whatever options they have available. Slowly, they will begin to realize that foreclosure is inevitable.

Set up a mailing campaign or use a schedule to either make quick phone calls or drop by in person on a weekly basis. Of course, if the homeowners threaten you or tell you to stop coming by, please honor their wishes. This is more for your safety than anything else. Besides, you should spend your time and energy on more promising properties.

Always follow through when contacting a homeowner. You may want to save your personal trips for properties that really get you excited and leave the rest of the properties for phone calls. At the same time, a well-scripted set of letters sent by mail can help to get the homeowner thinking of you as a possible solution. As serious as foreclosure is, many homeowners will freeze like deer in the headlights of a speeding car. They may not understand what their choices are, or they may be inundated with too many choices. Your job will be to develop "top of mind" presence within their brains. When or if the homeowners wake up and decide they better try to sell their property before foreclosure, you want them to be thinking about your name. The only way you will be able to do this is with multiple contacts. This is how you will beat out any competing investors who are looking for the same piece of pie.

HOW HOMEOWNERS WILL TRY TO STOP FORECLOSURES

Of course, the purpose of this book is to help you build wealth by investing in pre-foreclosure properties. Your role in the pre-foreclosure situation would be to "help" out a property owner only by buying the property before it forecloses. You do not really want to help homeowners to the point that you would be putting yourself out of business. However, you will benefit if you understand the different ways (other than selling the property) homeowners will try to stall or stop a foreclosure from happening. In essence, you need to understand what the homeowner is up to. This is not only so you can speak the language, but also so you can better gauge the chances that they will succeed in their actions. You want to limit your time and energy investments if it looks like the homeowner has a strong chance to beat the bank's foreclosure attempts.

The most common ways to beat a foreclosure are filing for bankruptcy (either by Chapter 7 or Chapter 13), giving a deed in lieu of foreclosure, refinancing the current loan, negotiating a new payment plan on the current mortgage, getting a forbearance, having the loan reinstated, getting an emergency loan from the FHA or the DVA, using the Soldiers and Sailors Act when it applies, and contesting the foreclosure.

As you read and learn more about how the typical homeowner can beat the lender's attempts at foreclosure, you may come up with an ethical dilemma. How much do you keep to yourself and how much do you share with the homeowner? Do not offer any information unless it is asked for. But if the homeowner does ask, be free with the "what" in your answers but not in the how. For example, if the homeowner asks you if you know any way they could beat the foreclosure, you could volunteer a couple of ways that might make sense given the circumstances (perhaps the Soldier and Sailor Act or maybe by declaring bankruptcy). If pressed for more information, you should demur, saying you have never had to use such a technique yourself (probably true unless you yourself have faced a foreclosure and successfully beat it) and you have never really looked into since it is not worth your time to really know how to do it. You may even want to say that doing so would be a conflict of interest since, clearly, you are interested in buying the property because it is in its pre-foreclosure period.

Some foreclosure "gurus" advocate helping homeowners as much as possible, knowing or hoping all along that they will not succeed. When the homeowners decide to sell the property, they are most likely going to turn to you, "their friend," for help. This approach does not seem that ethical. "Helping" becomes problematic in maintaining a professional line between you and the homeowner. As a consequence, the homeowner could end up taking advantage of you, either by using your time or even by blaming you when things don't work in his or her favor.

Share that you know just enough to point the homeowner in the right direction. The homeowner needs to be a hundred percent responsible for fighting the foreclosure. Stay out of that fight and only be interested in buying the property while it is in pre-foreclosure.

File for Bankruptcy Either by Chapter 7 or Chapter 13

We first talked about bankruptcies in Chapter 4: How to Locate Pre-Foreclosure Properties within the section Bankruptcy Proceedings. As a review, Chapter 7 is a liquidation of previous debts, basically wiping the debt slate clean. Chapter 13 is a reorganization of the debt scheduled over a period of three to five years, during which the homeowner can pay off any debts currently owed without losing anything he or she owns. The sneaky thing about a Chapter 7 bankruptcy is that, depending on state law, the homeowner might be able to keep his or her home! Florida law protects the homeowner's right to keep the home. Virginia law allows the homeowner to keep some equity built into the house ($5,000 plus $500 per dependent, or $10,000 if both the husband and wife file for bankruptcy together). The lender can still sell the house, but the homeowner will get to keep a certain amount of the equity before the lender takes it all.

We have not talked about Chapter 11 bankruptcy because this type of filing is mostly for corporations. But if the homeowner owes more than $750,000 in secured debt or $250,000 in unsecured debt (too much debt to use a Chapter 13) or if the homeowner is self-employed, the person can opt to file for a Chapter 11 bankruptcy. (You probably also will not hear about Chapter 12 bankruptcies too much because they are for family farmers.)

Bankruptcies in general mean bad business for a foreclosure because, if the homeowner can get the courts to allow a bankruptcy filing, in most cases, the home equity will be protected in the arrangement. If the homeowner is successful in getting a Chapter 13, he or she wins an automatic "stay" that prevents the lender from selling the house. The homeowner will usually get a time period to pay back the lender whatever payments were missed to start the foreclosure process in the first place.

Because of new laws, most people (in theory) are supposed to find it harder to file a Chapter 7 bankruptcy than a Chapter 13. That is because of the Bankruptcy Abuse Prevention and Consumer Protection Act of 2005 that went into effect October 17, 2005. This set of laws mandated stricter regulations before allowing people to file for Chapter 7. One was the implementation of the "means test," which determines whether a homeowner is able to settle his or her debts. Basically, if a person makes more than the state's median salary, the person is prohibited from filing Chapter 7 and, therefore, has to file a Chapter 13. You want this because, in most cases, a person's home is not protected in a Chapter 13 bankruptcy if he or she cannot make good on the mortgage payments as part of the debt restructuring.

Keep tabs on property owners who are filing for bankruptcy. The property may slip off the radar of other real estate investors. Three months down the line when the courts decide not to allow the homeowner to file for a Chapter 7 bankruptcy, you want to be there to help "restructure" the debt.

Deed in Lieu of Foreclosure

Sometimes, homeowners think if they move and just mail the keys back to the lender everything will be settled. But the problem with this is, even if the homeowners give back the keys, they may still owe money beyond the current worth of the mortgage. In other words, the homeowner may not have enough equity in the house to offset what was owed on the mortgage. This can be especially true if housing values have plummeted in that area or if the house has environmental issues or other required fixes making it cost more than it is worth.

If the homeowners try to do a deed in lieu of foreclosure, unless they work out a special agreement with the bank, they lose all of their equity and they may forfeit any claims they had against the bank. Selling the house to you might make more sense since the homeowners may gain some of their equity back. The lender likes the deed in lieu of foreclosure because it saves them litigation costs.

REFINANCE THE LOAN

The homeowners may try to refinance their loan in an attempt to lower their monthly obligation on the mortgage. The truth is, it is extremely hard for a homeowner to get a legitimate refinanced loan while the property is in foreclosure. Many people have scams to take advantage of homeowners trying to do this. If the homeowners are trying to refinance their loan, they are probably still in denial of what serious trouble they are in.

NEGOTIATING A NEW PAYMENT PLAN

Negotiating a new payment plan on the current mortgage can help the homeowner stay in the house and maybe pay the bank something instead of having to deal with a foreclosure. It is not quite like refinancing in that the homeowner is not shopping for a new mortgage loan. But the lender can revisit the current mortgage loan agreement and work something out so the homeowner can make the payments and keep the house. The lender might lengthen the schedule (say, from the remaining 25 years back to 30 years again), reduce the interest rate, or roll the money due into the total again and re-amortize the loan amount. Mortgage modification, in this case, is always a good thing for the homeowner.

FORBEARANCE

Forbearance is different from negotiating a new payment plan in that it is a temporary fix. With forbearance, the lender will work with the homeowner to help him or her find a way to pay back what is owed. This only works if the lender believes the homeowner can eventually settle the debt. Common ways banks accept forbearance include reducing the amount of payments due in a year, accepting reduced payments, extending the grace period, and skipping a payment. Forbearance is usually good for a 12- to 18-month period.

In order to qualify for forbearance, the homeowner usually has to demonstrate financial difficulties, such as a sudden increase in living expenses or a sudden decrease in income, and the ability to eventually overcome them.

Applying for Public Assistance

Applying for public assistance is another way homeowners may try to stretch their current means as a way to continue to keep the house. Public assistance includes tax abatement and supplementary Social Security.

Reinstatement of the Loan

Reinstatement of the loan may be possible. If the homeowners can get a lump sum together (maybe by cashing out a retirement plan) to bring their mortgage payments up to date and pay all incurred fees, then the bank will probably listen.

Getting an Emergency Loan from FHA or VHA

Getting an emergency loan from the FHA or the VHA might help the homeowners, especially if they can demonstrate they are turning things around with their financial situation. To qualify for the FHA loan, the homeowner must be at least four months late with the mortgage payments but no more than 12 months.

Soldiers and Sailors Act

The Soldiers and Sailors Act may help members of the military against foreclosure. This law is now known as the Servicemembers Civil Relief Act, passed in December 2003 by

President George W. Bush. Although you may be showing your age if you admit this, some of you may know parts of this law as the Soldiers and Sailors Civil Relief Act of 1940.

Homeowners do not have to be in the military themselves to get relief from the act. The homeowner could be the spouse of a servicemember or even the parent of a servicemember to whom he or she had depended on for money to help pay the mortgage. Using this act, the homeowner could get the foreclosure stopped and, at the very least, arrange for a reduction in the interest rate. The Servicemembers Civil Relief Act provides a number of solutions to foreclosure, including forbearance and mortgage modification.

Contesting the Foreclosure

Contesting the foreclosure may win the homeowners some time against the foreclosure, but it rarely stops the process permanently. First of all, the homeowner will need to demonstrate that the foreclosure is illegal. Eventually, the court will side with the lender if the lender can prove that it is acting in accordance with state and federal laws regarding foreclosure.

What to Do with This Information

By knowing and understanding the most common ways homeowners will try to stop a foreclosure, you can avoid wasting time pursuing a pre-foreclosure property when the homeowner has a good chance of stopping the foreclosure process. You will also be able to demonstrate your understanding of the foreclosure process to the homeowners so, in the case that their actions do not successfully stop the foreclosure, they may still be impressed with your knowledge.

Some investors will pretend to help homeowners with some of these methods, knowing they will not work and that the homeowners will ultimately fail in their attempts to stall foreclosure. Do not follow through with any of these activities for the following reasons:

1) You might be successful in helping the homeowner bid against foreclosure—and you eventually lose your time and efforts.

2) You might lose your objectivity if you start to care what happens to the homeowners. Your goal will most likely not be that compatible with their goals.

3) The homeowners may figure out that you are not really trying to help them and your actions may turn on you.

4) Even if you successfully fool one set of homeowners, you may develop a reputation locally for being a "two-faced" fake who is not to be trusted. Do not chance it. Bad word-of-mouth is a killer to your reputation.

When the Homeowner Is Interested in Talking with You

The homeowner has contacted you and they want to talk business. Great! Now what do you discuss with them? To save yourself time, you should prepare a checklist of questions you want to ask the homeowner; now that you have made first contact, you need to first qualify the contact and then focus on gathering as much information as you need to help you decide for how much you can purchase the house, if at all.

In terms of qualifying the contact, before you get too excited, make sure the person who has contacted you is worth your time. Here is a list of questions you could use to qualify people who contact you:

- How did you hear about me?

- Where do you live?

- Has an auction been scheduled yet?

- How many months of payments have been missed so far?

- How much do you owe the bank?

- What are you trying to do with your property (are they thinking about going forward with foreclosure, fighting foreclosure, or selling the house)?

- Are you the legal owner of the property? Is the title in your name? What about the mortgage loan?

- Are you interested in selling your property to me to avoid foreclosure?

If the person on the phone cannot answer these questions the way you want, it does not mean you hang up on them. Explain to them what you do. Keep a script with notes handy to make sure you cover all your bases. You could write something up that basically explains what you do and why you do it. Your notes could look something like this:

- I invest in real estate.

- I focus on properties facing foreclosure because I find motivated sellers and like working in quick timelines.

- I am not a financial consultant or foreclosure consultant in the sense that you would pay for my services.

- I understand foreclosure law in [insert your county and/ or state].

- Do you have any questions about what my role would be in this situation?

Warning: Do not take anything the homeowner says at face value. They may honestly not know all the pertinent information you need, not realize how necessary it is for you to know the information, or they could be withholding information from you on purpose. You must do complete title searches on properties before you start talking numbers. You must also make sure you are talking to the right people—just because somebody is living at the house does not mean the person has the legal right to sell the property.

CASE STUDY

Beau Betts, an Accredited Buyer Representative, helps represent buyers who want to invest in pre-foreclosures in the greater Seattle area. Beau maintains a real estate blog at www.beaubetts.com/news. You can reach Beau at (425) 744-5317.

Use a direct mail campaign to contact homeowners facing foreclosure

As a Realtor, I have been involved with pre-foreclosures by helping motivated sellers find investors who are interested in purchasing their properties. I've had good luck by sending out direct mailings to homeowners who are facing pre-foreclosures. I got their information by searching for Notice of Trustee Sales. These notices are usually posted for public access via county Web sites.

It was my experience that homeowners who contacted me were not too concerned about their credit ratings, so using "fear of a bad credit score" wouldn't work at all with my clients. However, most of them did not want to sit through a foreclosure and were open ears to options they had to get out of the foreclosures.

I used the short sale method to close most of these properties since with the homeowners that contacted me, they did not have a lot, if any, equity in the property. If a homeowner has considerable equity in their property, they are not going to want to go with a short sale since the bank doesn't give them any of their equity back after clearing any indebtedness. In the case that a homeowner does have a lot of equity in their house, you're going to want to go another route other than a short sale.

It's been my experience that using a direct mail campaign is an effective way to find motivated homeowners looking to avoid foreclosures. In terms of numbers, I would get about 10 percent of calls based on the mailings. Out of those phones calls, I qualified about 50 percent of the properties that I wanted to get involved with. Out of those properties, I was able to match up investors with homeowners about 30 percent of the time.

CASE STUDY

D.C. Fowler has been a real estate investor for over 15 years specializing in the area of pre-foreclosure/short sale investing. He has bought and sold homes in Georgia, Florida, Louisiana, Texas, and Tennessee using the same short sale techniques that he teaches in his best selling course, *Making Money with Short Sales: The Complete Guide to Acquiring Property Pre-Foreclosure,* which is available by calling toll free 800-939-5211 or visiting www.shortsaledeals.com. Mr. Fowler and his team can be reached at info@shortsaledeals.com.

Make a Good First Impression

I want to talk about what to say when you first speak with a homeowner facing foreclosure. What I've discovered is that while you may think you'll come across more professional by broadcasting your company's name; in fact, doing this might work against you. Many investors just starting out will form a company or decide to "do business as" with a company name, thinking it will give them more credibility when talking to homeowners.

The problem that I've found is that when I used my company name to try to convince a homeowner that I knew what I was doing, it often shifted the focus away from what I wanted (which was to find out more information about the homeowner in order to qualify their situation) to getting grilled about my company. Now instead of me getting my questions answered, I would have to spend the next few minutes placating the homeowner about what my company does, what my role is, how we found out about them, etc.

You ever hear the phrase, "Less is more"? Nothing could be truer in your first dealings with a homeowner facing foreclosure. Instead of providing information to them that will allow them to use preset filters to decide who they won't do work with, stick with their situation at hand to keep them talking about their upcoming foreclosure.

Stick with a simple greeting like "Good Morning, John speaking. How can I help you?" When the homeowner asks what you do, don't write a book. A straightforward "I'm a private investor that focuses on obtaining properties before they go to foreclosure" is often the best response.

7

EVALUATING PRE-FORECLOSURE PROPERTIES FOR VALUE

After you have found properties facing foreclosure and you have made first contact with the homeowners, you need to begin evaluating the properties for their value. Only with a thorough investigation will you know how much you can purchase a property for and still make a profit when you sell it.

When you are thinking about what you would pay for the property, you basically need to work backwards from an estimated sale price down the road, minus your profit and minus your costs to buy the house. When you put together a number to buy the house, make sure you are not just thinking about what the homeowner wants to satisfy the mortgage loan, but also include any secondary liens or repair costs you would have to pay in order to resell the property.

DUE DILIGENCE ON THE TITLE

Most practical real estate research begins with a thorough title search. This is mostly because you cannot rely on what the homeowner tells you in terms of who owns the property but also because you need to know how "cloudy" the title is. We have all heard of cloudy skies and cloudy water, but what does a cloudy title mean? With a full title search, you will be looking for current owner information, purchase price and date history, the mortgage amount, a copy of the current deed, comparable sales, any environmental information as well as any liens, judgments, or lawsuits involving the property.

What do you want to find out from the title search? Best-case scenario would be that the title is "clear." Clear of what? Clear of any liens, judgments, taxes, marriage issues, or probate issues. If a title search brings up any of these issues, the title is said to be "cloudy." Just because a title is cloudy does not mean you drop it like a hot potato. You just must consider any secondary liens on the property and weigh them against your profit margin. A house might seem like a great buy until you discover the second mortgages and tax liens on the property.

Just because they happened to the homeowner does not mean they stay with the homeowner when you buy the house. The secondary liens are against the property; so if you buy the property, you are also assuming any secondary liens. (We will go over secondary liens in detail in the section Understanding Junior Debts.)

Basically, the first mortgage on the house is the primary voluntary lien on the property. When people do not get money the homeowner owes them, they can legally place liens against the property; these liens are called junior liens or secondary liens. Most of these liens stay on the property even when the property is sold and ownership is transferred. (We will talk more about how to deal with junior liens in a later section. Suffice it to say that after you add those costs to the sale price, you may not have much of a bargain anymore.)

To actually perform a title search, you need to review the county records for the area where the property resides. When looking online, you may come across title searches for $40 or less. You will come across property details, possible valuation analyses, and area comp values. While these types of title searches can be helpful, keep in mind that they are not full title searches. Watch out what you pay for; in this case, you are only going to get a warmed-up version of property records you could probably find very easily online yourself.

A full title search confirms whether this is a first mortgage foreclosure and who is on the title. Why? Because you must verify the person who you are dealing with has the legal right to sell you the house and that you are, in fact, working out the first mortgage for the house and not a second one. You do not want to spend any extra time working a deal only to find out that not all of the owners are in agreement about selling the house or that they do not want to sell it to you. Maybe the people contacting you do not even know what the homeowner is up to (like an estranged spouse, a parent on extended holiday, etc.).

You are probably expecting us to say that you should not pay anybody else to perform a title search for you until you have flipped your first property. With this work, we are going to deviate from our usual advice and tell you to go ahead and get a good, local title insurance/research company to help you. Unless you are an expert at this, it makes sense to pay somebody else who knows how to conduct title searches.

If you are just starting out, you could think you are performing a thorough title check only to find out after you have purchased the property that there were additional liens against the property. Guess what? Just like with traffic stops, ignorance is no defense. Just because you did not know about a junior debt when you worked your numbers does not wipe the slate clean for you. You will still owe those junior debts. So instead of going it alone, pay somebody else to do your first couple of title searches. Full title searches are not cheap; depending on how the title research company packages its services, expect to pay $100 to $350. Since they cost so much, make sure you qualify the property before you pay for a title search. In other words, make sure that by using a best-case scenario, you could still make money on the property. Otherwise, there is no sense in spending money on title research or home inspections.

Be careful who you do business with when looking for top-notch title searches. People who conduct title research are often called title examiners, abstractors, and title searchers. Ask around for reputable referrals. Most states will have state-level associations of land title searchers. The American Land Title Association (**www.alta.org**) offers a list of members that can be filtered by city and state or by county.

What Is the House Worth?

The first thing you will need to figure out is how much the house worth, as is. Only with a valid number can you start to figure out if the property is worth your efforts. We have all heard about home prices rising or falling. Different numbers are associated with a house's worth. For starters, there is the mortgage loan payout amount, which is how much the homeowner needs to pay to the lender to fulfill the loan obligation. Most homeowners hope their properties appreciate in value due to demand and so that, over time, their equity builds up as they pay on the principal of the mortgage loan. Equity is the difference between the fair market value of the house and what the homeowner still owes on the property (first mortgage and any secondary liens).

Figuring out the fair market value is not too hard. For a quick number, you can use the latest city or county tax assessment. Most states charge personal property tax via the homeowner's property. For example, Travis County in Texas, which includes the city of Austin, breaks down the real estate tax rate by city. In Austin, the 2005 tax rate was .443 per $100 valuation. So if a house were assessed at $350,000, the personal property tax would be $1,550.50 for that year. You can bet that in Austin, just like in every other town in the United States, the assessment process gives a lot of homeowners' axes to grind with their local appraisals. The assessment value of the house determines how much the homeowner will owe in personal property taxes based on a city or county government appraisal. We basically have a love-hate relationship with our home appraisals. We are unhappy that they are high come tax time but real happy with those values when it is time to sell. You must get comfortable understanding appraisals, and hopefully you will get good at doing them yourself. The average cost for a single-family home appraisal will run you about $200 to $500 a home if you pay somebody else to do it. But before you pay for an appraisal, use the latest tax assessment to help you determine if it is worth your money to move forward with the house. You may also want to try your hand at appraising the property yourself to see how close you come to what the appraiser gives you. Do not do this yourself until you build up your appraisal skills. This is detail-oriented work and really forms the basis of your number workings (that is, trying to figure out if you can make money with this property).

ESTIMATE CURRENT MARKET VALUE OF PROPERTY

Realtors and investors use three ways to estimate the current value of a property: the cost approach, the comparable sales approach, and the income approach (used mostly for commercial-use properties). The cost approach makes sense when you have a unique property or you do not have enough comparable properties to use the comparable sales approach. Most people then go with the comparable sales approach unless they are dealing with a rental property.

COST APPROACH

With the cost approach, you figure out how much it would cost to build a property at today's prices. Subtract depreciation and then add the lot's current value. The amount you depreciate is really a subject call—it could be anywhere from 10 percent all the way to 100 percent! You could also try to itemize the necessary repairs to bring the house up to specs and up to date. To get a replacement cost estimate, you could try this yourself or contact an independent insurance broker to get a replacement cost quote.

To calculate the replacement cost, you would need the following information:

- Age of house

- Construction type

- Current use

- Heating and cooling system

- Number of stories

- Square footage

- Street address

- Type of roof

You can also use a construction replacement estimate calculator at one of these Web sites:

- Building-Cost.net (**www.building-cost.net**) helps you estimate your construction replacement costs in about five minutes.

- NRMA Insurance (**www.nrma.com.au/pub/nrma/home /calculator/building/index.shtml**) also provides an online calculator.

Comparable Sales Approach

While the cost approach would give you an idea of how much it would cost to build a new house (if you had the property to begin with), the comparable sales approach takes a more pragmatic method to estimate how much the property in question is worth. With this approach, you look at recent sales in the neighborhood to get an idea of what the property would probably sell for.

To save time and to prevent you from costing yourself an arm and a leg with the cost method should you miscalculate, use the comparison method. It's faster and takes into account the "sexiness" of a particular neighborhood within a city or a county.

When using the comp method, use a tactic commonly used in research studies: Throw out out-liers. An out-lier is a subject whose scores must raise the perfect bell curve for all the other scores. Scientists do not know why you always seem to have out-liers in a study, but they are in there and the best thing to do is throw them out. Otherwise, they will mess up your statistics. For a test study, maybe one of the subjects was a genius or on a new memory-enhancing medication. Maybe the person had developed a photographic memory at a young age. You never know why, but as tempting as it is to include the subject to skew your results favorably, you know you must throw out the subject's scores so your study will more accurately depict what really happened to the majority of your subjects.

If you have three properties that all sold for $185,000 and one property that sold for $300,000 in the same neighborhood with the same square footage, amenities, etc., do yourself a favor and throw the $300,000 house out of your comps sales comparison. At least throw it out while you work your numbers on this end of the deal. If you decide the numbers look good and you successfully purchase the house, there is no reason you cannot dream about selling the property for $300,000 as long as you realistically planned to sell it for about $185,000. If you have done all your work, you should be able to find out why one property sold for more in the same neighborhood. If you cannot, do not spend too much time on it. The point is not to account for all the differences in the property prices but to come up with a good idea of how much the target property is worth right now. Hopefully it will be worth your while!

Visit these online sources for comparable sales data:

- DataQuick (**www.dataquick.com**)

- HomeGain (**www.homegain.com**)

- HomeRadar (**www.homeradar.com**)

- Real-Comp (**www.real-comp.com**)

- Realtor.com (**www.realtor.com**)

You may also find information on comparable sales by city or county. For example, in Fairfax County, Virginia, you can find both assessed values and sales values for properties (**http://icare.fairfaxcounty.gov/Search/GenericSearch .aspx?mode=ADDRESS**).

Add to and subtract from the price for positive and negative features of the property that you are interested in (for example, second floor added, newer roof, pool in the backyard, etc.). Here is what you need to run comparable sales on properties near your target property:

- Sale date

- Location

- Property age

- Property condition

- Living area square footage

- Number of rooms, bedrooms, bathrooms

- Other buildings on the property

- Outside living areas

- Amenities

- Yard size

Do not stretch the location thing too far or you will risk messing up your comp results. What is true about computer programs is true for any algorithm you use. Garbage in equals garbage out! Make sure you are not taking an "as the crow flies" approach to location to find comparable properties. You must find properties in the same neighborhood or in a neighborhood where the sale prices are generally the same.

Fundamentally, the value of the land a house sits on depends on its demand. How do you really quantifiably put a value on a piece of land? If you are looking at a highly desirable suburb of New York, for example, you could put the same exact house on a property there or somewhere in the Appalachian Mountains. The home in the New York suburb will cost ten times, maybe twenty times more! While the housing costs may go up due to labor costs, the real value will probably be in the land appraisal. The best way to come up with the land value is probably to use comparable sales.

You will need to be organized about comparing similar properties. Take the information you gather for comparable sales and enter it into a spreadsheet. You can use the following table as a good starting point. Make pricing adjustments to resolve differences between the evaluation property and comparables properties.

Figure 21: Worksheet for Comparable Sales

FEATURE	EVALUATION PROPERTY	COMP #1	COMP #2	COMP #3
Address				
Selling Price				
Sell Date				
Property Size				

FEATURE	EVALUATION PROPERTY	COMP #1	COMP #2	COMP #3
Living Space				
Total Rooms				
Bedrooms				
Baths				
Condition				
Age				
Basement				
Garage				
Porch/Patio				
Net Adjustment				
Value				
Remarks:				

Income Approach

Using the income approach to estimate a property's current market value makes sense if you are looking to rent out the property. To use the income approach, you consider how much rent you could charge for the property and convert that into a capital value amount. To do this, you have to know rent values for similar and nearby properties and use them to find a gross rental multiplier (GRM).

To find out what the house is worth, find out what nearby houses rent for and sold for. Divide the sale prices by the monthly rent to get to the GRM. GRM = Sale Price/Monthly Rent. In the following table, we calculate the GRM based on what the most recent sale price was for a property and how much monthly rent was being charged for that house while it was rented out. Getting the rent rates is not as easy as finding sales data for real estate. You will need to do some snooping around to find out what the rental rates are for houses nearby the target property.

Table 2: Example GRM Calculations

PROPERTY	SALE PRICE	MONTHLY RENT	GRM
204 Peach Street	$280,000	$1,500	187
100 Washington	$400,000	$3,000	133
3058 Burke Station	$300,000	$2,500	120

Take the GRM values and multiply them by the monthly rent amounts that you believe you could get for the target house to give you an idea of what the house if worth to you.

Say you have a property on 300 Burke Station that is very close in appearance and location to the houses above. You would then take that property and multiply the rental amounts you could get by the GRM to determine the house's worth.

Table 3: GRMs Used to Predict House Value

GRM	MONTHLY RENT	VALUE OF THE HOUSE
187	$1,000	$187,000
133	$1,000	$133,000
122	$1,000	$122,000

Those set of equations give you a ballpark range of $122,000 to $187,000 for the property. Using the income method only makes sense if you are going to use the real estate as rental property. Otherwise, use the cost approach or the comparable sales method.

Finding Real Estate Data

Depending on your state laws and how Internet savvy your local government is regarding real estate data, you may find this information fairly easily yourself.

Public Records

Most states require public disclosure of real estate sales information. You will be able to find recent sales information and any more recent tax-assessed value yourself. Most states record this information and provide this online. If your state/ county does not provide this online, you may still obtain this information in person or by phone. Even if your local government is not Web-enabled, it may provide computer access if you trudge on down to its real estate or County Clerk's office.

If you need a little help finding out where to go for property records, try the following sites:

- BRB Publications has a free resource center (**www .brbpub.com/pubrecsitesStates.asp**) that lists online state, county, and city real estate records sites with annotations.

- NETR Online is a real estate information and public relations research site offering a public record online directory (**www.netronline.com/public_records.htm**) serving as a portal to state and local real estate information.

You can also pay for this service to get a copy online from a third party, but really, a third party will not be able to provide you with much more than what you can dig up yourself (as long as you live in a state requiring public disclosure of real estate sales information). You may not get those great results if the company is using a computer program to come up with your comps without any human intervention.

PRIVATE RECORDS

Six states do not require public disclosure of real estate sales information (Indiana, Kansas, Mississippi, New Mexico, Utah, and Wyoming). For these states, the only way you will be able to get sale price information is through the principals or the real estate agents who actually worked the deal. Your best bet in this case might be to look at current sale prices to try to get a feeling for what houses are really going for in the area of your target property.

HOW TO FURTHER EVALUATE A PROPERTY'S FUTURE EARNING VALUE

Besides looking at recent sale prices to get an idea of what your target house is worth, you will want to mull over some additional information. Consider how much the property will appreciate if you are going to hold onto it. For example, is it a single-family home, a trailer house, or a condo? Traditionally, single-family homes appreciate more over time because of the land value. According to an article by MSN's Liz Pulliam Weston, *Bidding Strategies for First-Time Homebuyers* (**http://moneycentral.msn .com/content/Banking/Homebuyingguide/P81710.asp**), condos have increased in value about 36 percent from their assessments in 2002 to 2005 while single-family home values only increased about half of that! Will this trend continue? It is hard to say.

Also look into the neighborhood crime rate, demographics,

economics, environmental hazards, and new construction (both housing and road) that could impact the salability of the house. You may have a feeling that a neighborhood is on the upswing or on its way down. Take note of your gut feelings because, oftentimes, they do capture some truth about the property that you may not be able to qualify now but will show later.

Now that you have an idea of what the property is worth to you now, consider what you would really have to pay for it if you decide to try to buy the property while it is in pre-foreclosure.

Find Out What You Have to Pay if You Buy the House

Buying a property is never as straightforward as you would hope. Even if you do not get a new mortgage from a bank, the following closing costs may apply to your purchase of the property: brokers' fees, third-party fees, and the mortgage costs.

Brokers Fees

If, for whatever reason, the homeowner decides to go with a broker, you may end up paying fees for the broker's services. According to Bankrate.com researchers Karen Christie and Debbie Carrick, the average amount of broker's fees for a $180,000 home purchase was $839. Sometimes, homeowners believe brokers do things for them that they cannot do for themselves. Whenever possible, go with the homeowner who is more than happy to go "FSBO" than use a real estate agent. You are going to be using a lawyer so everything will be legal. You do not really need to kiss some of your hard-earned money away to a real estate agent whose hand-holding you do not need.

Third-Party Fees

Third-party expenses include appraisal, attorney, or settlement fees; credit report; flood certification; pest and other types of inspection; survey; postage; title insurance and title work. For many of these things, you will have to go through the motions to get the property properly insured. According to Bankrate. com researchers Karen Christie and Debbie Carrick, the average amount for third-party fees for a $180,000 loan was $1,910. Do not forget to include these costs when you figure out what you will have to pay out to acquire the property.

Mortgage Costs

Mortgage costs are any late payments still due as well as any fees the lender may impose on you for your deal. The mortgage costs are straightforward when compared to junior debts. You should also consider how you are going to finance the property and how much your mortgage payments will be. It might seem weird to think about it this way, but how much you will have to pay while you are working on selling the house takes away from the profit you make when you do flip the property.

Understanding Junior Debts

First off, there is nothing "junior" about these debts. Before a house is actually foreclosed, if you take on the mortgage or otherwise buy the house, you may be responsible for any junior liens or judgments.

A lien is a legal claim against the owner's property that is made to secure debt payment. House mortgages and deeds of trust are liens, but the homeowner's property can also be the subject of many more liens.

Voluntary liens include the first mortgage or deed of trust and second mortgages and home equity loans. These liens are also called "equitable" or "consensual" liens. Homeowners agree to voluntary liens; they are part of the mortgage agreement that accompanies the mortgage loan.

Statutory liens or non-consensual liens are liens placed against the property as a result of legal action by somebody to whom the homeowner owes money. These liens are not something to which the homeowner agreed but is allowed by law so that the lender is allowed some way to collect from a debtor.

It might seem weird to you that the lien is conveyed with the property and does not stay with the original homeowner. It would seem more natural that the lien would be associated with the homeowner as opposed to the property, especially when the property transfers ownership. But the lien holder does not care who owns the property now — they just want a way to get back what the homeowner owed them to begin with. Placing a lien against the property was the only legal way the lien holder thinks they would ever get back what is owed.

Liens are prioritized based on the type of lien and when it was recorded. Generally, liens are applied in terms of seniority. Some types of liens, however, will take priority over other liens (for example, federal tax liens usually trump most other liens). Any lien placed after another would only get its money after the first lien was satisfied with any equity built up in the house.

What is a junior lien? A junior lien, also called a subordinate or secondary lien, is a form of lien that has been placed on the property subsequent to the first mortgage or the deed of trust. This type of lien is considered "junior" to the primary first mortgage lien. Just about all liens are going to be secondary to the primary or senior mortgage lien. Lien priority is mostly set at the state level. You will find that property taxes or other types of assessment taxes can be given higher status than other liens, including the first mortgage lien. Check your state laws on the matter.

Tip: We will cover this later in more detail, but almost all second liens (except for IRS or other federal liens) are extinguished — totally wiped out — in a foreclosure to satisfy a primary lien. Any second lien holder will simply not get its money if the property is foreclosed. This is all the more reason lien holders should be open to negotiation if you are trying to buy the property before it becomes foreclosed (while the liens are still assumable by the new owner). This means they can look forward to getting a little something in exchange for negotiating the amount down for you. Otherwise, if you do not buy the property pre-foreclosure and the property goes to auction, junior lien holders will get nothing!

Common Types of Liens

In just about any case where a homeowner could owe money, you would find subsequent law supporting liens against the property. If the house is purchased at auction, many of these liens are extinguished. In most cases, however, laws are written to give the junior lien holders a redemption period in which they can try to "tender the sale price" and get their money back. Common types of junior liens include:

- **Property tax liens,** which are liens a local government will place on a property when the homeowner is in default of the property taxes. Property tax liens are a big deal in terms of seniority. They will sometimes (depending on state law) even trump the first mortgage lien. Check out your state law. If the tax lien is not paid within a two- to three-year period (depends on state law), the tax collector can initiate tax foreclosure on the property.

- **Construction liens**, which are liens anybody can file for work done on the property but has not been paid for. This includes engineers, surveyors, and architects as well as mechanics and contractors. The construction lien is another interesting junior lien because it ends up being not that junior! Construction liens can even be held senior over the first mortgage lien if they pre-date the mortgage lien. One thing you can verify is whether the person who filed the construction lien was actually a licensed contractor. Otherwise, their lien is illegal and cannot be upheld in court. Once the foreclosure process has begun, additional construction liens cannot be placed on the house. Smart contractors should do title searches before doing any work on a house to make sure that the house is not in pre-foreclosure.

- **Mechanics' liens** are another common descriptor for construction liens.

- **Federal tax liens/IRS liens** are tricky because federal tax liens are not extinguished at auction. The IRS usually will not talk turkey with you about cutting the lien amounts down. The IRS figures it will get its money eventually. To find a federal tax lien against the property, look for a Form 668, Notice of Federal Tax Lien under Internal Revenue Laws, to be filed with either the county or state records or even the U.S. district court in which the property's judicial property is located.

- **State inheritance tax liens** are liens against the estate of the recipient. Death taxes are often confusing. The federal government does not tax inheritances. The IRS will impose an estate tax on the deceased. This estate tax is taken out of the inheritance money before it is doled out. You need to leave a sizable amount of money before the IRS comes looking for its inheritance tax. The idea behind this originally was to prevent American families from leaving huge sums of money to their heirs and thereby creating an American caste of royalty. For 2006, 2007, and 2008, the cut-off amount is $2,000,000. Your total assets (including properties, monies, etc.) would have to total $2,000,000 before you are taxed the estate tax on what is over and beyond the exemption amount. The estate tax is separate from the deceased person's final income taxes. This rate ranges from 18 percent to a hefty 46 percent for 2006, depending on how much money is being taxed. The maximum rate only goes down to 45 percent for 2007, 2008, and 2009. If the deceased person did leave a sizable estate but did not plan for paying estate taxes, a federal lien for estate taxes could be filed against the property. In this case, if you are looking into a property that is in probate, make sure you look into any federal or state death tax liens. In addition to this, states can impose an inheritance tax on the recipients of inheritances (Indiana, Kentucky, Maryland, Nebraska, New Jersey, Oregon, Pennsylvania, and Tennessee). If you live in one of these states, make sure the real estate property does not have a state inheritance tax lien placed against the property.

- **Homeowners' association liens** are for those nasty homeowner association fees. It is tough enough that they will not let you add on to your house or build out that deck, but homeowner associations can actually place liens and eventually foreclose on a property to get their fees. In some states, you will find that about half of the homes are part of a homeowner association — so liens can be common.

- **Child support liens** are unfortunately much more prevalent than you would like to know. In the state of Wisconsin, for example, nearly $2 billion are currently owed in unpaid child support plus interest. That is a lot of liens! In Wisconsin, you can find these liens by researching the Child Support Lien Docket. Most other states will have a similar system.

- **Spousal support liens** may also be known as a marital support lien, depending on the language used by the state. If, during divorce proceedings, the spouse agreed to make spousal support payments but did not make them, the receiving spouse can place a lien on the ex-spouse's assets, including real estate property. This is different from a divorce lien that is more like a "voluntary" lien the spouse agrees to so they can stay in the house while the other spouse has the security to eventually get back any equity that is in the house. A divorce lien is set up like a second mortgage between the two ex-spouses.

- **Public defender liens** are liens that local, state, or federal governments can place on a property when the homeowner owes court costs. The thing about public defenders is that people are usually assigned to them when they are insolvent (that is, could not afford a private attorney even through the sale of the property). But if the defendant is found guilty in court or pleads guilty, the court could impose a public defender lien to try to recover the costs. So, unlike what you might have heard or understood, a public defender lien does not go back to the attorney but to the court for miscellaneous costs incurred during the preparation and trial.

- **Welfare liens** are liens that state and federal governments will put against the homeowner if they discover that the homeowner collected welfare payments to which they were not entitled.

- **Code enforcement liens** are placed by local code enforcement boards when the homeowner fails to pay fines for incompliance with local enforcement laws. These local enforcement laws can be nuisance activities including graffiti, domestic violence, and disorderly conduct or code violations for grass and weeds, trash and junk, etc. Other types of code violations include zone violations and parking violations.

- **Bail bond liens** are liens courts will place against the homeowner when the property was pledged in order to let a person facing criminal charges out on bail.

- **Corporate franchise tax liens** are liens placed by the state when a corporation fails to pay its franchise taxes. The liens will be placed against any real estate property within the state where the corporation is located.

- **Mortgage and deed of trust liens** verify that only one mortgage or deed of trust lien exists for the property. Otherwise, you will need to worry about second mortgages or equity loans secured with the property's equity.

- **Hospital liens** are liens hospitals can place against the homeowner's properties.

- **Judgments liens** are liens resulting from lawsuits awarding the plaintiff monetary damages. Judgment liens can result in a "writ of execution" whereby the property is auctioned off to pay the debt.

- **Municipal liens** are liens for services a city or county did for the homeowner that the homeowner did not pay for (water, sewage, trash services, for example).

After looking at all the different kinds of liens that can be applied to the property, you can see why a thorough title search is necessary. So go with a well-known title abstractor to help you see what "clouds" are raining over your property.

INSPECTION TIME

If you are satisfied with the title search and believe you can still make a good profit on the house, make sure you have the house inspected for damages or needed repairs. Get a professional inspection done if you are new to the business. A home inspection will run you $250 to $750, depending on the size of the house. If you have the time, accompany the home inspector during the inspection so you can observe the inspector and see for yourself the problems with the house. After you get really busy with your house flipping, you should have developed a good rapport with a home inspector whose judgment you trust hands down.

Before you even get into a physical inspection, make sure you have checked out the following problems:

- **Location in flood zone.** The Federal Emergency Management Association (FEMA) (**www.fema.gov**) signifies different flood zone designations, many of which require mandatory flood insurance. For more information, check out FEMA's Web page on flood hazard mapping (**www.fema.gov/plan/prevent/fhm/index.shtm**). Flood insurance will run on the average about $350 to $400 a year. But the insurance cost is not the problem. The problem is with prospective homeowners who have an issue with flood zones. If you have two properties you are looking to work with and one is in a flood zone and the other is not, focus on the property on "high land."

- **Environmental hazards** can be on the property itself, come from next door, or even stem from a source miles away. Environmental hazards include asbestos, radon, lead, hazardous wastes, groundwater contamination, mold, and formaldehyde. If there is no record of environmental hazards from previous home inspections, it does not mean the house is in the clear. Often, a regular home inspection will not pick up all of the environmental hazards, so you will have to do a little research on property in the area; rule out any environmental hazards before you spend any more time or money on the property. Frequently, the cleanup of these environmental hazards can be cost-prohibitive for a real estate investor to take on.

- **Code violations** could be for something as innocent as uncut grass but could also include overhanging limbs, problems or safety issues with the structure, proper fencing and management of backyard pools or spas, or even illegally built rooftop decks.

For most home buyers, a sound home inspection will give them an opportunity to "look in the horse's mouth" before committing to a sale price. Usually with backup documentation, the home buyer can go to the homeowner and negotiate the sale price down. This will probably not be the case in your situation, although you can try it. Depending on how much equity the homeowner has in the property, he or she might be willing to "wheel and deal" based on the inspection results, but there is a good chance the homeowner does not have any equity in the house—otherwise, he or she would fight harder to keep the house.

COSTLY REPAIRS TO AVOID

While you are a real estate investor, you are not trying to buy properties you will "invest" a lot of your own money or time into. We want properties that make sense to flip, not money holes nobody else would touch. To save the comedy for the movies, try to avoid purchasing properties with the following problems:

- **Termite infestation.** Termite specialists often say that houses either are infested with termites or they will be. According to a report by the University of Florida's Institute of Food and Agricultural Sciences (IFAS), termite damage and control costs exceed $500 million annually in Florida alone. According to Focused Extermination (**www .focusedxterm.com/termites.html**), a rodent and pest control company in Merriam, Kansas, the average cost to control an active termite infestation is $1,000 to $3,000.

- **Safety, fire, electrical hazards.**

- **Mold problems** can indicate moisture problems in the house. Too much mold on the premises may indicate structural problems. If the mold is just on the surface of the walls, then the average cleanup cost should be under $200. If, however, the mold is found within the walls, cleanup costs can go up into the thousands. Toxic mold is extremely dangerous to one's health.

- **Dry-rot damage** occurs when moisture-loving fungi have attacked wood on the property. Lumber that is dry-rotted will need to be replaced. Depending on the cause of the dry-rot, the property may have moisture problems and any new lumber may need to be chemical-treated.

- **Water and sewer line problems.**

- **Roof damage.** Roof repairs typically run $4 to $8 per foot. Replacing an entire roof (3,000 square feet) could run you $12,000!

- **Water damage/leaks** (especially in basements).

- **Cracking/sinking foundations** mean big repair bucks. Centex House Leveling & Foundation Repair (**www.centexhouseleveling.com/repairFAQ.html**), a repair company operating out of Waco, Texas, has stated that the average foundation repair costs $6,000 and can range anywhere from $1,250 to $40,000 on a single-family home built with a pier and beam or a slab foundation.

- **Faulty electrical wiring.**

Repair Costs

Depending on your time availability and skills, you may decide to remedy many of the repairs yourself to save money. Even if you do the repairs yourself, you should record the estimated costs to help you figure out the total cost of ownership. If you do not know how much the repairs will cost, you will need to get quotes from contractors to do the work. You can go online to get a general estimate of the repair from these sites:

- Housemaster.com (**www.housemaster.com**)

- Pillar to Post (**www.pillartopost.com/resources /repair_cost_estimates.cfm**)

Tips

General tips when considering repairs on a pre-foreclosure property:

- Let professionals deal with plumbing and electrical problems.

- Tackle any problem areas that will scare away buyers such as water in the basement, a leaking roof, or mold on the walls.

- Do not take the time and money to tackle expensive projects. Consider lowering the price and letting somebody else deal with the problem. Sell the property as is if you can still make a healthy profit from it.

Repairs and Improvements—Improving Your Bottom Line

Temper any eagerness you may have to make repairs on the house since you could end up spending money you will not get back in the sale of the house. You should, however, consider improvements to the house that will pay you back more than they will cost for you to do yourself or pay somebody else to do. Here is a list of easy and relatively cheap improvements you should think about:

- Cleaning the property (inside and out).

- New paint (go with a neutral color throughout).

- Adding shelves to closets.

- Washing the old carpet or bringing in new carpet (carpets can re-bloom considerably after a good steam cleaning).

- Any repair that brings in more natural light (this might involve cutting down trees or bushes on the outside that block too much of the natural sunlight coming in).

- Eliminating negative views or improve sound barriers by planting trees and shrubs.

Be careful you do not over-improve the property so that you price it outside of its immediate neighborhood.

When dealing with contractors doing your repair work, use the following tips:

- Get bids in writing. Get more than one bid for a job, always, even if you can only swing two.

- Do not pay your contactors the entire payment before

they finish a job. Hold a certain amount until the job is complete (including cleanup work).

- Include per-day penalties for scheduled work so you do not end up having to sit on properties too long. Be reasonable when working with contractors. You want to build a good rapport so they will want to finish your work for you as soon as they can. Everybody gets sick or has problems with their car once in a while, right?

Use this worksheet to help you tally up estimated costs to repair the property. Copy the section for each bedroom the property has.

Table 4: Worksheet to Help Determine Repair Costs for Property

PART OF PROPERTY	NOTES	ESTIMATED COST TO REPAIR
Exterior		
Back Door		
Back Stoop		
Back Storm Door		
Chimney		
Fascia		
Front Door		
Front Stoop		
Front Storm Door		
Garage Door		
Painting		
Patio		
Roof		
Screened Porch		
Screens		
Soffit		
Siding/Shingles		

PART OF PROPERTY	NOTES	ESTIMATED COST TO REPAIR
Steps		
Window		
Other		
Grounds		
Drainage		
Driveway		
Fencing/Gates		
Lawn		
Outside Lighting		
Pot Holes		
Sink Holes		
Streets		
Trash Pickup		
Tree Cleanup		
Other		
Interior (by each room)		
Carpeting		
Ceiling		
Doors		
Electrical Outlets		
Hardwood Floor		
Lighting		
Mold		
Moldings		
Paint/Wallpaper		
Walls		
Other		
Kitchen		

PART OF PROPERTY	NOTES	ESTIMATED COST TO REPAIR
Stove		
Dishwasher		
Cabinets		
Ceiling		
Ceramic Tile		
Countertops		
Doors		
Electrical Outlets		
Floor		
Lighting		
Mold		
Oven		
Paint		
Pantry		
Plumbing		
Refrigerator		
Sink		
Walls		
Windows		
Other		
Bedroom		
Floor		
Walls		
Closet Doors		
Other		
Bathroom		
Bathtub		
Ceiling		
Ceramic Tile		

PART OF PROPERTY	NOTES	ESTIMATED COST TO REPAIR
Doors		
Electrical Outlets		
Floor		
Lighting		
Linen Closet		
Mirrors		
Mold		
Paint		
Sink		
Toilet		
Vanity		
Ventilation		
Walls		
Windows		
Other		
Basement		
Floor		
Walls		
Other		
Attic		
Air Ducts		
Ceiling Joists		
Floor		
Insulation		
Lighting		
Mold		
Pests		
Roof Rafters		

PART OF PROPERTY	NOTES	ESTIMATED COST TO REPAIR
Termite Damage		
Ventilation		
Wiring		
Other		
Garage/Carport		
Air-Conditioning		
Ceiling		
Doors		
Fascia		
Floor		
Heat		
Lighting		
Mold		
Paint		
Roof		
Soffit (underside of overhang)		
Walls		
Windows		
Other		
Electrical Inspection		
Capacity		
Circuit Breakers		
Electrical Meter		
Electrical Outlets		
Lighting		
Riser		
Service Panel		
Wiring		
Other		

PART OF PROPERTY	NOTES	ESTIMATED COST TO REPAIR
Plumbing Inspection		
Drains and Sewer Lines		
Hot Water Heater		
Mold		
Plumbing Fixtures		
Septic System		
Shower		
Sinks		
Toilets		
Tub		
Water Pipes		
Water Pressure		
Water Supply		
Water Supply Lines		
Other		
Heating and A/C Inspection		
Central Heat and Air		
Condenser Unit		
Heat Pump		
Mold		
Natural Gas		
Oil Furnace		
Solar Panels		
Vents		
Window and Wall Units		
Other		
Total Repairs Required:		

People historically underestimate the amount of time or money that is involved with home repairs. Since every dollar more that you spend over what you estimated affects your profitability, you must do a good job with your repair estimations. You can do a couple of things to help prevent yourself from losing money overestimating repairs:

- Give yourself a "soft" landing. Instead of going with your estimated repairs straight out of the calculator, add 10 percent or 15 percent to the numbers before you record them. This gives you a little bit of breathing room for either overestimations or underestimations.

- As you repair the property or have somebody else do the work, keep detailed records of your costs. Keeping track of how much things costs compared to what you thought they would cost should help hone your repair-estimating skills.

Whatever you do, make sure you keep a daily record of costs incurred while you get the property ready for sale to make sure you do not start eating into your profit margin.

Consider the big picture when looking at pre-foreclosure properties for investment purposes. How much will it cost you and how much can you get for it down the road? Will the difference make a profit worth the trouble? We explore these questions next.

CASE STUDY

Elaine Zimmermann is a national book author and columnist and owner of www.ipreforeclosures.com

Which Type of Pre-Foreclosure Owners to Avoid

It is almost impossible to deal with homeowners who face foreclosure and are in the middle of a divorce or are drug or alcohol addicts. And sometimes the owners who are divorcing are also drug and alcohol addicts, which make the situation even more impossible.

Where there is a divorce, there are usually lawyers. The addition of lawyers means you are no longer negotiating with the homeowners but their attorneys. This never is a good situation.

Lawyers bill by the hour, not by how quickly they solve their clients' problems. The settling of the real estate assets becomes a billable issue which they have no incentive to resolve quickly. You will waste a lot of your time and will never arrive at a deal financially feasible for you.

The same holds true for homeowners who are drug or alcohol addicts. You are not dealing with a reasonable person in a jam, but an addict who will waste your time and sanity.

And because these people work hard at being manipulative, you will find yourself mistreated no matter how hard you work in these peoples' interest. The horror stories that have resulted from investors trying to work with addicts are so numerous that I have now made it a hard-and-fast rule to never attempt to purchase a pre-foreclosure from any of them, no matter how lucrative the deal appears to be.

8

Do the Math

You found the perfect property. It's in a great location, the homeowners have bent over backwards in their eagerness to sell the house before foreclosure, and the house looks great. You make an offer that the homeowners readily accept. After paying off the secondary liens and making your repair costs, you realize that you'll need a good price to make a profit on the house. As the house sits on the market for the next six months, your monthly costs of ownership start putting your numbers in the red. What went wrong?

You must do your math before you make an offer. You cannot simply take the homeowner's house price, add a profit margin, and aim for that sale price a few months later. You need to consider all of the costs you will have to pay out while you have the house plus what you hope to sell the house for. That will give you an idea of the maximum you should pay out for a pre-foreclosure property with the intent to sell it as soon as possible. In effect, you must work backwards from a conservative sale price six months down the road.

We talked about comping properties to get an idea of current market value, what second or junior liens may be on the property, and what repairs you should consider when looking at a property to buy in the previous chapter, Chapter 7: Evaluating Pre-Foreclosure Properties for Value. Getting valid, accurate, and complete data is important. After you get that information, you need to put it into a formula to see if the numbers work in your favor.

Costs

Costs include:

- Repairs

- Mortgage costs

- Closing costs

- Brokers' fees

- Liens on the property

- Eviction

- Cost of ownership

Mortgage costs can include any fees still owed to the bank in addition to the current monthly payments. Depending on how you pay for the property, there may be sizable closing costs associated with buying the property. Brokers' fees may play a part in your number crunching if you decide to use a broker to sell the property. If the homeowners do not leave the premises on their own, you may need to pay for a proper eviction.

Many first-time investors do not properly consider the cost of ownership as they usually have a mythical idea of selling the property before the dust settles. Even if you sit on the property for a month, you will need to factor the cost of ownership into your formula. We are talking about monthly mortgages if the investor does not buy the property outright plus any real estate taxes and maintenance fees that the investor may incur while owning the property.

While holding the house before you sell it, you should consider the following costs:

- Personal property tax for six months

- Insurance

- Utilities (oil, gas, electric, water)

Selling costs often include the following:

- Real estate agent's commission

- Legal charges

- Stamps on the deed

- Mortgage satisfaction preparation

- Title closer

Real estate taxes are levied by local cities and counties, although each state sets maximum percentages that can be levied. Real estate taxes are often expressed in "mills" (1/1000 of a dollar), a percentage point, or a dollar amount ($1 per $100 of property).

For example, in Rhode Island, the average annual real estate tax is $15.32 per $1,000 of personal real estate property. If a house is appraised at $200,000 there, the annual real estate tax would be $15.32 x $200 or $3,064. Taken out monthly from the mortgage payments, this would equate to $255. In Arkansas, state law mandates that counties can levy up to 21 mills of property tax and cities can levy up to 20 mills of property tax. In Arkansas, real estate taxes can be levied up to $.21 per $1,000 of personal real estate property. According to *Retirement Living* (**www.retirementliving.com/RLtaxes.html**), the states with the lowest property tax per capita include Arkansas, Alabama, Kentucky, New Mexico, and Oklahoma. The states with the highest property tax per capita include New Jersey, Connecticut, New York, and Rhode Island. This information was interpolated from 2002 census data.

COST WORKSHEET

To be consistent, use a worksheet to help you figure out what the costs are to own the property until you sell it. Use the following worksheet as an example:

Table 5: Worksheet to Determine Real Cost of House

COST	AMOUNT	NOTES
Purchase Price		
Amount to Cure Default		
Liens		
Legal Costs		
Necessary Repairs		
Eviction Cost		
Cost of Ownership		

COST	AMOUNT	NOTES
Total Cost		
Selling Costs		
Profit Margin		
Final Selling Price/Market Value		

As a rule of thumb, you should only stick with pre-foreclosure properties with a debt-to-value ratio of at least 80 percent. You do not want to buy a property with too much debt owed on it compared to its market value. This is an inverse way of looking at what your profit will be after your total costs for the house.

For example, if the house has a current market value of $150,000 but the total debt owed on the house (including the first and second mortgage as well as liens and legal costs) is $100,000, the debt-to-value ratio for the house is only 67 percent. That is good! If you add your repairs, holding, and selling costs, you should still have a healthy 15 percent profit margin for your hard work.

If you limit yourself to looking at pre-foreclosure properties with debt-to-value ratios of 75 percent or below, you should give yourself enough padding for a healthy profit when you turn around and sell the house. When working out how high of an offering price you can offer the homeowner, it may be easier if you work backwards:

COST	AMOUNT	NOTES
Final Selling Price Market Value	$350,000	Based on reasonable comps.
Profit Margin	$52,250	Based on a 15% profit margin. You may decide to go lower if you still make enough money.
Selling Costs	$21,000	
Cost of Ownership	$10,000	Based on six months of ownership.
Necessary Repairs	$15,000	
Amount to Cure Default	$5,000	
Liens	$5,000	
Legal Costs	$2,000	
Eviction Cost	$1,000	
Total Costs	$59,000	
Total Costs + Profit	$111,250	
Purchase Price	$238,500	This is the highest you could go and still make a decent profit on the property.

You should also be considering the "path of least resistance" in terms of how to prioritize the houses you go after. For example, if two houses are up for foreclosure, with one having a homeowner who's been moved because of work and has not been able to sell the house, and the second one has homeowners in the middle of a messy divorce who are not on speaking terms, which one should you choose? This might seem like an overly simple comparison, but the truth is that you will be up against decisions along this continuum the entire time you look at properties to qualify them. Get comfortable about dropping any qualms you may have on the house you could have worked. Instead, focus on the property that provides the most likely scenario for you to make the most money and with the least amount of work and time.

Do not be blinded by a house that presents itself as a really great opportunity for profit if it just requires too much work in terms of baby-sitting or hand-holding the homeowners. There might not be bigger fish in the sea, but they will be a whole heck of a lot easier to catch.

Also, even if the numbers look good enough to pursue, consider whether you can find a house that would be even better to pursue. When you start doing the math, you should start categorizing the potential wins for yourself. For example, if a house is worth a potential $25K profit, you could categorize it as an A+ house to pursue. What if, after you do the math, it looks like you would only net $5K? Is it worth going after? It might be.

As an example, say after all the costs and considering the real estate market that the house is in, you would only get $5K like in the example above. What is your hourly rate right now? You can either use what you get paid on your regular job or you could use another system in terms of targets and goals to figure out what you should be earning per house.

To look at the numbers, say you currently earn $50,000 on your regular day job. That will roughly equal $25 an hour, before taxes. It is not exact, but if you use the $XK/2K formula, you will get to an hourly rate much more quickly (meaning you can do this in your head) than if you were to try to find your real hourly rate. Plus, we are not covering all of your insurance and benefits, just your straight hourly rate; so if you could work overtime at your current job, you would earn this amount.

To figure out if a house is worth your effort, you must first keep track of how many hours you spend on the average to go from finding a house to selling it. This does not have to be fancy. You can write down your efforts in a notebook or use a spreadsheet. Record how much time you spend per activity to give you an idea of whether you should hire out some of the work.

Say you discover that you spend 20 hours a week for five weeks over three properties only to see one through — the other two you lost before you could buy them. Twenty hours x five weeks = 100 hours. 100 hours x $25 = $2,500. So it looks like, right now, it would be worth it for you to pursue the house that would net you a $5,000 profit. Your break-even point in this example is $2,500. Do not be overly optimistic in your cost estimates, or you will end up spending more time to earn less money.

Document how you spend your time on projects. When you first start out, it pays to do everything yourself because you have more time than money. But after you get the ball rolling, you may discover you spend too much time on certain tasks that you might be better off having somebody else do for you. In this case, continue to do the street work only if you have more time than money. Most people do not really have more time than money once they become fairly successful in real estate investing. Figure out how much of your time it would take to pursue a house and then give yourself a break-even point.

Even if you think you could live with a $5K profit, consider that you might want to put the house aside as a possible purchase; you do not want to tie up your investments in a property with such little profit when you could put your money and time in a house across town that will net you a $25K profit.

Put the "question mark" house on the back burner until you

have exhausted all of your other possibilities. You will probably run out of time before you can visit your troubled house, but there is just as good a chance that the property will still be in the foreclosure market.

Another way to look at what your profit margin should be is to use a percentage of the total house cost. Shoot for a minimum 15 percent profit margin to make up for the time and risk that you take on with any property. If you look at a property that you value at $180,000 after repairs, then your target profit margin should be $27,000.

Here is how to figure out the least amount you should spend on a property: Take the estimated value of the house after repairs based on either cost or comparable sales. Take that amount and subtract the following: repairs, overhead, and holding costs (10 percent); selling costs (6 percent); and profit (15 percent). After that, you will have the net balance that is the maximum amount you can offer and still make your profit. Do not forget to look at back mortgages and liens when considering what the net balance is that you can offer for a house.

Focus on houses that will return a good profit and ones that offer a solid-looking chance that you can buy them before foreclosure (with the owners being open to selling before foreclosure and the lenders being agreeable to you acquiring the property).

AVOID ANALYSIS PARALYSIS

Develop good judgment when deciding which houses to pursue in a fast-moving, competitive market. You want to give your all to properties that, if you buy them, will net you the highest profits in return.

Do not fall victim to analysis paralysis, where you hide between hours and hours of research but never make it to the next step of "working the deal." At some point, you have got to get up from behind the desk and make an offer. What is the worst that can happen? The homeowner can say no. In order to make a sale down the road, you must go out and, beyond actually contacting people about their properties, convince somebody to sell you the property at a price that makes sense for you.

You can analyze all you want, but eventually you will become a Monday-night quarterback as opposed to somebody actually playing on live TV on Sunday. Get out and "work the deal." Real estate investing is not for the faint of heart. If you do not have the courage to get out and talk to people, the thick skin to face rejection, or the level of comfort that nothing is guaranteed, you will never enjoy the vast wealth-making opportunities that investing in real estate can bring to you.

CASE STUDY

D.C. Fowler has been a real estate investor for over 15 years, specializing in the area of pre-foreclosure/short sale investing. He has bought and sold homes in Georgia, Florida, Louisiana, Texas, and Tennessee using the same short sale techniques that he teaches in his best-selling course, *Making Money with Short Sales: The Complete Guide to Acquiring Property Pre-Foreclosure,* which is available by calling toll-free 800-939-5211 or visiting www.shortsaledeals.com. Mr. Fowler and his team can be reached at info@shortsaledeals.com.

Prioritize Your Short Sales by Looking at Your Exit Strategies

Once you find a homeowner willing to do a short sale and their situation looks promising that the bank will go ahead with one, oftentimes it's easy to stumble over yourself in your excitement to close the deal.

But what I like to stress is that you must always go fast forward to selling the property (not literally, but in terms of planning), to what your exit strategy will be for that property to make sure you've found a property that will really work for you down the road.

Short sales are a lot of work. There's a lot of information that has to go into a short sale packet. Each lender has their requirements for what has to be included. Typically, documents include a hardship letter, purchase and sales contract, ECOR, settlement statement (HUD 1), net sheet, pay stubs, bank statements, and personal financial sheet (a monthly budget).

So it makes even more sense for you to work backwards from your exit strategy before you start on any of the short sale paperwork to make sure you even want to pursue a particular property. At the very least, use your exit strategies to help you prioritize your pre-foreclosure deals.

9

Swimming Through Pre-Foreclosure Negotiations

The property meets your approval. You did the numbers and decided that "YES! I want this property." This chapter deals with how you go about pre-foreclosure negotiations to make sure you get the property that you want.

Controlling the Pre-Foreclosure Process

At this point, we have already decided that the property is a good bet since you've performed due diligence on the property, worked out your comps, and did your math on what you need to buy the property for to sell it at a profit down the road.

Make sure you understand the timeline that you are working against with each pre-foreclosure property that you focus on. More often than not, you will find yourself running out of time on a really hot property. You have some ways to slow down the foreclosure process legally — but not frivolously — to give you more time to work the deal if you need it. Do not suggest to the homeowner to contest the foreclosure frivolously to forestall the process. If you are negotiating a short payoff sale, ask the lender to adjourn the sale for a couple of weeks to give you time to get a short payoff sale package approved. The borrower can also ask that the sale be adjourned, but you can go ahead and ask the bank first — it will not hurt. The lender is not limited to how many times it can adjourn the sale, so make sure you stay on the lender's good side to get its fullest cooperation while you work your pre-foreclosure deal. The lender may agree to adjourn the sale for a couple of weeks if you make a payment on the property.

If you run out of time and the bank refuses to grant any more adjournments, you may be able to get the courts to grant an adjournment to the sale as long as you get the owner to go with you and present your case well — that is, show how close you are to getting your pre-foreclosure deal finished, which would help the homeowner avoid a foreclosure.

Working with Homeowners

When working with homeowners, consider what state laws may be in effect that could impact your dealings with the homeowner, think twice about dealing with "problem" homeowners, and hone your negotiation skills with the homeowner.

Does your state have a Home Equity Sales Contract Statute? If it does, what impact does it have on you as a real estate investor? Generally speaking, these statutes are enacted to prevent buyers from taking unfair advantage of homeowners via high-pressure sales tactics. Many states have Home Equity Sales Contract Statutes giving homeowners a chance to back out of a purchase agreement. For example, the California Department of Consumer Affairs (**www.dca.ca.gov/legal/k-6.html**) reports that consumers have five days to cancel a house sale made during the pre-foreclosure period.

You should qualify the homeowners as well. Do not invest much time or energy into a property with a homeowner who is too difficult. Do not be so blinded by your own ambition to buy a house at pre-foreclosure that you agree to things or believe whatever the homeowner says. Homeowners will always do what they think is in their best interest. They may string you along thinking you will bail them out without ever giving you anything in exchange. If the homeowner is dealing with an ugly divorce (not that many divorces end amicably) or has substance abuse issues, you will invest a lot of extra time trying to close a deal on a property that may not be worth your efforts. Put "problem" homeowners on the bottom of your hot property list and spend your energy on another property first. You might be smiling to yourself at this point, wondering if one would not view all homeowners facing foreclosure as "problem" homeowners? Good point, but some will be easier to work with than others. Stick with the rational ones who have straightforward financial problems.

Another problem that can drain your resources is homeowners trying to declare bankruptcy or get a second mortgage to pay their first one (based on the equity in the house). Do not pursue properties whose owners are trying last-ditch efforts to fight foreclosure—efforts that don't include selling the property to you. While bankruptcy will definitely forestall foreclosure, it may not work in your favor when the owner does successfully file bankruptcy; the person's possessions, including the property you want, may be tied up in bankruptcy court or protected by bankruptcy laws.

If a property is really nice but the homeowner is pursuing

bankruptcy, you can keep the property at the bottom of your list and still keep in touch with the owner. If you want to keep track of pre-foreclosure properties whose owners decided to file for bankruptcy, you can go online to view their statuses at any time. Bankruptcy docket information is available online via the PACER (Public Access to Court Electronic Records) system (**http://pacer .psc.uscourts.gov**). You will need to register to gain access to the system. The site will charge you $.08 per page that is accessed. To learn more about bankruptcy law in general, check out these sites:

- Bankruptcy Action (**www.bankruptcyaction.com**)

- BankruptcyData (**www.bankruptcydata.com**)

- American Bankruptcy Institute (**www.abiworld.org**)

Avoid working with homeowners who have already listed their properties with a Realtor. The sellers will end up having to pay the Realtor a sales commission for nothing! Do not contact the seller in person, and do not have any dealings with the Realtor. Tell the sellers in a letter to contact you if they do not sell their house after their listing with the Realtor expires. You will not have to pay anything directly, but any amount of the sale price that the seller has to pay the broker could have been split between you and the sellers—hopefully in your favor.

When talking to the homeowners, back up your asking price by documenting any necessary repairs you may need to do. Be prepared to walk away if you cannot get the price you need in order to make your profit margin.

Make sure you do not give the seller any serious money in this time period. If you want to offer $50 or $100 as goodwill to keep the seller from dealing with other real estate investors, that is your choice; however, it's not necessary, and you will lose it if the homeowner gets cold feet or decides to go with somebody else.

Have the homeowner give you a written authorization allowing the bank to release the loan information to you; this way, you can discuss the loan directly with someone in the Loan Loss Mitigation Department instead of having to go exclusively through the homeowner.

Do not be sarcastic or use scare tactics to try to pressure the homeowner into selling the house to you. Most homeowners facing foreclosure will be like rats backed into a corner and will not appreciate getting extra pressure from you. If your tactics do work, they may only work for the short-term. In some states, the homeowner can rescind on the agreement with you.

Keep a professional distance from the homeowner. When all is said and done, you really are trying to benefit from another person's financial problems. If you want to rationalize your actions with the sanctimonious rhetoric of some real estate "gurus," go ahead, but the truth is, we are not "saving" homeowners or doing them any great favors. You cannot be a "friend" to the homeowner; a true friend would not buy somebody's house when the person's only alternative would be foreclosure. That does not mean you are the enemy in this case; you simply are not a friend. So keep your distance and try to remember everybody's role in this situation. Stay objective and do not get all buddy-buddy. The problem with getting buddy-buddy is that you lose your perspective on the situation.

Also try not to be rude or condescending. It can be hard at times since homeowners facing foreclosure can try your patience after a while. You just have to remember that their foreclosure is a combination of their behavior and their situation—some of which was beyond their control.

If the homeowners come back after telling you twice that they weren't interested, do not gloat. Even if you were going for a little light humor, most homeowners will not appreciate your comedic side. This is not a funny time for them. Try to be considerate without crossing over into the "friend" territory. Ask the homeowners what you can do to help them decide or close on the house. If you think the request is reasonable and falls within professional parameters (like making copies as opposed to picking up their grandmother), then go ahead and do it. You are just trying to help move things along.

How to Successfully Negotiate with Lenders

Why would lenders want to talk to you? Lenders do not want to assume the loan. They plan to get rid of the property at auction. If you can motivate them to let you assume the loan so they will receive their monthly mortgage payments again, that is all they want. They do not want to be in the business of owning property, and they do not want their money tied up in real estate.

In order to have a successful relationship with a lender, you must be professional and knowledgeable about what you are doing. The lender will not hold your hand or tell you what you need to do. In fact, lenders don't want to deal with novices at all, so make sure you have done your homework.

All banks have a special department or somebody in charge who deals with properties that the bank is trying to foreclose. Typically, this group is called the Lost Mitigation Department. They are also called:

- Collection Department

- Default Management Department

- Foreclosure Department

- Loan Resolution Department

- Loan Workout Department

- Nonperforming Assets Department

- Special Loans Department

Before the bank can talk with you, the homeowner usually must give the bank written permission to deal with you on the homeowner's behalf. You can ask for discounts on what is due, but do not get crazy. You want to help the homeowners solve their problems as well. Taking a hostile attitude with the lender will guarantee that you will not get the property at pre-foreclosure.

Also make sure you have the homeowner request an Estoppel Letter from the foreclosing lender so you have written proof of any information that the lender sends you regarding the mortgage.

Negotiating Successfully with Junior Lien Holders

If the title to a property is cloudy, you must work with junior lien holders to reduce the amount of money you would owe them if you buy the house. Why would junior lien holders want to talk with you? Because, for the most part—except for some federal liens like the ones the IRS will put on a property—most junior liens are extinguished when a house is foreclosed. If the house goes to auction, the junior lien holder loses everything.

Before you begin negotiations, confirm that you have identified all liens by having an exhaustive title search done on the property. Consider what the impact will be if you can reduce the liens by 50 percent and if the property would still be an attractive buy. If the collective amount of liens is too great, you will find that there won't be enough of a difference between what you can pay for the property and what you can sell it for. In this case, do not begin negotiating with the junior lien holders; walk away from the property and do not look back. If, however, after doing the math, you think that keeping 50 percent of the current liens would still work for you, you can do the following:

- Contest fraudulent liens. In most states, unlicensed contractors do not have the authority to place liens against the property. Also make sure that all liens were placed before the foreclosure process began. Otherwise, they probably cannot be upheld in court.

- Do not try to negotiate federal, state, or local government liens; they will not do business.

- You might get somewhere with the IRS if you write a hardship letter for the homeowner (you can probably get it down to 60 to 80 percent of the original liens). You must get the homeowner's authorization to contact the IRS on the matter.

- Negotiate purchase liens down. Get the homeowners' permission to contact the lien holder on their behalf. Use the tactic that, at least through you, the lien holder will get something; otherwise, you will not be interested in buying the property and the lien holder will end up with nothing.

- If the original lien holder is no longer in business, you may be able to file a lawsuit to "quiet title." Do not do this unless you have worked out the cost savings and find that a lawsuit saves you money over what the amount is should the subordinate lien holder show up again.

If you do not have extensive title search experience yourself, please save yourself the headaches of possibly missing something and have a professional group do it for you. Title searches will run you anywhere from $100 to $500, with $200 being the average fee.

All junior liens (except for local or federal taxes) will be wiped out after the foreclosure. So any liens put into place after the property was put into foreclosure will be eliminated. Any liens existing before the property was put into foreclosure will still be valid. Given this, you should be able to convince junior lien holders to discount the amount owed if it makes the property more attractive to you and helps you to buy the property before foreclosure.

When you talk to lien holders, tell them you have met the homeowner and you are negotiating a purchase of the property. If more than one lien exists on the property, let the lien holders know so they will not think you are trying to cheat them out of what the homeowner owes them but that, totaled up, the liens would not be doable. Start at 20 or 25 percent of the original lien amount and take it from there. Continue going up 10 percent higher each time until you reach an offer they accept. At any point, if this relationship does not look like it is working for you, you can walk away from the deal. Whatever you do, do not pay off any liens until the title to the property has been transferred to your name. Otherwise, you are just doing a "good deed" without actually getting the deed you want!

General Negotiating Tips

You do not want to begin negotiations until you have everything you need to make an educated offer for the property. Get all the information you need from the homeowner, a title search that includes a search on secondary liens, and an inspection on the house. You also need to do your comps so you have a good idea of what you could sell the property for down the road.

Keep your cards close to the table. Do not share or divulge information you do not need to share. For example, do not say, "Oh, I will not make my 15 percent profit margin with a price like that." Keep it vague: "That amount will not let me hit my target numbers for this property." The reason you want to do this is that most people on the other side will not be sympathetic to your needs and wants. If you want a 15 percent profit margin and share that information, the homeowners may decide that 10 percent or even 5 percent should be enough for you. Their reality is not the same as yours.

Ask questions. If the person responds no, do not let it go. Ask why or why not to find out the reasoning. You may be able to resolve issues with creative bargaining.

Ask what if in an attempt to bridge no responses to yes responses. Find out how far the other person's target numbers are from yours. You might be able to negotiate on points so that both you and the other person are happy with the deal.

Use the range technique to try to slide the money amount in the direction you want. This is a sales tactic that many high-visibility real estate "gurus" advocate. Use a subtle difference in the direction that you want from what the other person just said. For example, if the other person says $200,000, try to change it subtly from $200,000 to $190,000. See if you can continuously get away with this. You will know this is working if the other person does not flinch; you will know it's not working if the person braces and repeats, "No, I said $200,000."

See if you can work out a couple of different deal options for the seller to choose from. This tactic may increase the chances the seller will say yes to one of them. One option might be to offer less money but pay it up in a quicker time frame. Another option might be to pay more money but stretch the payments out over a six-month period. Offer doing a short sale if possible, but explain the limitations of this solution to the homeowner.

Before you agree to any numbers with the lien holders or bank, ask, "Well, can you do any better than that for me?" You never know what they might be willing to give into if you hold your ground for a few more seconds.

Do not offer a value amount first. Whoever goes first shows his or her cards. Wait and see if you can turn around a request for a hard number by asking what the other person's range is for the same item.

Use reverse psychology or at least open-ended questioning to see if the other person will open up about his or her decision-making process. Instead of trying to lead the other person by asking him or her to go with what you proposed, ask the question in a more open-ended way. For example, "Did you get a chance to think about my proposition? Do you want to go with it, or did you come across something better in the meantime?" By not pressuring the other person, you increase the chances that the person will come to you and reduce the chances that your tactics will push them away. People do not like feeling forced into a decision. They like to feel like they have come around to it on their own.

Do not come across as too needy, pushy, or highfalutin. At the same time, if the deal looks like it might be successful, do not ingratiate yourself with the sellers or lenders or come across as egotistical about the solution.

Remember to slow down and not be afraid of silence. It will give the other person time to consider what you are saying and also reflect on his or her own decision making. Going too fast, even when you know where you want to go with a conversation, can end up shutting down the other party due to feeling that he or she is not getting the chance to talk. You may also be folding your cards too soon just because you are not used to the sound of silence. Take a "wait and see" approach to find out what the other person is thinking.

Build rapport. Do not come across as fake friendly, but do not build a hostile relationship between you, the homeowners, or the lenders. Be respectful and polite in all dealings with all parties involved with the property. You do not want to get a reputation for being a jerk to work with.

Perfect Your Negotiation Skills

Lawyers often win not because they have the best information but because they put on the best show in court. Just enough emotion to sway the jury without so much melodrama that they have people rolling their eyes or feeling manipulated. Likewise, you must perfect your tone, attitude, and ability to negotiate. Read books on negotiation. Here are a few favorites:

- *Getting to Yes: Negotiating Agreement Without Giving In* by Roger Fisher, William L. Ury, and Bruce Patton. Published by Penguin Books in 1991. ISBN: 0140157352. $15

- *Getting Past No: Negotiating Your Way from Confrontation to Cooperation* by William Ury. Published by Bantam Books in 1993. ISBN: 0553371312. $17

- *Secrets of Power Negotiating* by Roger Dawson. Published by Career Press in 2000. ISBN: 1564144984. $15.99

Using a Purchase Agreement

Use a purchase agreement or a purchase contract to stipulate in simple language the terms of your agreement to buy the property from the current owners. Make sure you include a "subject to" clause to get you out should anything unplanned happen. Include a "pack up" date—a date the current owners and all their belongings need to vacate the premise. Do not let the current owners stay on past this date; you may end up having to pay to have them legally evicted. Make sure your purchase contract lists all primary and secondary liens and the amounts due. Get the current owners and all lien holders to agree to the purchase contract as well. If the purchase agreement involves the bank, make sure the bank is on board with the contract.

Do not use state real estate licensee forms, because they are tailored to the real estate broker and not to the seller or the buyer.

Get Legal Help

Make sure you have crossed all your t's and dotted all your i's legally. Do not get this far only to have things fall apart because you did not have everything legally ready.

Get a good attorney who deals with real estate and has

experience dealing with purchasing properties in foreclosure. If you cannot get a referral, you can find a good lawyer online:

- FindLaw (**http://lawyers.findlaw.com**) lets you browse by state, city, and by specialty (includes real estate as a specialty).

- Lawyers.com (**www.lawyers.com**) is another online directory that lets you find lawyers near you.

- Case Post (**www.casepost.com**) is a little different in that after you post a description of your needs, a lawyer will contact you.

10

COMING UP WITH THE MONEY

You have passed the hurdles of finding a property that is workable; now you will need to decide how you are going to buy the property. When working your way though the pre-foreclosure process, you will probably need to seriously consider how you should go about actually buying the property. With every property that you evaluate, you'll need to answer the following three questions:

- How to buy the property (that is, if you don't pay for the house outright with cash, what type of arrangement will you work out with the homeowner)?

- How much cash do you need to buy the property?

- How to come up with cash for the purchase (even if you are refinancing the house, you will need to come up with extra cash to maintain the house until you sell it as well as come up with money for repairs).

How to Buy the Property?

You have a number of options when buying a pre-foreclosure property. Let's look at popular options:

- **Assuming the mortgage.**

- **Wrap-around mortgage.**

- **Payoff of the loan.**

- **Getting a new mortgage.**

- "**Subject to**" is one of those topics that is simply not extinguishable. We've devoted a complete chapter to assuming mortgages with "subject to" agreements in Chapter 11: "Subject To" Deal.

- **Short payoff sale** is the golden ring in successfully negotiating a pre-foreclosure property sale. With a short payoff sale, you ethically convince the bank to let the homeowner off the hook on some part of the mortgage, thereby allowing you to buy the property at (hopefully) below market value. This topic is such a big one that we pull it out into its own chapter, Chapter 12: Short Payoff Sale.

What Kinds of Loans Can You Assume?

Although most mortgage agreements are written so that any change in ownership can "trigger" a "due on sale" clause, there are some mortgage agreements that are assumable:

- **Department of Veterans Affairs (VA) loans.** Military veterans apply for VA-guaranteed loans because they can then buy a house without having to put any money down. In order to qualify for a VA loan, the homeowner must have some proof of having served in the military. You can assume a Department of Veterans Affairs-guaranteed loan without being a military veteran yourself. The Department of Veterans Affairs, however, will not give the original veteran new eligibility beyond until the original mortgage has been paid off (even if it was assumed by somebody else) or if the first mortgage is transferred to another veteran (who is willing to use his or her own eligibility to guarantee the loan). If you refinance the mortgage to a conventional mortgage or if you sell the property to another veteran, you should avoid any problems with tying up the original homeowner's eligibility to get another VA-guaranteed loan.

- **Federal Housing Administration (FHA)-insured loans**. The Federal Housing Administration insures mortgage loans to help homeowners buy property without putting the traditional 20 percent down on the house. Getting qualified for an FHA-backed loan usually involves a rigorous credit check. Before 1986, FHA loans were assumable without any extra work. Now, in order for a new homeowner to assume an FHA-backed loan, he or she would also have to go through a rigorous credit check.

In theory, you cannot assume an FHA loan unless you will be an "owner-occupant" of the property. Rigid rules for proving you are an owner-occupant do not exist, but you will still need to be creditworthy.

Formally Assuming the Mortgage

For many mortgages, you cannot assume the mortgage without the bank's approval or notice. That does not mean you cannot assume the mortgage agreement ever but that you cannot do it without the bank's participation. Banks have the right to know with whom they are dealing. The bank went into a mortgage agreement with the original homeowner, not you. So why not tell the bank? Many investors fear the bank would act on the "due on sale" clause of the mortgage agreement that entitles the bank to request the entire amount due on the mortgage. Whether or not this is legal, ethical, or smart, is covered in Chapter 11: "Subject To" Deal.

Wrap-Around Mortgage

A wrap-around mortgage is like a second mortgage except that the new owner does not lose the interest rate that is already on the original mortgage. The seller keeps the original mortgage and the buyer now pays the seller a monthly payment that the seller uses to pay his or her own monthly mortgage payments to the bank.

Why would a buyer want a wrap-around mortgage? Because of three reasons:

1. Criteria from the bank for assuming the loan can be strict.

2. The bank will usually charge the new homeowner current interest rates (which should be higher for any of this to matter).

3. The bank will charge an assumption fee of $500 or more.

A wrap-around mortgage is not valid to use on a non-assumable mortgage, so watch out if the lender finds out what you are doing. The lender could decide to exercise the "due on sale" clause. For that reason alone, do not use the wrap-around mortgage to try to buy a property if the homeowners have a non-assumable mortgage. You would be better off finding another way to buy the property.

The other problem with wrap-around mortgages is that you must make sure the person you are paying the mortgage to is actually using this money to pay off his or her first mortgage. You can do this by setting up a joint account with the seller where both your and the seller's signatures are required for withdrawals and have an automatic deposit set up to pay off the first mortgage with monies you deposit into the account.

In some states, escrow companies are required by law to inform the original lender of what you are doing, so make sure you are not violating the original mortgage agreement between the lender and the first mortgage owner. Wrap-around mortgages are illegal in some states and are prohibited with clauses in some mortgages. So make sure you have all your paperwork done between you and the homeowner if you decide to use a wrap-around mortgage. The homeowner gets to sell the house and still get a little bit of monthly profit out of it. The real estate investor gets the property without any money down.

Pay Off the Loan

After you are successfully flipping your properties, you may want to orchestrate a complete payoff of the loan. The advantage to this process is that you will not have to go through any lengthy approval process with the bank. The downside is that you will tie up your money pretty quickly if you use this process every time you buy pre-foreclosure property.

If you cannot find a quick and easy way to secure financing and if you have the cash available, there is no reason why you should not use your own money to buy a property. It is an option and, as such, will be included here, but most people do not have that kind of liquidity or bank account to buy properties outright.

Get a New Mortgage

Ever notice how you never read about just going out and getting a new mortgage to finance your payment of a pre-foreclosure house? Getting a new mortgage just isn't sexy enough or interesting enough to make for good copy. But really, if you have decent credit, why not go this route? You will need to find a mortgage lender who can work fast with you; otherwise, you risk tying up your mortgage money in bureaucracy that will not work with your tight time frame.

How Much Money Do You Need?

How much money do you need for your new property? Besides the actual purchase price, you should consider money for repairs as well as ownership costs you'll incur until you sell the property. Use the numbers you crunched in Chapter 8: Do the Math, to help you decide how much money you need to secure to buy the property.

Where Can You Get the Money?

Where you get the money to finance your new investment depends partially on how much money you require. Options include downsizing your spending, personal investment funds, home equity lines of credit, credit cards, finance companies, conventional mortgage loans, hard money lenders, private investors, and wholesale flipping of properties to get more cash.

Downsizing

Depending on how much money you need, you may be able to squeeze it out of your current income, downsize your spending habits. Look at how you currently spend your money and decide if you should be saving more to invest more. Can you shave $300 to $500 off of your monthly expenditures? Is that enough to cover your mortgage payment until you sell the property? It may not be enough to pay for the house, but it may be enough for ownership costs and repairs.

Personal Investments Funds

Instead of going to complete strangers and asking them to back your venture, you could partner with your friends, family, or business acquaintances. The plus is that you will not have to worry about a credit check. The downside is that just asking can be tenuous on your relationships, and if you fail to provide a return on their investment or you end up in the hole, you could damage your personal relationships beyond repair.

Home Equity Lines of Credit (HELOC)

A home equity line of credit (HELOC) is a great thing to have in your tool belt when financing pre-foreclosure investments. A HELOC is like a second mortgage, although the first mortgage could already be paid off. Instead of a one-time loan, the HELOC is a secured line of credit that is good for a set period.

With a HELOC, you must have equity in a property to use it. You can normally only borrow up to 75 or 80 percent of the equity amount, and you lose whatever you put up for equity should you default on the HELOC payments.

The great thing about HELOCs is that you can use them more than once. You can actually borrow to the maximum of your HELOC, pay it back, and then borrow it all over again as many times as you need it for the period the HELOC is good for. An average payback period might be ten years. Using a HELOC can, therefore, be an easy way to finance your real estate investments, just as long as you pay back the HELOC from your profits when you turn around and sell a house.

What to consider when shopping for a HELOC:

- Interest rate

- Introductory period

- How much you can borrow (usually 75 to 85 percent of the equity in your house minus any you still owe on your first mortgage)

Shopping for a HELOC has never been easier with the advent of the Internet. Try the following sites to find a good HELOC:

- Bank Rate (**www.bankrate.com/brm/rate/loan_home.asp**)

- Price Line (**www.plmhomeequity.com**)

- E-LOAN (**https://www.eloan.com/helocapp/intro/equity ?user=ggl&sid=y5T8ep5ZYz9tiLJWrpwm33C1AM &mcode=gglkw3cs9&context=equity**)

Low-Interest Lines of Unsecured Credit

We will not recommend that you try to finance the entire house using your credit cards, but you could use them to finance repairs and ownership costs until you sell the property. Good sources online for credit cards include:

- E-LOAN (**https://www.eloan.com/s/show/creditcards /credit_cards?context=personalloans&linksrc=PLccsubnav &sid=QR2nwG9SqNG9X4rBsAEFJr-hAOg&user =&mcode=**)

- Bank Rate (**www.bankrate.com/brm/rate/cc_home.asp**)

- Love to Know's page on best credit card sites (**www.lovetoknow.com/top10/credit-cards.html**)

FINANCE COMPANIES

Another choice the real estate investor has is to get a regular loan, either secured with cash or equity or unsecured. You do not have to tell the finance companies that you want the loan to buy a house; or else, you may end up inviting the lender to do its own appraisal or even put a lien on the property for the amount it will lend you. Finance companies will not provide a rate as good as a mortgage company will, but if you flip the property relatively quickly, you will not need to worry about that. Look into the bank that you currently do your banking with, or check out the following companies that provide small loans:

- Beneficial (**https://www.beneficial.com/learn /HomeNewUser.jst**)

- CitiFinancial (**www.citifinancial.com**)

MORTGAGE COMPANIES

Mortgage companies can be a good source for financing instead of using a bank. Many mortgage companies are private companies, so there is not as much regulation or bureaucracy.

Applications are approved much more quickly than with government-regulated agencies.

Hard Money Lenders

For many investors new to real estate, hard money lending seems mythical or dangerous. In truth, hard money lending is much more common than one would realize. Hard money lending basically means a source of money that is usually available with fewer questions asked in exchange for a higher interest rate and usually a shorter time period for payoff.

Hard money financing is a good bet if the real estate investor does not want to work with banks, has bad credit, a poor work history, or is self-employed. Make sure you go with a legitimate one and not some kind of criminal loan shark or scam artist. Expect high interest rates and short periods. Most hard money loans have pay periods of six months to one year. Approval will be much easier than with any other kind of loan. Hard money loans are fairly common for properties in remote areas or for houses made out of unusual materials — two things that regular lenders will not touch with a ten-foot pole.

According to a recent article on Bankrate.com, hard money loans typically have interest rates in the range of 12 to 18 percent. They offer balloon payments that come due after one to two years, and the loan must be for a first mortgage. They will not cover second mortgages. The load ratio can be anywhere in the range of 50 to 70 percent, but also expect to shell out between four to eight points on the deal.

Hard money lenders can be private investors or they can be business entities in the business of lending money out at a high interest rate. Finding good hard money lenders can be difficult on your own—this is an area where having a mentor or good friends in the business can really make a difference. Ask around with settlement attorneys, title companies, insurance agents, accountants, and mortgage brokers.

PRIVATE INVESTORS

Private investors are different than hard money lenders in that private investors are all about security. They will lend you the money, but they will not like it if you lose it for them. In fact, you will have a hard time getting private investing again if you mess up even once! They are not as speculative as you would think, and they are not interested in a really high interest rate. You may want to hold off on getting private investments until you have done this for a while and have confidence in your own abilities as well as a fat portfolio that you can show potential private investors. Ask around with settlement attorneys, title companies, insurance agents, accountants, and mortgage brokers to find a private investor willing to work with you.

WHOLESALE FLIPPING

If you absolutely cannot come up with financing on your own, you may want to consider wholesale flipping to make money until you have enough for your own investments. With wholesale flipping, you arrange the whole deal, basically acting like a broker between the homeowner and an investor who has the money. You are acting like a super-charged-up bird dog in this case. You should be able to make at least a couple of thousand dollars on each deal. Do not waste your time arranging the deal without having a qualified buyer in place.

You are not doing anything illegal when you flip a property. Flipping simply means that you're buying and selling a property very quickly (basically flipping it from one homeowner to another). Just like in any real estate specialty, scam flipping occurs when the investor uses unethical practices to get the homeowner to sell his or her property way below market value or when an investor in cahoots with an appraiser sets the property's value too high and takes advantage of a unknowing home buyer. (For example, "Hey, buddy, I've got some swamp land I'd like to sell you down in Florida!") In the real estate market that we have now, you will usually have a hard time finding a homeowner who will sell his or her property for below market value. We focus on pre-foreclosure property because, in this case, we are dealing with a motivated seller who is facing extraordinary circumstances and who really needs to sell the property as soon as possible.

Wholesale flipping refers to you brokering deals between homeowners facing foreclosures and investors who have the money but not the time to broker their own deals. Bird dogs are on one end of the continuum of wholesale flipping. In this case, you serve as the middleman, the "dealer," in a pre-foreclosure situation.

While this is a reasonable way for you to make a little extra money, as soon as you have enough to invest on your own, do so. The rewards will be much more than the "tip" you get from wholesale flipping each property.

11

"SUBJECT TO" DEAL

Entire books could be written about acquiring real estate property with "subject to" agreements. The phrase "subject to" refers to the fact that the deed transfer is "subject to" transfer of current financing on the house. The investor is assuming the loan by taking the current mortgage over from the original homeowner along with the deed for the property.

Most mortgages are written so banks do not have to allow for a transfer on the mortgage and can act on the "due on sale" clause. The "due on sale" clause should actually be interpreted more liberally as a "due on transfer" clause because the bank can call the total amount due whenever the property is transferred (with or without a bona fide sale). Many banks will waive the "due on sale" clause if the new owner has a good credit history and makes good on the monthly mortgage payments.

Just because it is not kosher doesn't mean that assuming the mortgage "subject to" is not one of the bread and butters of pre-foreclosure investing. Why would an investor go for a "subject to" deal with a pre-foreclosure property? The same reasons as they would for a wrap-around mortgage:

- The bank's criteria for assuming the loan can be as strict as applying for a new loan outright.

- The bank will charge the new homeowner current interest rates. Interestingly enough, this may not even matter given how low current rates are.

- The bank can charge an assumption fee of $500 or more.

Are "subject to" agreements legal, ethical, or smart? First of all, contrary to what some real estate "gurus" will tell you, "subject to" agreements are not illegal in the slightest. What can happen is that the bank, when it discovers that the property has been transferred, may act on the "due on sale" clause, but most people would not want to have happen to their mortgage. The real estate investor will not go to jail just for assuming a "non-assumable" loan. Now if you try to cover up what you are doing, it is possible that you will be doing something illegal. John T. Reed has a fascinating Web page regarding the legality, ethics, and history of the "subject to" deal and the correlated "due on sale" clause on his Web site (**www.johntreed.com/dueonsale.html**).

In terms of ethics, there is nothing inherently unethical about going with a "subject to" agreement to purchase a property from the original homeowner. In theory, the bank should have the right to discern with whom they do business. The original mortgage agreement was with the original homeowner. So the bank has a right to be involved in the transfer of the property, not because of pure greed in terms of getting closing costs again, but because the bank should be afforded the opportunity to decide if it wants to enter into a mortgage agreement with the real estate investor. You have the right to try to get a property without going through the bank, but the bank has its right to remedy the situation.

In terms of whether a "subject to" deal is a smart move on the investor's part, it really depends on the situation. Buying the property "subject to" existing financing lets you purchase the property without having to obtain financing on your own. If you are going to do this, you will need to "take title" after reinstating the loan.

While some real estate "gurus" will tell you to keep things hush-hush, most investors will advise you to try to get the lender's permission. Oftentimes, you will not hear a peep back from the bank. If you do assume the original mortgage, you may be able to sell the house to be clear of the mortgage agreement before the bank decides if it should make good on the "due on sale" clause.

About the "Due on Sale" Clause

While some real estate "gurus" will tell you that the "due on sale" clause was originally written into the mortgage to remedy situations in the 1960s where people were transferring old mortgages left and right and taking advantage of old interest rates without giving banks their fair share, the truth goes back further than that. The "due on sale" clause simply gives banks the right to know with whom they are doing business. They want to be kept in the loop with a mortgage agreement, and they don't think that their mortgage agreements should be passed around without their say in the matter.

With the current trend in mortgage rates, the property you are interested in probably has an existing mortgage rate with a higher or very similar rate to what is available now. The bank really does not stand to lose much (if anything) if you were to assume the current mortgage. Instead of trying to evade or "pull one over" on the bank, go ahead and write them a letter that states you want to assume the mortgage. As long as you have a good credit history, you have a pretty good shot at being able to assume the mortgage without the bank calling in the "due on sale" clause of the original mortgage.

If the bank decides it wants you to pay the entire amount, you usually have 30 days to pay the balance before you get into any real trouble with the property (that is, the bank decides to foreclose the property on you). Make sure you get an attorney, preferably one specializing in foreclosures, to help you with the deal. If you can sell the property in the 30-day time period before the bank says the mortgage amount is due, you should stay out of trouble.

The only kinds of loans assumable without the lender's permission are FHA and DVA loans. These types of mortgage agreements do not have "due on sale" clauses written into them. However, they will require credit checks on the new mortgage holder.

Truthfully, this method of buying a pre-foreclosure house has real estate investors very divided. Some investors would rather go the "subject to" route and say nothing to the lenders, planning on flipping the property before ever facing any serious "due on sale" clause, while other investors claim being upfront with a lender is the best policy and nothing negative has ever come out of them telling the bank before. You may want to try either or both approaches when dealing with attractive-looking mortgages on a pre-foreclosure house until you figure out what you like to do. If you are short on cash or in a market you think will take longer than 30 days to either get the property ready to sell or to actually sell, you may want to go ahead and tell the lender first and see what happens. If, on the other hand, you have plenty of cash available should the bank exercise the "due on sale" clause or you are very confident you will be able to sell the house before you run into any legal problems with the bank, by all means, try buying the property "subject to."

Keeping the lender in the dark is not a criminal act, depending on the level that you stoop to. You will not go to jail if the lender finds out you assumed the current mortgage without its approval, as long as you did not break any laws in your eagerness to conceal the truth from the bank. The problem is the bank then has the right to exercise the "due on sale" clause. If you cannot pay off the mortgage in full at this time, you will end up facing foreclosure with the same property!

The real difference occurring with a "subject to" and assuming the loan is that with the "subject to," the real estate investor is just taking on the mortgage payments but they have done nothing to update the promissory note. If you formally assume the loan, you will also be updating paperwork to say you will be legally responsible for repayment of the loan via an updated promissory note.

SETTING UP A "SUBJECT TO" DEAL

To set up a "subject to" deal correctly, put together the following documents:

- Limited power of attorney.

- Letter from seller acknowledging that he or she sold the house to you but that the mortgage is not paid yet and, as such, may impact his or her home-buying ability in the future (the person may not be in any position to even think about buying another property for some time, so this may not be a big deal).

- Deed conveying property to you.

- Undated Payoff Request from the seller to an unnamed lender.

- Letter from seller to lender explaining that you will be "managing" the property from now on (only go this route if you plan to be secretive; otherwise, be upfront with the bank).

(This information is from Vena Jones-Cox (**www.regoddess.com**) as quoted in Dempsey and Beitler's *The Complete Idiot's Guide to Buying Foreclosures*.)

If you take over the mortgage without telling the lender, chances are somebody will notice when they get updated information from the insurance company that there has been a change with the homeowner information. You could try to not have the policy converted in your name, but then you will not have the coverage; the original homeowner will have it. You could try to add yourself as co-insured, but some insurance companies have a problem with this. Again, it is your call whether you are going to tell the bank at all, what you are going to tell the bank, and what you will end up doing if the bank exercises the "due on sale" clause.

Using Land Trusts

One way that real estate investors try to take on the "subject to" deal is with the land trust. By putting the property into a trust, the seller and investor hope to sidestep the "due on sale" clause because, by federal law, the lender cannot call the loan due because of the transfer of ownership. John Reed feels that there are loopholes in this line of thinking (**www.johntreed.com /dueonsale.html**).

WHAT IS IN IT FOR THE HOMEOWNER?

What is in it for the homeowner? If the homeowner is concerned about his or her credit score, he or she may not want a foreclosure on record. The homeowner may not want to pursue a bankruptcy to clear the house debt but are not ready or interested in trying to work with the bank to come up with a suitable payment plan. The homeowner may really just want to walk away from the whole mess (maybe there isn't enough equity built up in the house yet) but cannot because he or she still owes more on the house than it is worth. If you are dealing with a homeowner such as just described, then you have a good shot with a "subject to" deal.

PROBLEMS WITH THE "SUBJECT TO" DEAL

Besides the "due on sale" clause problem, you have got to consider the following problems you may encounter with a "subject to" deal:

- The original homeowner can still go into bankruptcy even if the deed is in your name. The lender still has its original lien against the house and, even if the loan is current, it can initiate a foreclosure.

- The homeowner may want you to pay off the mortgage as soon as possible so he or she can buy another car, house, etc. If you go with the "subject to" deal, try to make it a short-term solution for financing so you do not have past homeowners hounding you to free them from their obligations on paper.

- Probably the biggest problem you are going to have with the "subject to" deal is the ethics of it. A "subject to" deal is not illegal in and of itself, but it is really hard to say how lenders will react if they find out— "if" being the operative word. And depending on your judgment and what you actually do to try to conceal what you are doing from the lender, you could get yourself in trouble.

Negotiating the Forbearance

If you want to take on the existing financing, you need to make the lender happy in order to stop the foreclosure. One way to do this is to work out a forbearance agreement with the lender to take care of past-due amounts (payment in arrears). Work out the forbearance agreement on paper and have the lender sign it and acknowledge that it will stop the foreclosure proceedings. Otherwise, you do not have any guarantee that the house will not actually get auctioned off.

Bottom Line with Buying "Subject To"

Taking a pre-foreclosure property by buying it "subject to" will save you money if you can assume the loan. You still need to pay points and loan fees. If you obtain a new loan, you will definitely pay more in closing costs (amortization of the loan starts over), plus you will need to qualify.

If the original mortgage interest rate is higher than current rates, it is highly unlikely the lender would exercise the "due on sale" clause because it can make more money with the older mortgage than by making you take on a new one.

Advice is very polarized about whether you should tell the bank you are going to buy the property "subject to" or if you should try to present yourself as just a "friend" of the homeowner who is not actually "buying" the property.

If you are prepared to deal with the bank exercising its "due on sale" clause, then go ahead with a "subject to" deal. If the idea of having to fork over the entire mortgage amount in 30 days makes you squeamish, then you should probably find another way to finance the property.

12
Short Payoff Sale

If you have spent any time researching pre-foreclosure investing yourself, you are sure to have come across somebody's success story of a short payoff sale. A short payoff sale—the jackpot for the real estate investor—occurs when the lender agrees to accept less than what the homeowner owes and calls the mortgage payment even. That's right, this is that magical agreement where the lender will actually agree to cut its losses and let the homeowner off the hook. But getting the short payoff sale can be a lot of work and requires that the homeowner actually qualify for it. You also have to find a homeowner who will go for it. There are limitations to the short payoff sale from the homeowner's point of view, which we will soon cover.

Just because the mortgage debt is more than what the property is worth does not mean the house is not a prospect. If you can convince the lender to do a short payoff sale of the property, you may be in the end zone.

A short payoff sale can be hard to pull off, but this is what everybody involved in pre-foreclosures is so hyped up about because you can get such a good deal (you are getting the house for less than what it would cost the homeowner to reinstate the mortgage). You must put together much more paperwork to show that the home buyer qualifies to do a short payoff sale, but you will find them to be lucrative deals since you end up paying less than what the homeowner currently owes on the property.

How much of a short sale can you expect? Fannie Mae and Freddie Mac will accept 85 to 90 percent of the fair market value, and HUD will accept as low as 82 percent. You might be able to get less from a lender—it does not hurt to ask.

Reasons That Lenders Allow for Short Payoff Sales

You usually need to work with one of the following factors to get a short payoff deal:

- The homeowner's financial circumstances

- The property's condition

- The current local real estate market

The Homeowner's Financial Circumstances

You need to convince the bank that the homeowner passes its hardship test. One of the following will usually qualify the homeowner for a hardship test:

- The homeowner's spouse has just divorced him or her or has died.

- The homeowners or an immediate family member has a very serious illness affecting their financial situation.

- Active military duty.

- The homeowner has a disabling injury that is keeping him or her from making the amount of money made before.

- Local economic conditions beyond the homeowner's control makes employment seem impossible.

- The homeowner is in jail and cannot make enough money to keep the house.

- The homeowner has had to move because of work and has not been able to successfully rent or sell the property.

The Property's Condition

This is not as hard to do as you might think if the house legitimately requires a lot of repairs in order to be sellable. Put together a list of all the repairs you need, including quotes for some of the larger projects. Make sure you do not estimate what it would cost you to do the repairs but rather put down how much it would cost you to hire somebody else to do the repairs.

The Current Local Real Estate Market

You may have trouble with the current local real estate market until the real estate bubble really bursts. You may have some luck if you can find a number of comparable sales in the neighborhood that, for whatever reason, are lower than what the bank wants for the foreclosure property.

Limitations to the Short Sale Approval

As good as the short payoff sale sounds, there are always limitations that even out one's enthusiasm for it.

Cash

You almost always must have cash to do a short sale. You must have enough money to buy the whole property with a hundred percent cash. You cannot do a short payoff sale with another mortgage or by trying to assume the loan. In this case, the lender wants out, a hundred percent of the way, with the property.

Arm's-Length Transaction

Short sales cannot be made with family members or close friends. Lenders will use an arm's-length transaction as a guideline for whom they will allow to participate in a short sale. If the lender finds out otherwise, it will likely file a lawsuit to rescind the sale.

No Proceeds from Sales

Brakes! So far, we were speeding along with the other limitations. But this one should really get you to put your hand on your chin and say "Hmmmm!" Homeowners do not like short payoff sales when they find out they do not get any equity from the sale. Lenders will not give them any proceeds in a short sale.

Make this limitation work for you. Target homeowners who would not face to receive much equity in an auction anyway — if they have large second liens, did not put a lot of money down on the house, have not been in the house for long, etc. If the homeowner does not have any equity in the house yet, then they will not mind going the "short payoff sale" route.

Tax Consequences for the Property Owner

The debt you can cancel with the short payoff will be seen as ordinary earned income that the homeowner will have to pay the IRS (the only exception being if the person declares bankruptcy).

So the difference between what the homeowner owes the lender and what the lender accepts for the house will be seen as income. The bank may "forgive" the homeowner, but the IRS will see that difference as real money that should be taxed.

WHAT TO WATCH OUT FOR WITH A SHORT SALE

Just because the bank agrees to the short sale does not have any impact on any secondary liens on the property or what other property costs you may have (repairs, improvements) to get the house into selling condition. Work your negotiations with any secondary liens to make sure the property still works for you. Many homeowners will usually balk at a short sale when it is proposed early on in the pre-foreclosure period. But if they are facing getting evicted either way, they may go for a short payoff sale to avoid foreclosure and move on.

NOTES ON SHORT SALES LINGO

Different lending institutions refer to the short sale as:

- Pre-Foreclosure Sale (FHA)

- Compromise Sales (DVA)

WHY DO LENDERS ACCEPT SHORT SALES?

If doing a short payoff sale means that the lender loses up to 20 percent of the mortgage agreement that it backed the homeowner, why would a lender accept a short sale at all? Possible reasons include the following:

- They face losing more on the house at the auction or down the road with the property as an REO.

- They face the costs of going through a foreclosure on their end.

- They face the costs of owning the property as an REO until they have the opportunity to sell it.

- They face strict regulations by federal laws stipulating the ratio of bad loans they have on their books and how much cash they have to balance this. The less bad loans they have on their books, the less money they have to keep liquid as a consequence.

As long as the homeowner qualifies for a short sale, your main problem will not be getting the lender to go along, it will be to get the homeowner to get along — the homeowner faces receiving zero equity in the short payoff sale, and any difference in the sale between what the homeowner owed and what is paid will be seen as income by the IRS.

Negotiating with Lenders for the Short Sale

Tips on negotiating with lenders for the short sale include:

- Talk to the person in the Loss Mitigation Department who has the authority to make the decisions you need made. Find out right away if lender can accept a short sale. If not, who do you need to talk to?

- Do not waste your time with a loan-servicing company as an intermediary. Find out who the bank is and who in the bank you need to talk to about your short sale offer.

- Make it easy for the lender by doing all your homework. Make sure your short sale packet is complete, accurate, and well organized.

- If you work with someone who does not like to accept short sales on principal, gently remind the person of what he or she stands to lose by going forward with the foreclosure. You can even talk about bankruptcy if the homeowner has talked about this as a possible "end game" to his or her financial problems.

- How to make it real easy for the lenders to accept? Offer fast closings (under 30 days), cash only, and without any contingencies.

WHAT GOES IN A SHORT SALE PACKET?

You will need to check with each bank, but typically you will need to include the following in a short sale packet to submit to the lender as part of your negotiation for a short sale:

- Cover letter

- Purchase agreement (the seller/homeowner cannot make any money with a short sale)

- Low comps list

- List of repairs with quotes for bids

- Photos of problems with the house

- Seller's hardship letter

- Net sheet (HUD-1)

- Financial information on seller (W-2s, tax returns, etc.)

- Your offer to buy the property (set a limited time for acceptance and your justification for the offer)

If you are facing a property that you think could qualify for a short payoff sale, send some feelers to the home buyer to find out how open he or she may be to participating in a short payoff sale. It never hurts to look into and can always offer you a property that you may not have otherwise been able to buy and still make a profit on down the road.

CASE STUDY

Beau Betts, an Accredited Buyer Representative, helps represent buyers who want to invest in pre-foreclosures in the greater Seattle area. Beau maintains a real estate blog at www.beaubetts.com/news. You can reach Beau at (425) 744-5317.

Work with Banks When Pushing Through a Short Sale

As a realtor, I've had much success going the short sale route when the situation warrants it. When you have a homeowner without a lot of equity in the house, who has financial problems, oftentimes the first thing you should consider is setting up a short sale with their lender.

The thing to watch out about going the short sale route is that you still have to battle with the banks on what the house can sell for. They will bring in their own appraiser and try to mandate that the house not go for below market value. In that case, don't think you have to walk away with a lost deal. All you need to do is a little of your own work. Look for nearby comps that demonstrate the neighborhood isn't as hot as the bank would like to think. Also, properly document any necessary repairs that the house is facing along with price quotes for those repairs to show you know what you're talking about. If house prices fall, you can also use this to defend a lower selling price.

Overall, you must also be prepared to follow through as much as necessary with both the homeowners and the bank. You will need to call on a daily basis, sometimes a couple times a day to get answers and to push through the paperwork. Even when you are successfully pushing through a short sale packet, the foreclosure timeline still ticks. The bank doesn't put a foreclosure auction on hold just because you have a short sale packet in the works. So you must keep track of what the status is at all times and do what you need to do to push it forward.

Given the opportunity to buy the house at below-market value, short sales are a great way to approach homeowners facing foreclosure. Just be prepared to put a little "sweat equity" into your workings with the bank before you get the property.

CASE STUDY

D.C. Fowler has been a real estate investor for over 15 years specializing in the area of pre-foreclosure/short sale investing. He has bought and sold homes in Georgia, Florida, Louisiana, Texas, and Tennessee using the same short sale techniques that he teaches in his best-selling course, *Making Money with Short Sales: The Complete Guide to Acquiring Property Pre-Foreclosure,* which is available by calling toll-free 800-939-5211 or visiting www.shortsaledeals.com. Mr. Fowler and his team can be reached at info@shortsaledeals.com.

Short Sales and Wholesale Flipping

If you're just starting out in the business, you may find the idea of working pre-foreclosure deals and then flipping them over to another investor who has the cash or credit liquidity to pick up the house as a good way for you to get your experience and build up money so you can eventually begin investing in the properties yourself.

If you've studied pre-foreclosure investing at all, you know how lucrative the short sale deal can be for the investor since the bank is willing to extend "forgiveness" to the homeowner for a good chunk of what they owe the bank. Instead of selling the property at market prices, the bank may agree to cut their losses up to 20 percent or so.

The problem with short sales and wholesale flipping is that you've got to be careful with the paperwork when you put it together. You cannot "assign" a short sale. What that means is you cannot do the deal and then a week later transfer the property to another investor who's got the money to keep the property until they sell it.

You can successfully work short sales with investors but you must have your investor ready and available when you put the paperwork together. You need their name on the paperwork, not yours. Before you commit yourself to the work and paperwork involved with a short sale, make sure you have your investor ready if you aren't planning to keep the property yourself.

SELLING REAL ESTATE WITH LESS TIME AND EFFORT

Successful real estate investors who plan to sell a property rarely hold onto it for more than three or four months. Otherwise, they will spend money to keep the house but do not have tenants to help pay monthly payments while they search for a buyer. What is the key to their success? They sell properties fast.

In this chapter, we focus on how to sell your property fast and easy. Topics include whether to use a broker or not; marketing tools; how to prepare the property for a fast sale; and how to screen interested home buyers, build healthy competition, and keep them interested.

BROKER OR GO IT ALONE?

Going with a broker or selling on your own is a time-versus-money issue. If you are just beginning, it might make more sense to go it alone rather than give a cut of your profit to a real estate broker. If you do not have enough time, do not enjoy selling, or perhaps, you find that you can make more money brokering the pre-foreclosure deal than you can showing the property once you have bought it, then by all means, go with a broker.

Perform a cost-savings analysis to determine what makes the most sense. You do not need a broker since you will use an attorney to help you draw up everything correctly. If you go with a broker, make sure you sign for a short-term contract (three months or less) and do not sign anything that will not allow you to market your property yourself. Make sure the broker will list your property in the Multiple Listing Service (MLS). We should not overlook the effectiveness of the MLS. While the Internet has opened up the listings for viewing by the public, in order to list with the MLS, one must either be a Realtor or work through a Realtor. There is no actual one MLS. There are multiples that span the United States with individual Realtor® members.

PRICING THE PROPERTY

By now, the concept of pricing the property will not be new to you. You should already have a good idea from your cost pricing earlier when you decided whether to buy the property or not. Your comparable sales listing should fortify you with a good selling price. Now that you have completed any repairs or improvements, you may want to revisit the comps list. To refresh your memory on comps, go back to Chapter 7: Evaluating Pre-Foreclosure Properties for Value. The section titled Estimate Current Market Value of Property covers how to comp properties.

Marketing the Property

Chapter 5: Effective Marketing: Getting Homeowners and Home Buyers to Come to You, already covers many of the marketing tools you can use to let people know about your services and properties:

- Newspaper advertising

- Online advertising

- Business cards

- Magnetic car signs

- E-mail signatures

- Bandit signs

- Co-op mailing campaigns

- Fliers

- Local cable TV ads

- Web sites

In this section, we will talk about marketing tools that work just on the selling part, not to find homeowners:

- "House for Sale" sign

- Pictures

- Detailed descriptions

- Maps

- Voice mail ads

- Online property ads

"House for Sale" Sign

You know from personal experience that nothing will stop a house-hunter dead in his or her tracks than a good old-fashioned "House for Sale" sign. Make sure it says "By Appointment Only" and include your contact phone number. Keep the sign simple. Include fliers in a waterproof flier box with all the relevant information on the property.

Pictures

Buyers want to SEE, SEE, and SEE! How many times have you visited a Web site selling properties and only clicked on properties that included pictures but skipped the ones that did not have any pictures? This is because people want to know what they are getting into. Nobody likes blind dates! So take plenty of pictures of the property to put on your Web site and flyers.

Get a digital camera. The digital camera does not have to be expensive; you will not need to produce blow-ups of the interior and exterior shots.

Detailed Descriptions

People are rarely simply buying a roof to put over their heads. People hunt for homes looking for specific neighborhoods, zip codes, school zones, square footage, age of the house, fireplaces, bedrooms, bathrooms, fenced-in yard, recent remodeling, additions, and so on. Whatever features the house has that will help sell it, make sure you include as many as possible when you market the property. Tell people what they need to know in order to fall in love with that property before they ever see it in person.

Go online to find examples of property descriptions that work. Here is one that looks good:

- Audrie's Advice (**www.audrie.com**) offers a good example of an Internet property description (**http://sell-home411.com/pa/property.php?propid=9999**).

Maps

Make it easy for people to find your property. Use online mapping software to provide directions. Offer GPS coordinates for the "techy" buyers. Provide landmarks that people know. Include in your description "nice to know" spots (for example, use the Augusta Towncenter instead of the gas station on the corner) when including landmarks.

Online mapping software sites include:

- AOL provides a link (**www.mapquest.com**) to MapQuest so that users can click on the property description online and see a detailed map.

- Microsoft's MapPoint also provides information (**www.microsoft.com/mappoint/default.mspx**) on how you can link maps to your site.

Voice Mail Ads

For each property that you want to sell, have the advertisement list a voice mail number. In the message, describe the property, the benefits, and features it has, and how much the person needs to move in and pay on a monthly basis. Then let interested people leave their phone numbers for you to call back. This message helps save you time off the phone and helps to qualify persons interested in your property.

Advertise Properties Online

Besides basic newspaper-style advertising that you can do online, you can also hook up with various Web site portals that serve as online storefronts for people selling and buying real estate property. Look into these sites:

- For Sale by Owner (**www.forsalebyowner.com**) will charge you monthly. Different plans are available.

- Total Real Estate Solutions (**www.totalrealestatesolutions .com/property/list/signup.cfm**) gives you pricing options from monthly to yearly packages.

- NeoRealEstate (**www.neorealestate.com/pyproperty /userlogin.asp**) lets you post your property for free.

- Home for Salez (**http://usa.homesalez.com/index.htm**) offers online postings for $49.95 until the property is sold.

- Flat Fee MLS Listings (**www.flatfeemlslisting.com**) offers MLS coverage for most of the states (42) starting at $399.

- Save on MLS (**www.saveonmls.com/default.htm**) also offers MLS coverage starting at $399.

Preparing the Property

Make sure that the property is clean. The carpet should be recently cleaned and the walls washed. The kitchen should be sparkly clean.

Have absolutely no clutter. You may want a small hall table in the foyer where you keep additional flyers on the property. The house should be empty of any furniture, storage, clutter, etc.

Have the power and water turned on. Turn all the lights on, even in the middle of the day. Bring in additional lighting if the house does not have sufficient overhead lighting.

Do not forget smells. Make sure your property smells as clean as it looks. If you need to bring in a couple of wall plug-ins, go ahead.

Screen Interested Parties

It is always exciting when somebody contacts you about a property that you are trying to sell. Do not stumble over yourself in your haste to sell a property so much that you do not take the time to qualify interested home buyers.

You do not want to waste their time and especially your time. Ask plenty of questions during that first phone call, including:

- Do you own a house now?

- Have you been pre-approved for a loan?

- If not, what is your current debt-to-income ratio?

- How much money do you have to put down?

- How much of a monthly mortgage can you afford?

- What will your debt-to-income ratio be with this property?

- How soon are you looking to move in?

- Where do you live now?

You do not have to decide whether somebody is a good candidate to buy your house right then and there, but you may decide between which parties you will make special appointments to show them the house.

CREATE COMPETITION

Never show the property to just one person or family. Whenever possible, schedule appointments with several interested parties for the same time. This way, you will naturally create competition for your properties. Just tell the parties involved that you have a busy day or week and would not be able to fit everybody in if you scheduled one-on-ones with every interested party.

KEEP THEM TALKING

The more you can have buyers talk about their wants and needs, the better. If you find that you are talking more than the buyer, shut up! Ask them questions and get them talking. The more the buyer talks about the property, the more they become aligned with the property. After you point out the benefits, do not use any hard-pressure sales tactics on the buyers. Just remember what they tell you about their lives and their wants and needs for a new property.

You might want to try parroting what they say to make sure you understand their point of view. Buyers will love that. Keep crib notes if you have to in order to keep your prospective buyers straight.

Do not be afraid to ask them outright if they want to buy the house. If they hedge, find out what their reservations are. Hopefully you can resolve them. If not, be polite but send the prospective buyers on their way. You do not need to sell the house at a discount; you are waiting for the right opportunity to offload your new property at a sweet profit. In fact, you may need to consider the market climate when budgeting your ownership costs for the property. It may not be feasible for you to "flip" the property in a month or two. You may decide to keep the house for longer if it means getting the numbers you want. Work out various scenarios so that you have an exit strategy that will work for you no matter what.

CASE STUDY

Marc Rasmussen sells Sarasota real estate (www.hesarasotamls.com) and Bradenton real estate (www.realestate-bradenton.com). You can e-mail Marc at marc@thesarasotamls.com or call him at 866-308-6766.

Buying a House at Pre-Foreclosure in Sarasota, Florida

The last home I purchased that was in foreclosure was in September 2003. The red-hot real estate market in Sarasota, Florida, has made it tough to find motivated sellers the last few years. It has been very easy for homeowners in trouble to sell their home.

My method of finding people in foreclosure was to query my local official county records and look for people who have had a "Lis Pendens" filed against them by a bank or mortgage lender. I would then contact these people via letter to see if I could help them out.

I am a Realtor, so I could either buy the home directly from them or list the home and sell it. I would really leave it up to the homeowner and do what is best for them. Sometimes they do not want to deal with putting their house on the market and would rather just have me buy it. If they have been in foreclosure for awhile and the clock is ticking, sometimes it is best to have me or one of my investor clients to purchase the home. If the foreclosure process just started, they may decide for me to list the home because they will usually net more.

In September 2003, I received a call from one of my letters. The gentleman was in foreclosure and needed help. Since there are many investors going after people in foreclosure, I made sure to make an appointment with him immediately.

I met with the homeowner that day. We sat and discussed what happened to him and why he was in that situation. He had some financial troubles with his job. His house was in total disarray and needed a lot of work. He had started some projects around the house but they were never finished. Much of the dry wall in the home had been removed. The home needed a lot of work.

He wanted to get the whole process over and behind him to get a fresh new start.

We agreed that listing the home was not a good idea and that I should buy it. He had already spoken with an investor who offered him $60,000 for the home. He owed around $62,000. I offered to put $6,500 in his pocket, pull him out of foreclosure, and buy the home subject to his mortgage. I figured the house was worth around $95,000 in its present dumpy condition.

We wrote a contract that spelled out the details of the transaction. I like buying homes subject to other people's mortgages. This way I don't have to go through the whole mortgage process and pay the fees.

At closing, I paid the seller $6,500, sent the money to the foreclosing attorney to reinstate the mortgage, and now I own the house. It came to just over $13,000 to get the home. I spent about $20,000 fixing up the home.

After the home had been repaired, it looked great. I found a local bank to refinance the house for me. At the time of the refinance, I had owned the home about 3 months. Many lenders will not allow a refinance unless you owned the home at least a year. So I borrowed $99,000 to pay myself back for most of the repairs and costs to purchase the home and the pay off the previous owner's mortgage.

After the repairs were completed, I figured that I could have sold the home between $130k and $140k. Fortunately, I decided to keep it and rent it. Since the market has gone up, it is now worth from $265,000 to $275,000

14

What Do You Need to Get Started?

The great thing about real estate investing when it comes to dealing with pre-foreclosures is that, more than anything else, you need time and energy. People don't call it "sweat equity" for nothing!

Time

With pre-foreclosures, more than with any other type of real estate investing, you have really got to have the time to commit to this business. Not only do you have to have enough hours in the week, you must constantly race against the clock to file your paperwork and close the deal before the house goes into foreclosure.

You will need enough time during "banking hours" to take care of business. Not everyone is open over the weekend, and most people that you need to talk to (other than the property owners) are not going to be available after regular business hours.

Office Equipment

You don't need a lot of office equipment. You probably have most of this stuff in your home already: desk, filing system, computer, and printer. You will probably find a fax machine a great help to have around as well as an office shredder to get rid of any documentation that you would not want to fall into the wrong hands. If you do not own a computer desk, you can work at your dining table for a while until you start making money on your investments. In terms of a filing system, a couple of boxes will do fine when you are just starting out. You just need someplace to keep your papers organized. If you do not already own a computer, consider this an important purchase as you will find it easiest and quickest to get much of your data online. You do not need anything fancy with your computer; something under $1,000 should be sufficient. Do not skimp too much on your printer; stay away from the budget models. You will be printing off a lot of paper, some of it legal documentation. Look at something that costs in the range of $100 to $200 when just starting out.

Mobile Phone

A mobile phone is one of those must-haves for anybody investing in real estate. You simply have to make it easy for people to contact you whenever they need to, no matter where you are. You will be out on the road a lot looking at properties. While other businesses might survive with an answering machine, real estate investing is one that would not.

KEEPING RECORDS

Keeping records is an important aspect of any business. The real estate investor needs to keep records to make sure that he or she is still making money, an actual profit and not just letting a lot of property and money change hands.

Another reason that keeping records benefits the real estate investor is that, by keeping careful records of time and money spent on various tasks and repairs on properties, the investor can better estimate the level of effort for flipping properties. All those little repairs tend to slip by unless diligent effort is made to record them.

Finally, even if you hate keeping records and have vowed not to record them for yourself at all, consider that you will need to keep them for tax purposes. The IRS wants to know what you are doing when you say you are "investing in real estate." Records of what you spend and what you earn is of paramount interest to the IRS.

A basic understanding of accounting can go a long way. If, after picking up a book or two, you still do not feel like you get it, enroll in a class (either online or in person). Most community colleges offer continuing education or non-credit courses on business accounting for new business owners. Look for a course that focuses on the pragmatic day-to-day recordkeeping that you need to know about, not a course that looks at accounting from a pedantic point of view.

Don't put off your recordkeeping for months on end. The best approach is to look at your expenses and profits on a daily basis. At the very least, use a weekend afternoon to update your records.

What you use to keep your records is up to you. You can get a paper ledger book at a local office supply store or you can go high-tech with accounting software. Many people just starting out will use a paper ledger book or an Excel spreadsheet until they reach a point where the cost and learning curve for accounting software becomes worth the effort.

For recordkeeping, you must specify when your "year" starts and ends. For most small businesses, the calendar year suffices. Sometimes, businesses will use fiscal years and short tax years. A fiscal year is any 12-month period that the business chooses to manage its records. A fiscal year could go from February 1 to January 31 of the next year. Likewise, a fiscal year could start September 1 and end August 31 of the next year. Setting a fiscal calendar is solely for the benefit of the business's operations. A short tax year is what you use the first year you are in business or in the event that you are switching from a calendar year to a fiscal year system, or vice versa.

Another major decision you will need to settle on is what accounting method you will use to record your business income and expenses. The most common methods are the cash method and the accrual method. The cash method is straightforward:

1. You record payments when you actually receive them.

2. You record expenses when you actually pay them.

The accrual method works like this:

1. You record income the year you earn it, regardless of when you are actually paid.

2. You record expenses when you actually incur them, regardless of when you actually pay them.

If you had a business where you kept merchandise and, therefore, maintained an inventory, you would have to use the accrual system. Other than that stipulation, the IRS does not care which method you use. If you incorporate and gross more than $5 million a year, you cannot use the cash method.

Making This a Legal Business

Even though you are not receiving some type of W-2, rest assured that the IRS will hear about your real estate deals; therefore, you need to keep documentation of all of your workings. You do not have to incorporate your business to make it legal. Many small operations nationwide exist as sole proprietorships.

Many people consider incorporation when they want to limit liabilities' reach into one's personal assets. If you want to incorporate, wait until you make your first sale and you are sure you want to get into this business for the long haul. Do not spend too much time "getting set up for business" as opposed to just working the deals! You do not need a lot up front to get started. If you decide you like investing in pre-foreclosures, you do it well and often enough, then go ahead and take the resources and time to set up a corporation for tax and liability.

Understanding Taxes

Most of us are used to working for "the man" and having our taxes taken out before we get them in our paycheck. When you work for yourself, you must get in the habit of withholding enough of your earnings to pay taxes. When you make enough, the IRS will expect you to start paying your taxes in a quarterly or monthly fashion; you will not have until next year to pay your income taxes. Make sure you have healthy accounting practices and do not spend money that you are not entitled to spend — the IRS is expecting it.

Take into account self-employment tax. Self-employment tax is an additional 15 percent that you will need to pay the IRS on any profit you make on your investments. That 15 percent is broken down into Social Security tax (12.4 percent) and Medicare tax (2.6 percent). You do not have to pay yourself the money in order to get the IRS's attention. Anything you make over any costs gets taxed regular and incurs self-employment tax, even if you do not plan to pay yourself a salary.

The great thing about being in business for yourself is that you now get to deduct all of your business costs. As long as you are making money or can show that your efforts qualify your activity as work and not a hobby, just about all of your business costs can help to lower the amount that the IRS will tax you.

Getting the Right Amount of Insurance

Make sure you have enough business insurance to cover anything that happens to your properties while you are doing repairs as well as showing people the homes. You also want to make sure you have enough car insurance. If something catastrophic happens or if you get sued, you do not lose your house or your other investments. While many people incorporate to limit liability to their business ventures, simply incorporating should not be seen as a fix-all to catastrophic problems at work. Business and home insurance are invaluable when bad things happen!

SET UP AN EMERGENCY FUND

With all of these business dealings, you might think you have enough cash to take care of business, but occasionally things take a turn for the worse. Mother Nature can be especially hard to grapple with when you run a new business. Besides saving money for your long-term retirement plans, make sure you set aside a certain amount of your profit, maybe up to 10 percent, for a short-term emergency reserve. You will thank yourself if you ever find yourself caught up in something that requires more cash than you have coming in. The last place you want to find yourself is at the wrong end of a foreclosure (for example, the homeowner who is losing his or her house as opposed to the investor who is picking up a great deal). Setting up a short-term emergency fund is especially important if you should decide to quit your regular job and go into real estate investing full-time.

15

How to Build Wealth Through Real Estate Pre-Foreclosures

Now that you understand how investing in the pre-foreclosure market system works and you have a good base knowledge, this chapter serves as a sort of blueprint for you to use to begin building wealth.

When investing in pre-foreclosures, your process should be:

1. Find as many pre-foreclosures as possible.

2. Qualify the pre-foreclosures so that you spend your time and money only on those that show a good potential for maximum returns.

3. Work those deals.

4. Sell the properties.

Besides understanding what you need to do to be successful in your real estate business, you must work out a plan of attack and work that plan. Have goals with targets and measures that you want to try to reach. For example, you might say your goal is to buy and sell one foreclosure property a month for the next year. In order to do that, you must contact thirty properties a month (this statistic is based on your personal results). Or, you might want to target your net profit. You want to make $100,000 a year investing in pre-foreclosures and take it from there, for example. You must have goals and targets. From there, you can create initiatives that you hold on to that should be broken down into daily and even hourly tasks.

Learn from your mistakes. Keep a "Lessons Learned" document or notebook where you track your costs, mistakes, errors with estimations—whatever has cost you money in a previous deal—and do not let them bite you on your bottom again. Improve your standard operating procedures based on what you have learned so far.

Understanding the Numbers

Do not invest in your business until you understand what you need to do and until you have successfully bought and sold your first house. Do not spend money on getting an assistant, incorporating, building a huge Web site, etc., until you have seriously committed yourself to this as a business. Otherwise, you are just spending a lot of money on a very expensive hobby. Likewise, once you start making money on your ventures, take recordkeeping very seriously, as the IRS will.

You are a real estate investor. Never buy a property for an amount greater than what your numbers on paper tell you make sense. To do so is just bad business for you. Do not let your love of closing the deal overshadow your better judgment. You spent the time preparing what your maximum offer should be;

now, do not budge, or if you do, budge very little. There is a reason that nobody else is willing to take a house at the price that the lender wants before parting with it. The lender doesn't expect to make any money on the property either. Sure, the demand and, therefore, the price of real estate is going up. We cannot make more real estate. But at the same time, keep your appraisals conservative so you do not run the risk of becoming too speculative for your income.

FIND A MENTOR OR MAKE NEW FRIENDS

Do not get into a new venture entirely on your own. This business can cost way too much to a newbie who blindly enters into pre-foreclosure deals. If you have questions, do not sit in the dark. Find answers.

Go online to find new associates or mentors who have answers to your questions. Going online can be a great way to find people willing to share their experiences and tips without risking competition (since you probably will not be in the same zip code).

Attend a seminar or attend a class on real estate investing. Try to meet up with the lecturer or the instructor.

Do not fall for those late-night infomercials where so-called real estate "gurus" tell you how they flipped properties with no money down or for pennies on the dollar. If it were that simple and easy, everybody and their mothers would be doing it! The following Web sites report critical opinions on many of the so-called real estate "gurus" out there. Keep in mind that each of these sites is probably trying to sell their own real estate investing tips. Reading their reviews, however, can be eye-opening:

- John Treed (**www.johntreed.com/Reedgururating.html**)

- Foreclosures.com (**www.foreclosures.com/pages /gurus_to_avoid.asp**)

Big Picture

When working your numbers, always look at the big picture. If you make "X" amount of profit on the average and it takes you one month's work, working 80 hours a month, figure out what your hourly rate is. Focus on the big picture. You could be flipping 20 houses a month, but if you do not watch what your profit margin is, you could be making as much money flipping burgers! Do not mistake being busy for being profitable.

Good Luck!

Congratulations! You made it to the end of our book on investing in pre-foreclosure homes. Armed with the information in this book, you should feel confident in your understanding of the steps you will need to take to successfully invest in pre-foreclosures. You also have a keen understanding that it is not just what steps you take but also how well you work as you dig up pre-foreclosures and negotiate with all the parties involved.

Ultimately, our advice is to think big but start out small. Be conservative in your expenditures when you first start out. Do not jump in without having a good understanding of the numbers. But once you have crunched the numbers, do not fall victim to analysis paralysis and let good, qualified properties slip through your fingertips. This is a great business to have a long-distance mentor or friend who you bounce your ideas off of.

The great thing about investing in pre-foreclosures is that houses will always get foreclosed. There will always be an opportunity for you to find that "motivated seller" facing inevitable foreclosure. Now you know how to take that opportunity and turn it into profit for yourself. Do not be afraid to take the first step and roll your sleeves up for a little "sweat equity!"

Bibliography

Online Sources

1. Article (**www.realtor.org/rmomag.NSF/pages /bizincomeexpensesurveyaug01**) by Realtor® Online Magazine

2. The Mortgage Bankers Association of America (**http: //mbaa.org/**) releases National Delinquency Surveys

3. MBAA's recent survey (**http://mbaa.org/news/2005 /pr1214.html**)

4. Plunkett Research (**www.plunkettresearch.com /Industries/BankingMortgagesCredit /BankingMortgagesCreditStatistics/tabid/233/Default.aspx**)

5. Federal Housing Administration (**www.hud.gov/offices /hsg/fhahistory.cfm**).

6. ForeclosureLink.com (**http://foreclosurelink.com**

/statelink_page.htm)

7.   United States Foreclosure Network (USFN) (**www.usfn .org**)

8.   Freddie Mac (**www.freddiemac.com**)

9.   Fannie Mae (**www.fanniemae.com**)

10. HUD (**www.hud.gov/offices/hsg/hsgabout.cfm**)

11. FHA (**www.hud.gov/offices/hsg/hsgabout.cfm**)

12. DVA (**www.va.gov**)

13. SBA (**www.sba.gov**)

14. Gomortgageonline.com (**www.gomortgagesonline.com /prequalify.cfm**)

15. Site hosted by Cornell listing current federal bankruptcy laws (**http://www4.law.cornell.edu/uscode/html/ uscode11/usc_sup_01_11.html**)

16. **http://pacer.psc.uscourts.gov/index.html**

17. **www.bankruptcyaction.com**

18. **www.bankruptcydata.com**

19. **www.abiworld.org**

20. Nolo (**www.nolo.com/resource.cfm/catid /462a9501-9b21-4e09-a08c5a7b8af51a79/213/161/**)

21. Cornell's Wex site (**www.law.cornell.edu/wex/index**

.php/Bankruptcy)

22. American Bankruptcy Institute (**www.abiworld.org**)

23. ForeclosureNet.net (**www.foreclosurenet.net**)

24. Foreclosure.com (**www.foreclosure.com**)

25. Foreclosures.com (**www.foreclosures.com**)

26. RealtyTrac (**www.realtytrac.com**)

27. Reozone (**www.reozone.com/index.php**)

28. Internet Retailer (**www.internetretailer.com /dailyNews.asp?id=15847**)

29. Google AdWords (**https://adwords.google.com/select**)

30. AdBrite (**www.adbrite.com**)

31. Open Directory (**http://dmoz.org**)

32. Yahoo.com (**www.yahoo.com**)

33. LookSmart (**www.looksmart.com**)

34. Yahoo Yellow Pages (**http://yp.yahoo.com**)

35. Verizon SuperPages (**www.superpages.com**)

36. Craig's List (**www.craigslist.org**)

37. OvernightPrints.com (**www.overnightprints.com**)

38. VistaPrint (**www.vistaprint.com**)

39. Business Entity Name Availability Check and Reservation—Registration Service site (**https://www.state.nj.us/njbgs/njbgsnar.htm**).

40. Chapter 22 of Title 15 (**http://www.law.cornell.edu/uscode/html/uscode15/usc_sup_01_15_10_22.html**)

41. U.S. Patent and Trademark Office (**www.uspto.gov**)

    TEAS index page (**www.uspto.gov/teas/index.html**)

42. MagneticSignsOnTime.com (**www.magneticsignsontime.com**)

43. Speedy Signs (**www.speedysigns.com/signs/magnetic.asp**)

44. Accent Signs and Graphics (**http://store.yahoo.com/accentgraphics/magneticsigns.html**)

45. AA Instant Sign (**www.aainstantsign.com/magnetic.htm**)

46. Kinko's (**www.kinkos.com**)

47. Staples (**www.staples.com**)

48. Office Depot (**www.officedepot.com**)

49. 1&1 (**http://order.1and1.com**)

50. GoDaddy.com (**www.godaddy.com**)

51. BlueHost.com (**www.bluehost.com**)

52. TransUnion (**www.transunion.com**)

53. Experian (**www.experian.com**)

54. Equifax (**www.equifax.com**)

55. Fair Isaacs & Co (**www.fairisaac.com/fairisaac**)

56. myFico.com (**www.myfico.com**)

57. CAN-SPAM LAW (**www.ftc.gov/bcp/conline/pubs /buspubs/canspam.htm**)

58. White Pages (**www.whitepages.com**) is a free service you can use

59. Anywho.com (**www.anywho.com**)

60. KnowX.com (**www.knowx.com**)

61. Intelius.com (**www.intelius.com**)

62. American Land Title Association (**www.alta.org**)

63. Building-Cost.net (**www.building-cost.net**)

64. NRMA Insurance (**www.nrma.com.au/pub/nrma /home/calculator/building/index.shtml**)

65. **www.dataquick.com**

66. **www.homegain.com**

67. **www.homeradar.com**

68. **www.real-comp.com**

69. www.realtor.com

70. Fairfax County, Virginia, both assessed values and sales values for properties (**http://icare.fairfaxcounty.gov /Search/GenericSearch.aspx?mode=ADDRESS**)

71. BRB Publications has a Free Resource Center (**www.brbpub.com/pubrecsitesStates.asp**)

72. NETR Online public record online directory (**www.netronline.com/public_records.htm**)

73. MSN's Liz Pulliam Weston, Bidding strategies for first-time homebuyers (**http://moneycentral.msn.com /content/Banking/Homebuyingguide/P81710.asp**)

74. Federal Emergency Management Association (FEMA) (**www.fema.gov**)

    FEMA's Web page on flood hazard mapping (**www .fema.gov/fhm/fq_gen13.shtm**)

75. Focused Extermination (**www.focusedxterm.com /termites.html**)

76. Centex House Leveling & Foundation Repair (**www.centexhouseleveling.com/repairFAQ.html**)

77. Pillar to Post (**www.pillartopost.com/resources /repair_cost_estimates.cfm**)

78. According to Retirement Living (**www.retirementliving .com/RLtaxes.html**)

79. California Department of Consumer Affairs (**http://www.dca.ca.gov/legal/k-6.html**)

80. PACER (**http://pacer.psc.uscourts.gov**)

81. **www.bankruptcyaction.com**

82. **www.bankruptcydata.com**

83. FindLaw (**http://lawyers.findlaw.com**)

84. Lawyers.com (**www.lawyers.com**)

85. Case Post (**www.casepost.com**)

86. Bank Rate (**www.bankrate.com/brm/rate/loan_home.asp**)

87. Price Line (**www.plmhomeequity.com**)

88. E-LOAN (**https://www.eloan.com/helocapp/intro/equity?user=ggl&sid=y5T8ep5ZYz9ti-LJWrpwm33C1AM&mcode=gglkw3cs9&context=equity**)

89. E-LOAN (**https://www.eloan.com/s/show/creditcards/credit_cards?context=personalloans&linksrc=PLccsubnav&sid=QR2nwG9SqNG9X4rBsAEFJr-hAOg&user=&mcode=**)

90. Bank Rate (**www.bankrate.com/brm/rate/cc_home.asp**)

91. Love to Know's page on best credit card sites (**www.lovetoknow.com/top10/credit-cards.html**)

92. Beneficial (**https://www.beneficial.com/learn/HomeNewUser.jst**)

93. CitiFinancial (**www.citifinancial.com**)

94. John T. Reed's Web site (**www.johntreed.com/dueonsale.html**)

95. Audrie's Advice (**www.audrie.com**) offers a good example of an Internet property description (**http://sell-home411.com/pa/property.php?propid=9999**)

96. AOL provides a link (**www.mapquest.com/features/main.adp?page=lf_main**)

97. Microsoft's MapPoint (**www.microsoft.com/mappoint**)

98. For Sale by Owner (**www.forsalebyowner.com**)

99. Total Real Estate Solutions (**www.totalrealestatesolutions.com/property/list/signup.cfm**)

100. NeoRealEstate (**www.neorealestate.com/pyproperty/userlogin.asp**)

101. Home for Salez (**http://usa.homesalez.com/index.htm**)

102. Flat Fee MLS Listings (**www.flatfeemlslisting.com**)

103. Save on MLS (**www.saveonmls.com/default.htm**)

104. Realty Trac (**www.realtytrac.com/foreclosure_laws.asp**)

105. Foreclosure University (**www.foreclosureuniversity.com/studycenter/foreclosurelaws/alabama.php**)

106. Lender Mediation (**www.lendermediation.com /ForeclosureLaws.html?afid=sneedfinancial**)

BOOK SOURCES

1. Lucier, Thomas. *The Pre-Foreclosure Property Investor's Kit.* John Wiley & Sons, Inc.: Hoboken, New Jersey.

2. Conti, Peter and Finkel, David. *Making Big Money Investing in Foreclosures.* Dearborn Trade Publishing: Chicago, IL.

3. Dallow, Theodore. *How to Buy Foreclosed Real Estate for a Fraction of Its Value.* Adams Media Corporation: Holbrook, MA.

4. Posner, Jeffrey. *The Foreclosure Handbook.*

5. Friedman, Jack and Harris, Jack. *Keys to Buying Foreclosed and Bargain Homes.* Barron's Educational Series: Hauppauge, NY.

6. Dempsey, Bobbi and Beitler, Todd. *The Complete Idiot's Guide to Buying Foreclosures.* Penguin Group: New York, NY.

CD SOURCES

1. Sheets, Carleton. How to Skyrocket Your Profits with Distressed and Foreclosed Properties. Professional Education Institute.

2.   Real Estate Wealth Series

3.   No Down Payment CDs

GLOSSARY

401(k)/403(b) An investment plan sponsored by an employer that enables individuals to set aside pre-tax income for retirement or emergency purposes. 401(k) plans are provided by private corporations. 403(b) plans are provided by non-profit organizations.

401(k)/403(b) Loan A type of financing using a loan against the money accumulated in a 401(k)/403(b) plan.

Abatement Sometimes referred to as free rent or early occupancy. A condition that could happen in addition to the primary term of the lease.

Above Building Standard Finishes and specialized designs that have been upgraded in order to accommodate a tenant's requirements.

Absorption Rate The speed and amount of time at which rentable space, in square feet, is filled.

Abstract or Title Search The process of reviewing all transactions that have been recorded publicly in order to determine whether any defects in the title exist that could interfere with a clear property ownership transfer.

Accelerated Cost Recovery System A calculation for taxes to provide more depreciation for the first few years of ownership.

Accelerated Depreciation A method of depreciation where the value of a property depreciates faster in the first few years after purchasing it.

Acceleration Clause A clause in a contract that gives the lender the right to demand immediate payment of the balance of the loan if the borrower defaults on the loan.

Acceptance The seller's written approval of a buyer's offer.

Ad Valorem A Latin phrase that translates as "according to value." Refers to a tax that is imposed on a property's value that is typically based on the local government's evaluation of the property.

Addendum An addition or update for an existing contract between parties.

Additional Principal Payment Additional money paid to the lender, apart from the scheduled loan payments, to pay more of the principal balance, shortening the length of the loan.

Adjustable-Rate Mortgage (ARM) A home loan with an interest rate that is adjusted periodically in order to reflect changes in a specific financial resource.

Adjusted Funds From Operations (AFFO) The rate of REIT performance or ability to pay dividends that is used by many analysts who have concerns about the quality of earnings as measured by Funds From Operations (FFO).

Adjustment Date The date at which the interest rate is adjusted for an adjustable-rate mortgage (ARM).

Adjustment Period The amount of time between adjustments for an interest rate in an ARM.

Administrative Fee A percentage of the value of the assets under management, or a fixed annual dollar amount charged to manage an account.

Advances The payments the servicer makes when the borrower fails to send a payment.

Adviser A broker or investment banker who represents an owner in a transaction and is paid a retainer and/or a performance fee once a financing or sales transaction has closed.

Agency Closing A type of closing in which a lender uses a title company or other firm as an agent to finish a loan.

Agency Disclosure A requirement in most states that agents who act for both buyers or sellers must disclose who they are working for in the transaction.

Aggregation Risk The risk that is associated with warehousing mortgages during the process of pooling them for future security.

Agreement of Sale A legal document the buyer and seller must approve and sign that details the price and terms in the transaction.

Alienation Clause The provision in a loan that requires the borrower to pay the total balance of the loan at once if the property is sold or the ownership transferred.

Alternative Mortgage A home loan that does not match the standard terms of a fixed-rate mortgage.

Alternative or Specialty Investments Types of property that are not considered to be conventional real estate investments, such as self-storage facilities, mobile homes, timber, agriculture, or parking lots.

Amortization The usual process of paying a loan's interest and principal via scheduled monthly payments.

Amortization Schedule A chart or table that shows the percentage of each payment that will be applied toward principal and interest over the life of the mortgage and how the loan balance decreases until it reaches zero.

Amortization Tables The mathematical tables that are used to calculate what a borrower's monthly payment will be.

Amortization Term The number of months it will take to amortize the loan.

Anchor The business or individual who is serving as the primary draw to a commercial property.

Annual Mortgagor Statement A yearly statement to borrowers which details the remaining principal balance and amounts paid throughout the year for taxes and interest.

Annual Percentage Rate (APR) The interest rate that states the actual cost of borrowing money over the course of a year.

Annuity The regular payments of a fixed sum.

Application The form a borrower must complete in order to apply for a mortgage loan, including information such as income, savings, assets, and debts.

Application Fee A fee some lenders charge that may include charges for items such as property appraisal or a credit report unless those fees are included elsewhere.

Appraisal The estimate of the value of a property on a particular date given by a professional appraiser, usually presented in a written document.

Appraisal Fee The fee charged by a professional appraiser for his estimate of the market value of a property.

Appraisal Report The written report presented by an appraiser regarding the value of a property.

Appraised Value The dollar amount a professional appraiser assigned to the value of a property in his report.

Appraiser A certified individual who is qualified by education, training, and experience to estimate the value of real and personal property.

Appreciation An increase in the home's or property's value.

Appreciation Return The amount gained when the value of the real estate assets increases during the current quarter.

Arbitrage The act of buying securities in one market and selling them immediately in another market in order to profit from the difference in price.

ARM Index A number that is publicly published and used as the basis for interest rate adjustments on an ARM.

As-Is Condition A phrase in a purchase or lease contract in which the new tenant accepts the existing condition of the premises as well as any physical defects.

Assessed Value The value placed on a home that is determined by a tax assessor in order to calculate a tax base.

Assessment (1) The approximate value of a property. (2) A fee charged in addition to taxes in order to help pay for items such as water, sewer, street improvements, etc.

Assessor A public officer who estimates the value of a property for the purpose of taxation.

Asset A property or item of value

owned by an individual or company.

Asset Management Fee A fee that is charged to investors based on the amount of money they have invested into real estate assets for the particular fund or account.

Asset Management The various tasks and areas around managing real estate assets from the initial investment until the time it is sold.

Asset Turnover The rate of total revenues for the previous 12 months divided by the average total assets.

Assets Under Management The amount of the current market value of real estate assets that a manager is responsible to manage and invest.

Assignee Name The individual or business to whom the lease, mortgage, or other contract has been re-assigned.

Assignment The transfer of rights and responsibilities from one party to another for paying a debt. The original party remains liable for the debt should the second party default.

Assignor The person who transfers the rights and interests of a property to another.

Assumable Mortgage A mortgage that is capable of being transferred to a different borrower.

Assumption The act of assuming the mortgage of the seller.

Assumption Clause A contractual provision that enables the buyer to take responsibility for the mortgage loan from the seller.

Assumption Fee A fee charged to the buyer for processing new records when they are assuming an existing loan.

Attorn To agree to recognize a new owner of a property and to pay rent to the new landlord.

Average Common Equity The sum of the common equity for the last five quarters divided by five.

Average Downtime The number of months that are expected between a lease's expiration and the beginning of a replacement lease under the current market conditions.

Average Free Rent The number of months the rent abatement concession is expected to be granted to a tenant as part of an incentive to lease under current market conditions.

Average Occupancy The average rate of each of the previous 12 months that a property was occupied.

Average Total Assets The sum of the total assets of a company for the previous five quarters divided by five.

Back Title Letter A letter that an attorney receives from a title insurance company before examining the title for insurance purposes.

Back-End Ratio The calculation lenders use to compare a borrower's gross monthly income to their total debt.

Balance Sheet A statement that lists an individual's assets, liabilities, and net worth.

Balloon Loan A type of mortgage in which the monthly payments are not large enough to repay the loan by the end of the term, and the final payment is one large payment of the remaining balance.

Balloon Payment The final huge payment due at the end of a balloon mortgage.

Balloon Risk The risk that a borrower may not be able to come up with the funds for the balloon payment at maturity.

Bankrupt The state an individual or business is in if they are unable to repay their debt when it is due.

Bankruptcy A legal proceeding where a debtor can obtain relief from payment of certain obligations through restructuring their finances.

Base Loan Amount The amount that forms the basis for the loan payments.

Base Principal Balance The original loan amount once adjustments for subsequent fundings and principal payments have been made without including accrued interest or other unpaid debts.

Base Rent A certain amount that is used as a minimum rent, providing for rent increases over the term of the lease agreement.

Base Year The sum of actual taxes and operating expenses during a given year, often that in which a lease begins.

Basis Point A term for 1/100 of one percentage point.

Before-Tax Income An individual's

income before taxes have been deducted.

Below-Grade Any structure or part of a structure that is below the surface of the ground that surrounds it.

Beneficiary An employee who is covered by the benefit plan his or her company provides.

Beta The measurement of common stock price volatility for a company in comparison to the market.

Bid The price or range an investor is willing to spend on whole loans or securities.

Bill of Sale A written legal document that transfers the ownership of personal property to another party.

Binder (1) A report describing the conditions of a property's title. (2) An early agreement between seller and buyer.

Biweekly Mortgage A mortgage repayment plan that requires payments every two weeks to help repay the loan over a shorter amount of time.

Blanket Mortgage A rare type of mortgage that covers more than one

of the borrower's properties.

Blind Pool A mixed fund that accepts capital from investors without specifying property assets.

Bond Market The daily buying and selling of thirty-year treasury bonds that also affects fixed rate mortgages.

Book Value The value of a property based on its purchase amount plus upgrades or other additions with depreciation subtracted.

Break-Even Point The point at which a landlord's income from rent matches expenses and debt.

Bridge Loan A short-term loan for individuals or companies that are still seeking more permanent financing.

Broker A person who serves as a go-between for a buyer and seller.

Brokerage The process of bringing two or more parties together in exchange for a fee, commission, or other compensation.

Buildable Acres The portion of land that can be built on after allowances for roads, setbacks, anticipated open spaces, and unsuitable areas have been made.

Building Code The laws set forth by the local government regarding end use of a given piece of property. These law codes may dictate the design, materials used, and/or types of improvements that will be allowed.

Building Standard Plus Allowance A detailed list provided by the landlord stating the standard building materials and costs necessary to make the premises inhabitable.

Build-Out Improvements to a property's space that have been implemented according to the tenant's specifications.

Build-to-Suit A way of leasing property, usually for commercial purposes, in which the developer or landlord builds to a tenant's specifications.

Buydown A term that usually refers to a fixed-rate mortgage for which additional payments can be applied to the interest rate for a temporary period, lowering payments for a period of one to three years.

Buydown Mortgage A style of

home loan in which the lender receives a higher payment in order to convince them to reduce the interest rate during the initial years of the mortgage.

Buyer's Remorse A nervousness that first-time homebuyers tend to feel after signing a sales contract or closing the purchase of a house.

Call Date The periodic or continuous right a lender has to call for payment of the total remaining balance prior to the date of maturity.

Call Option A clause in a loan agreement that allows a lender to demand repayment of the entire principal balance at any time.

Cap A limit on how much the monthly payment or interest rate is allowed to increase in an adjustable-rate mortgage.

Capital Appreciation The change in a property's or portfolio's market value after it has been adjusted for capital improvements and partial sales.

Capital Expenditures The purchase of long-term assets, or the expansion of existing ones, that prolongs the life or efficiency of those assets.

Capital Gain The amount of excess when the net proceeds from the sale of an asset are higher than its book value.

Capital Improvements Expenses that prolong the life of a property or add new improvements to it.

Capital Markets Public and private markets where individuals or businesses can raise or borrow capital.

Capitalization The mathematical process that investors use to derive the value of a property using the rate of return on investments.

Capitalization Rate The percentage of return as it is estimated from the net income of a property.

Carryback Financing A type of funding in which a seller agrees to hold back a note for a specified portion of the sales price.

Carrying Charges Costs incurred to the landlord when initially leasing out a property and then during the periods of vacancy.

Cash Flow The amount of income an investor receives on a rental property after operating expenses and loan payments have been deducted.

Cashier's Check A check the bank draws on its own resources instead of a depositor's account.

Cash-on-Cash Yield The percentage of a property's net cash flow and the average amount of invested capital during the specified operating year.

Cash-Out Refinance The act of refinancing a mortgage for an amount that is higher than the original amount for the purpose of using the leftover cash for personal use.

Certificate of Deposit A type of deposit that is held in a bank for a limited time and pays a certain amount of interest to the depositor.

Certificate of Deposit Index (CODI) A rate that is based on interest rates of six-month CDs and is often used to determine interest rates for some ARMs.

Certificate of Eligibility A type of document that the Department of Veterans Affairs issues to verify the eligibility of a veteran for a VA loan.

Certificate of Occupancy (CO) A written document issued by a local government or building agency that states that a home or other building is inhabitable after meeting all building codes.

Certificate of Reasonable Value (CRV) An appraisal presented by the Department of Veterans Affairs that shows the current market value of a property.

Certificate of Veteran Status A document veterans or reservists receive if they have served 90 days of continuous active duty (including training time).

Chain of Title The official record of all transfers of ownership over the history of a piece of property.

Chapter 11 The part of the federal bankruptcy code that deals with reorganizations of businesses.

Chapter 7 The part of the federal bankruptcy code that deals with liquidations of businesses.

Circulation Factor The interior space that is required for internal office circulation and is not included in the net square footage.

Class A A property rating that is usually assigned to those that will generate the maximum rent per square foot, due to superior quality and/or location.

Class B A good property that most potential tenants would find desirable but lacks certain attributes that would bring in the top dollar.

Class C A building that is physically acceptable but offers few amenities, thereby becoming cost-effective space for tenants who are seeking a particular image.

Clear Title A property title that is free of liens, defects, or other legal encumbrances.

Clear-Span Facility A type of building, usually a warehouse or parking garage, consisting of vertical columns on the outer edges of the structure and clear spaces between the columns.

Closed-End Fund A mixed fund with a planned range of investor capital and a limited life.

Closing The final act of procuring a loan and title in which documents are signed between the buyer and seller and/or their respective representation and all money concerned in the contract changes hands.

Closing Costs The expenses that are related to the sale of real estate including loan, title, and appraisal fees and are beyond the price of the property itself.

Closing Statement See: Settlement Statement.

Cloud on Title Certain conditions uncovered in a title search that present a negative impact to the title for the property.

Commercial Mortgage-Backed Securities (CMBS) A type of securities that is backed by loans on commercial real estate.

Collateralized Mortgage Obligation (CMO) Debt that is fully based on a pool of mortgages.

Co-Borrower Another individual who is jointly responsible for the loan and is on the title to the property.

Cost of Funds Index (COFI) An index used to determine changes in the interest rates for certain ARMs.

Co-Investment Program A separate account for an insurance company or investment partnership in which two or more pension funds may co-invest their capital in an individual property or a portfolio of properties.

Co-Investment The condition that occurs when two or more pension funds or groups of funds are sharing ownership of a real estate investment.

Collateral The property for which a borrower has obtained a loan, thereby assuming the risk of losing the property if the loan is not repaid according to the terms of the loan agreement.

Collection The effort on the part of a lender, due to a borrower defaulting on a loan, which involves mailing and recording certain documents in the event that the foreclosure procedure must be implemented.

Commercial Mortgage A loan used to purchase a piece of commercial property or building.

Commercial Mortgage Broker A broker specialized in commercial mortgage applications.

Commercial Mortgage Lender A lender specialized in funding commercial mortgage loans.

Commingled Fund A pooled fund that enables qualified employee benefit plans to mix their capital in order to achieve professional management, greater diversification, or investment positions in larger properties.

Commission A compensation to salespeople that is paid out of the total amount of the purchase transaction.

Commitment The agreement of a lender to make a loan with given terms for a specific period.

Commitment Fee The fee a lender charges for the guarantee of specified loan terms, to be honored at some point in the future.

Common Area Assessments Sometimes called Homeowners' Association Fees. Charges paid to the homeowners' association by the individual unit owners, in a condominium or planned unit development (PUD), that are usually used to maintain the property and common areas.

Common Area Maintenance The additional charges the tenant must pay in addition to the base rent to pay for the maintenance of common areas.

Common Areas The portions of a building, land, and amenities, owned or managed by a planned unit development (PUD) or condominium's homeowners' association, that are used by all of the unit owners who share in the common expense of operation and maintenance.

Common Law A set of unofficial laws that were originally based on English customs and used to some extent in several states.

Community Property Property that is acquired by a married couple during the course of their marriage and is considered in many states to be owned jointly, unless certain circumstances are in play.

Comparable Sales Also called Comps or Comparables. The recent selling prices of similar properties in the area that are used to help determine the market value of a property.

Compound Interest The amount of interest paid on the principal balance of a mortgage in addition to accrued interest.

Concessions Cash, or the equivalent, that the landlord pays or allows in the form of rental abatement, additional tenant finish allowance, moving expenses, or other costs expended in order to persuade a tenant to sign a lease.

Condemnation A government agency's act of taking private property, without the owner's consent, for public use through the power of eminent domain.

Conditional Commitment A lender's agreement to make a loan providing the borrower meets certain conditions.

Conditional Sale A contract to sell a property that states that the seller will retain the title until all contractual conditions have been fulfilled.

Condominium A type of ownership in which all of the unit owners own the property, common areas, and buildings jointly, and have sole ownership in the unit to which they hold the title.

Condominium Conversion Changing an existing rental property's ownership to the condominium form of ownership.

Condominium Hotel A condominium project that involves registration desks, short-term occupancy, food and telephone services, and daily cleaning services, and is generally operated as a commercial hotel even though the units are individually owned.

Conduit A strategic alliance between lenders and unaffiliated organizations that acts as a source of funding by regularly purchasing loans, usually with a goal of pooling and securitizing them.

Conforming Loan A type of mortgage that meets the conditions to be purchased by Fannie Mae or Freddie Mac.

Construction Documents The drawings and specifications an architect and/or engineer provides to describe construction requirements for a project.

Construction Loan A short-term loan to finance the cost of construction, usually dispensed in stages throughout the construction project.

Construction Management The process of ensuring that the stages of the construction project are completed in a timely and seamless manner.

Construction-to-Permanent Loan A construction loan that can be converted to a longer-term traditional mortgage after construction is complete.

Consultant Any individual or company that provides the services to institutional investors, such as defining real estate investment policies, making recommendations to advisers or managers, analyzing existing real estate portfolios, monitoring and reporting on portfolio performance, and/or reviewing specified investment opportunities.

Consumer Price Index (CPI) A measurement of inflation, relating to the change in the prices of goods and services that are regularly purchased by a specific population during a certain period of time.

Contiguous Space Refers to several suites or spaces on a floor (or connected floors) in a given building that can be combined and rented to a single tenant.

Contingency A specific condition that must be met before either party in a contract can be legally bound.

Contract An agreement, either verbal or written, to perform or not to perform a certain thing.

Contract Documents See: Construction Documents.

Contract Rent Also known as Face Rent. The dollar amount of the rental obligation specified in a lease.

Conventional Loan A long-term loan from a non-governmental lender that a borrower obtains for the purchase of a home.

Convertible Adjustable-Rate Mortgage A type of mortgage that

begins as a traditional ARM but contains a provision to enable the borrower to change to a fixed-rate mortgage during a certain period of time.

Convertible Debt The point in a mortgage at which the lender has the option to convert to a partially or fully owned property within a certain period of time.

Convertible Preferred Stock Preferred stock that can be converted to common stock under certain conditions that have been specified by the issuer.

Conveyance The act of transferring a property title between parties by deed.

Cooperative Also called a Co-op. A type of ownership by multiple residents of a multi-unit housing complex in which they all own shares in the cooperative corporation that owns the property, thereby having the right to occupy a particular apartment or unit.

Cooperative Mortgage Any loan that is related to a cooperative residential project.

Core Properties The main types of property, specifically office, retail, industrial, and multi-family.

Co-Signer A second individual or party who also signs a promissory note or loan agreement, thereby taking responsibility for the debt in the event that the primary borrower cannot pay.

Cost-Approach Improvement Value The current expenses for constructing a copy or replacement for an existing structure, but subtracting an estimate of the accrued depreciation.

Cost-Approach Land Value The estimated value of the basic interest in the land, as if it were available for development to its highest and best use.

Cost-of-Sale Percentage An estimate of the expenses of selling an investment that represents brokerage commissions, closing costs, fees, and other necessary sales costs.

Coupon The token or expected interest rate the borrower is charged on a promissory note or mortgage.

Courier Fee The fee that is charged at closing for the delivery of documents between all parties concerned in a real estate transaction.

Covenant A written agreement, included in deeds or other legal documents, that defines the requirements for certain acts or use of a property.

Credit An agreement in which a borrower promises to repay the lender at a later date and receives something of value in exchange.

Credit Enhancement The necessary credit support, in addition to mortgage collateral, in order to achieve the desired credit rating on mortgage-backed securities.

Credit History An individual's record which details his current and past financial obligations and performance.

Credit Life Insurance A type of insurance that pays the balance of a mortgage if the borrower dies.

Credit Rating The degree of creditworthiness a person is assigned based on his credit history and current financial status.

Credit Report A record detailing an individual's credit, employment, and residence history used to determine the individual's creditworthiness.

Credit Repository A company that records and updates credit applicants' financial and credit information from various sources.

Credit Score Sometimes called a Credit Risk Score. The number contained in a consumer's credit report that represents a statistical summary of the information.

Creditor A party to whom other parties owe money.

Cross-Collateralization A group of mortgages or properties that jointly secures one debt obligation.

Cross-Defaulting A provision that allows a trustee or lender to require full payment on all loans in a group, if any single loan in the group is in default.

Cumulative Discount Rate A percentage of the current value of base rent with all landlord lease concessions taken into account.

Current Occupancy The current percentage of units in a building or property that is leased.

Current Yield The annual rate of return on an investment, expressed as a percentage.

Deal Structure The type of agreement in financing an acquisition. The deal can be un-leveraged, leveraged, traditional debt, participating debt, participating/convertible debt, or joint ventures.

Debt Any amount one party owes to another party.

Debt Service Coverage Ratio (DSCR) A property's yearly net operating income divided by the yearly cost of debt service.

Debt Service The amount of money that is necessary to meet all interest and principal payments during a specific period.

Debt-to-Income Ratio The percentage of a borrower's monthly payment on long-term debts divided by his gross monthly income.

Dedicate To change a private property to public ownership for a particular public use.

Deed A legal document that conveys property ownership to the buyer.

Deed in Lieu of Foreclosure A situation in which a deed is given to a lender in order to satisfy a mortgage debt and to avoid the foreclosure process.

Deed of Trust A provision that

allows a lender to foreclose on a property in the event that the borrower defaults on the loan.

Default The state that occurs when a borrow fails to fulfill a duty or take care of an obligation, such as making monthly mortgage payments.

Deferred Maintenance Account A type of account that a borrower must fund to provide for maintenance of a property.

Deficiency Judgment The legal assignment of personal liability to a borrower for the unpaid balance of a mortgage, after foreclosing on the property has failed to yield the full amount of the debt.

Defined-Benefit Plan A type of benefit provided by an employer that defines an employee's benefits either as a fixed amount or a percentage of the beneficiary's salary when he retires.

Defined-Contribution Plan A type of benefit plan provided by an employer in which an employee's retirement benefits are determined by the amount that has been contributed by the employer and/or employee during the time of employment, and by the actual investment earnings on those

contributions over the life of the fund.

Delinquency A state that occurs when the borrower fails to make mortgage payments on time, eventually resulting in foreclosure, if severe enough.

Delinquent Mortgage A mortgage in which the borrower is behind on payments.

Demising Wall The physical partition between the spaces of two tenants or from the building's common areas.

Deposit Also referred to as Earnest Money. The funds that the buyer provides when offering to purchase property.

Depreciation A decline in the value of property or an asset, often used as a tax-deductible item.

Derivative Securities A type of securities that has been created from other financial instruments.

Design/Build An approach in which a single individual or business is responsible for both the design and construction.

Disclosure A written statement, presented to a potential buyer, that lists information relevant to a piece of property, whether positive or negative.

Discount Points Fees that a lender charges in order to provide a lower interest rate.

Discount Rate A figure used to translate present value from future payments or receipts.

Discretion The amount of authority an adviser or manager is granted for investing and managing a client's capital.

Distraint The act of seizing a tenant's personal property when the tenant is in default, based on the right the landlord has in satisfying the debt.

Diversification The act of spreading individual investments out to insulate a portfolio against the risk of reduced yield or capital loss.

Dividend Yield The percentage of a security's market price that represents the annual dividend rate.

Dividend Distributions of cash or stock that stockholders receive.

Dividend-Ex Date The initial date on which a person purchasing the stock can no longer receive the most

recently announced dividend.

Document Needs List The list of documents a lender requires from a potential borrower who is submitting a loan application.

Documentation Preparation Fee A fee that lenders, brokers, and/or settlement agents charge for the preparation of the necessary closing documents.

Dollar Stop An agreed amount of taxes and operating expenses each tenant must pay out on a prorated basis.

Down Payment The variance between the purchase price and the portion that the mortgage lender financed.

DOWNREIT A structure of organization that makes it possible for REITs to purchase properties using partnership units.

Draw A payment from the construction loan proceeds made to contractors, subcontractors, home builders, or suppliers.

Due Diligence The activities of a prospective purchaser or mortgager of real property for the purpose of confirming that the property is as represented by the seller and is not subject to environmental or other problems.

Due on Sale Clause The standard mortgage language that states the loan must still be repaid if the property is resold.

Earnest Money See: Deposit.

Earthquake Insurance A type of insurance policy that provides coverage against earthquake damage to a home.

Easement The right given to a non-ownership party to use a certain part of the property for specified purposes, such as servicing power lines or cable lines.

Economic Feasibility The viability of a building or project in terms of costs and revenue where the degree of viability is established by extra revenue.

Economic Rent The market rental value of a property at a particular point in time.

Effective Age An estimate of the physical condition of a building presented by an appraiser.

Effective Date The date on which the sale of securities can commence once a registration statement becomes effective.

Effective Gross Income (EGI) The total property income that rents and other sources generate after subtracting a vacancy factor estimated to be appropriate for the property.

Effective Gross Rent (EGR) The net rent that is generated after adjusting for tenant improvements and other capital costs, lease commissions, and other sales expenses.

Effective Rent The actual rental rate that the landlord achieves after deducting the concession value from the base rental rate a tenant pays.

Electronic Authentication A way of providing proof that a particular electronic document is genuine, has arrived unaltered, and came from the indicated source.

Eminent Domain The power of the government to pay the fair market value for a property, appropriating it for public use.

Encroachment Any improvement or upgrade that illegally intrudes onto another party's property.

Encumbrance Any right or interest

in a property that interferes with using it or transferring ownership.

End Loan The result of converting to permanent financing from a construction loan.

Entitlement A benefit of a VA home loan. Often referred to as eligibility.

Environmental Impact Statement Legally required documents that must accompany major project proposals where there will likely be an impact on the surrounding environment.

Equal Credit Opportunity Act (ECOA) A federal law that requires a lender or other creditor to make credit available for applicants regardless of sex, marital status, race, religion, or age.

Equifax One of the three primary credit-reporting bureaus.

Equity The value of a property after existing liabilities have been deducted.

Employee Retirement Income Security Act (ERISA) A legislation that controls the investment activities, mainly of corporate and union pension plans.

Errors and Omissions Insurance A type of policy that insures against the mistakes of a builder or architect.

Escalation Clause The clause in a lease that provides for the rent to be increased to account for increases in the expenses the landlord must pay.

Escrow A valuable item, money, or documents deposited with a third party for delivery upon the fulfillment of a condition.

Escrow Account Also referred to as an Impound Account. An account established by a mortgage lender or servicing company for the purpose of holding funds for the payment of items, such as homeowner's insurance and property taxes.

Escrow Agent A neutral third party who makes sure that all conditions of a real estate transaction have been met before any funds are transferred or property is recorded.

Escrow Agreement A written agreement between an escrow agent and the contractual parties that defines the basic obligations of each party, the money (or other valuables) to be deposited in escrow, and how the escrow agent is to dispose of the money on deposit.

Escrow Analysis An annual investigation a lender performs to make sure they are collecting the appropriate amount of money for anticipated expenditures.

Escrow Closing The event in which all conditions of a real estate transaction have been met, and the property title is transferred to the buyer.

Escrow Company A neutral company that serves as a third party to ensure that all conditions of a real estate transaction are met.

Escrow Disbursements The dispensing of escrow funds for the payment of real estate taxes, hazard insurance, mortgage insurance, and other property expenses as they are due.

Escrow Payment The funds that are withdrawn by a mortgage servicer from a borrower's escrow account to pay property taxes and insurance.

Estate The total assets, including property, of an individual after he has died.

Estimated Closing Costs An estimation of the expenses relating to the sale of real estate.

Estimated Hazard Insurance An estimation of hazard insurance, or homeowner's insurance, that will cover physical risks.

Estimated Property Taxes An estimation of the property taxes that must be paid on the property, according to state and county tax rates.

Estoppel Certificate A signed statement that certifies that certain factual statements are correct as of the date of the statement and can be relied upon by a third party, such as a prospective lender or purchaser.

Eviction The legal removal of an occupant from a piece of property.

Examination of Title A title company's inspection and report of public records and other documents for the purpose of determining the chain of ownership of a property.

Exclusive Agency Listing A written agreement between a property owner and a real estate broker in which the owner promises to pay the broker a commission if certain property is leased during the listing period.

Exclusive Listing A contract that allows a licensed real estate agent to be the only agent who can sell a property for a given time.

Executed Contract An agreement in which all parties involved have fulfilled their duties.

Executor The individual who is named in a will to administer an estate. Executrix is the feminine form.

Exit Strategy An approach investors may use when they wish to liquidate all or part of their investment.

Experian One of the three primary credit-reporting bureaus.

Face Rental Rate The rental rate that the landlord publishes.

Facility Space The floor area in a hospitality property that is dedicated to activities, such as restaurants, health clubs, and gift shops, that interactively service multiple people and is not directly related to room occupancy.

Funds Available for Distribution (FAD) The income from operations, with cash expenditures subtracted, that may be used for leasing commissions and tenant improvement costs.

FAD Multiple The price per share of a REIT divided by its funds available for distribution.

Fair Credit Reporting Act (FCRA) The federal legislation that governs the processes credit reporting agencies must follow.

Fair Housing Act The federal legislation that prohibits the refusal to rent or sell to anyone based on race, color, religion, sex, family status, or disability.

Fair Market Value The highest price that a buyer would be willing to pay, and the lowest a seller would be willing to accept.

Fannie Mae See: Federal National Mortgage Association.

Fannie Mae's Community Home Buyer's Program A community lending model based on borrower income in which mortgage insurers and Fannie Mae offer flexible underwriting guidelines in order to increase the buying power for a low- or moderate-income family and to decrease the total amount of cash needed to purchase a home.

Farmer's Home Administration (FMHA) An agency within the U.S. Department of Agriculture that provides credit to farmers and other rural residents.

Federal Home Loan Mortgage Corporation (FHLMC) Also known as Freddie Mac. The company that buys mortgages from lending institutions, combines them with other loans, and sells shares to investors.

Federal Housing Administration (FHA) A government agency that provides low-rate mortgages to buyers who are able to make a down payment as low as 3 percent.

Federal National Mortgage Association (FNMA) Also known as Fannie Mae. A congressionally chartered, shareholder-owned company that is the nation's largest supplier of home mortgage funds. The company buys mortgages from lenders and resells them as securities on the secondary mortgage market.

Fee Simple The highest possible interest a person can have in a piece of real estate.

Fee Simple Estate An unconditional, unlimited inheritance estate in which the owner may dispose of or use the property as desired.

Fee Simple Interest The state of owning all the rights in a real estate parcel.

Funds From Operations (FFO) A ratio that is meant to highlight the amount of cash a company's real estate portfolio generates relative to its total operating cash flow.

FFO Multiple The price of a REIT share divided by its funds from operations.

FHA Loans Mortgages that the Federal Housing Administration (FHA) insures.

FHA Mortgage Insurance A type of insurance that requires a fee to be paid at closing in order to insure the loan with the Federal Housing Administration (FHA).

Fiduciary Any individual who holds authority over a plan's asset management, administration or disposition, or renders paid investment advice regarding a plan's assets.

Finance Charge The amount of interest to be paid on a loan or credit card balance.

Firm Commitment A written agreement a lender makes to loan money for the purchase of property.

First Mortgage The main mortgage on a property.

First Refusal Right/ Right of First

Refusal A lease clause that gives a tenant the first opportunity to buy a property or to lease additional space in a property at the same price and terms as those contained in an offer from a third party that the owner has expressed a willingness to accept.

First-Generation Space A new space that has never before been occupied by a tenant and is currently available for lease.

First-Loss Position A security's position that will suffer the first economic loss if the assets below it lose value or are foreclosed on.

Fixed Costs Expenses that remain the same despite the level of sales or production.

Fixed Rate An interest rate that does not change over the life of the loan.

Fixed Time The particular weeks of a year that the owner of a timeshare arrangement can access his or her accommodations.

Fixed-Rate Mortgage A loan with an unchanging interest rate over the life of the loan.

Fixture Items that become a part of the property when they are permanently attached to the property.

Flat Fee An amount of money that an adviser or manager receives for managing a portfolio of real estate assets.

Flex Space A building that provides a flexible configuration of office or showroom space combined with manufacturing, laboratory, warehouse, distribution, etc.

Float The number of freely traded shares owned by the public.

Flood Certification The process of analyzing whether a property is located in a known flood zone.

Flood Insurance A policy that is required in designated flood zones to protect against loss due to flood damage.

Floor Area Ratio (FAR) A measurement of a building's gross square footage compared to the square footage of the land on which it is located.

For Sale By Owner (FSBO) A method of selling property in which the property owner serves as the selling agent and directly handles the sales process with the buyer or buyer's agent.

Force Majeure An external force that is not controlled by the contractual parties and prevents them from complying with the provisions of the contract.

Foreclosure The legal process in which a lender takes over ownership of a property once the borrower is in default in a mortgage arrangement.

Forward Commitments Contractual agreements to perform certain financing duties according to any stated conditions.

Four Quadrants of the Real Estate Capital Markets The four market types that consist of Private Equity, Public Equity, Private Debt, and Public Debt.

Freddie Mac See: Federal Home Loan Mortgage Corporation.

Front-End Ratio The measurement a lender uses to compare a borrower's monthly housing expense to gross monthly income.

Full Recourse A loan on which the responsibility of a loan is transferred to an endorser or guarantor in the event of default by the borrower.

Full-Service Rent A rental rate that includes all operating expenses and real estate taxes for the first year.

Fully Amortized ARM An ARM with a monthly payment that is sufficient to amortize the remaining balance at the current interest accrual rate over the amortization term.

Fully Diluted Shares The number of outstanding common stock shares if all convertible securities were converted to common shares.

Future Proposed Space The space in a commercial development that has been proposed but is not yet under construction, or the future phases of a multi-phase project that has not yet been built.

General Contractor The main person or business that contracts for the construction of an entire building or project, rather than individual duties.

General Partner The member in a partnership who holds the authority to bind the partnership and shares in its profits and losses.

Gift Money a buyer has received from a relative or other source that will not have to be repaid.

Ginnie Mae See: Government

National Mortgage Association.

Going-In Capitalization Rate The rate that is computed by dividing the expected net operating income for the first year by the value of the property.

Good Faith Estimate A lender's or broker's estimate that shows all costs associated with obtaining a home loan including loan processing, title, and inspection fees.

Government Loan A mortgage that is insured or guaranteed by the FHA, the Department of Veterans Affairs (VA), or the Rural Housing Service (RHS).

Government National Mortgage Association (GNMA) Also known as Ginnie Mae. A government-owned corporation under the U.S. Department of Housing and Urban Development (HUD) that performs the same role as Fannie Mae and Freddie Mac in providing funds to lenders for making home loans, but only purchases loans that are backed by the federal government.

Grace Period A defined time period in which a borrower may make a loan payment after its due date without incurring a penalty.

Graduated Lease A lease, usually long-term, in which rent payments vary in accordance with future contingencies.

Graduated Payment Mortgage A mortgage that requires low payments during the first years of the loan, but eventually requires larger monthly payments over the term of the loan that become fixed later in the term.

Grant To give or transfer an interest in a property by deed or other documented method.

Grantee The party to whom an interest in a property is given.

Grantor The party who is transferring an interest in a property.

Gross Building Area The sum of areas at all floor levels, including the basement, mezzanine, and penthouses included in the principal outside faces of the exterior walls without allowing for architectural setbacks or projections.

Gross Income The total income of a household before taxes or expenses have been subtracted.

Gross Investment in Real Estate (Historic Cost) The total amount of equity and debt that is invested in a piece of real estate minus proceeds from sales or partial sales.

Gross Leasable Area The amount of floor space that is designed for tenants' occupancy and exclusive use.

Gross Lease A rental arrangement in which the tenant pays a flat sum for rent, and the landlord must pay all building expenses out of that amount.

Gross Real Estate Asset Value The total market value of the real estate investments under management in a fund or individual accounts, usually including the total value of all equity positions, debt positions, and joint venture ownership positions.

Gross Real Estate Investment Value The market value of real estate investments that are held in a portfolio without including debt.

Gross Returns The investment returns generated from operating a property without adjusting for adviser or manager fees.

Ground Lease Land being leased to an individual that has absolutely no residential dwelling on the property; or if it does, the ground (or land) is the only portion of the property being leased.

Ground Rent A long-term lease in which rent is paid to the land owner, normally to build something on that land.

Growing-Equity Mortgage A fixed-rate mortgage in which payments increase over a specified amount of time with the extra funds being applied to the principal.

Guarantor The part who makes a guaranty.

Guaranty An agreement in which the guarantor promises to satisfy the debt or obligations of another, if and when the debtor fails to do so.

Hard Cost The expenses attributed to actually constructing property improvements.

Hazard Insurance Also known as Homeowner's Insurance or Fire Insurance. A policy that provides coverage for damage from forces such as fire and wind.

Highest and Best Use The most reasonable, expected, legal use of a piece of vacant land or improved property that is physically possible, supported appropriately, financially feasible, and that results in the highest value.

High-Rise In a suburban district, any building taller than six stories. In a business district, any building taller than 25 stories.

Holdbacks A portion of a loan funding that is not dispersed until an additional condition is met, such as the completion of construction.

Holding Period The expected length of time, from purchase to sale, that an investor will own a property.

Hold-Over Tenant A tenant who retains possession of the leased premises after the lease has expired.

Home Equity Conversion Mortgage (HECM) Also referred to as a Reverse Annuity Mortgage. A type of mortgage in which the lender makes payments to the owner, thereby enabling older homeowners to convert equity in their homes into cash in the form of monthly payments.

Home Equity Line An open-ended amount of credit based on the equity a homeowner has accumulated.

Home Equity Loan A type of loan that allows owners to borrow against the equity in their homes up to a limited amount.

Home Inspection A pre-purchase examination of the condition a home is in by a certified inspector.

Home Inspector A certified professional who determines the structural soundness and operating systems of a property.

Home Price The price that a buyer and seller agree upon, generally based on the home's appraised market value.

Homeowners' Association (HOA) A group that governs a community, condominium building, or neighborhood and enforces the covenants, conditions, and restrictions set by the developer.

Homeowners' Association Dues The monthly payments that are paid to the homeowners' association for maintenance and communal expenses.

Homeowner's Insurance A policy that includes coverage for all damages that may affect the value of a house as defined in the terms of the insurance policy.

Homeowner's Warranty A type of policy homebuyers often purchase to cover repairs, such as heating or air-conditioning, should they stop working within the coverage period.

Homestead The property an owner uses as his primary residence.

Housing Expense Ratio The percentage of gross income that is devoted to housing costs each month.

HUD (Housing and Urban Development) A federal agency that oversees a variety of housing and community development programs, including the FHA.

HUD Median Income The average income for families in a particular area, which is estimated by HUD.

HUD-1 Settlement Statement Also known as the Closing Statement or Settlement Sheet. An itemized listing of the funds paid at closing.

HUD-1 Uniform Settlement Statement A closing statement for the buyer and seller that describes all closing costs for a real estate transaction or refinancing.

HVAC Heating, ventilating, and air-conditioning.

Hybrid Debt A position in a mortgage that has equity-like features of participation in both

cash flow and the appreciation of the property at the point of sale or refinance.

Implied Cap Rate The net operating income divided by the sum of a REIT's equity market capitalization and its total outstanding debt.

Impounds The part of the monthly mortgage payment that is reserved in an account in order to pay for hazard insurance, property taxes, and private mortgage insurance.

Improvements The upgrades or changes made to a building to improve its value or usefulness.

Incentive Fee A structure in which the fee amount charged is based on the performance of the real estate assets under management.

Income Capitalization Value The figure derived for an income-producing property by converting its expected benefits into property value.

Income Property A particular property that is used to generate income but is not occupied by the owner.

Income Return The percentage of the total return generated by the income from property, fund, or account operations.

Index A financial table that lenders use for calculating interest rates on ARMs.

Indexed Rate The sum of the published index with a margin added.

Indirect Costs Expenses of development other than the costs of direct material and labor that are related directly to the construction of improvements.

Individual Account Management The process of maintaining accounts that have been established for individual plan sponsors or other investors for investment in real estate, where a firm acts as an adviser in obtaining and/or managing a real estate portfolio.

Inflation Hedge An investment whose value tends to increase at a greater rate than inflation, contributing to the preservation of the purchasing power of a portfolio.

Inflation The rate at which consumer prices increase each year.

Initial Interest Rate The original interest rate on an ARM which is sometimes subject to a variety of adjustments throughout the mortgage.

Initial Public Offering (IPO) The first time a previously private company offers securities for public sale.

Initial Rate Cap The limit specified by some ARMs as the maximum amount the interest rate may increase when the initial interest rate expires.

Initial Rate Duration The date specified by most ARMs at which the initial rate expires.

Inspection Fee The fee that a licensed property inspector charges for determining the current physical condition of the property.

Inspection Report A written report of the property's condition presented by a licensed inspection professional.

Institutional-Grade Property A variety of types of real estate properties usually owned or financed by tax-exempt institutional investors.

Insurance Binder A temporary insurance policy that is implemented while a permanent policy is drawn up or obtained.

Insurance Company Separate Account A real estate investment vehicle only offered by life insurance companies, which enables an ERISA-governed fund to avoid creating unrelated taxable income for certain types of property investments and investment structures.

Insured Mortgage A mortgage that is guaranteed by the FHA or by private mortgage insurance (PMI).

Interest Accrual Rate The rate at which a mortgage accrues interest.

Interest-Only Loan A mortgage for which the borrower pays only the interest that accrues on the loan balance each month.

Interest Paid over Life of Loan The total amount that has been paid to the lender during the time the money was borrowed.

Interest Rate The percentage that is charged for a loan.

Interest Rate Buy-Down Plans A plan in which a seller uses funds from the sale of the home to buy down the interest rate and reduce the buyer's monthly payments.

Interest Rate Cap The highest interest rate charge allowed on the monthly payment of an ARM during an adjustment period.

Interest Rate Ceiling The maximum interest rate a lender can charge for an ARM.

Interest Rate Floor The minimum possible interest rate a lender can charge for an ARM.

Interest The price that is paid for the use of capital.

Interest-Only Strip A derivative security that consists of all or part of the portion of interest in the underlying loan or security.

Interim Financing Also known as Bridge or Swing Loans. Short-term financing a seller uses to bridge the gap between the sale of one house and the purchase of another.

Internal Rate of Return (IRR) The calculation of a discounted cash flow analysis that is used to determine the potential total return of a real estate asset during a particular holding period.

Inventory The entire space of a certain proscribed market without concern for its availability or condition.

Investment Committee The

governing body that is charged with overseeing corporate pension investments and developing investment policies for board approval.

Investment Manager An individual or company that assumes authority over a specified amount of real estate capital, invests that capital in assets using a separate account, and provides asset management.

Investment Policy A document that formalizes an institution's goals, objectives, and guidelines for asset management, investment advisory contracting, fees, and utilization of consultants and other outside professionals.

Investment Property A piece of real estate that generates some form of income.

Investment Strategy The methods used by a manager in structuring a portfolio and selecting the real estate assets for a fund or an account.

Investment Structures Approaches to investing that include un-leveraged acquisitions, leveraged acquisitions, traditional debt, participating debt, convertible debt, triple-net leases, and joint ventures.

Investment-Grade CMBS Commercial mortgage-backed securities that have ratings of AAA, AA, A, or BBB.

Investor Status The position an investor is in, either taxable or tax-exempt.

Joint Liability The condition in which responsibility rests with two or more people for fulfilling the terms of a home loan or other financial debt.

Joint Tenancy A form of ownership in which two or more people have equal shares in a piece of property, and rights pass to the surviving owner(s) in the event of death.

Joint Venture An investment business formed by more than one party for the purpose of acquiring or developing and managing property and/or other assets.

Judgment The decision a court of law makes.

Judicial Foreclosure The usual foreclosure proceeding some states use, which is handled in a civil lawsuit.

Jumbo Loan A type of mortgage that exceeds the required limits set by Fannie Mae and Freddie Mac each year.

Junior Mortgage A loan that is a lower priority behind the primary loan.

Just Compensation The amount that is fair to both the owner and the government when property is appropriated for public use through eminent domain.

Landlord's Warrant The warrant a landlord obtains to take a tenant's personal property to sell at a public sale to compel payment of the rent or other stipulation in the lease.

Late Charge The fee that is imposed by a lender when the borrower has not made a payment when it was due.

Late Payment The payment made to the lender after the due date has passed.

Lead Manager The investment banking firm that has primary responsibility for coordinating the new issuance of securities.

Lease A contract between a property owner and tenant that defines payments and conditions under which the tenant may occupy the real estate for a given period of time.

Lease Commencement Date The date at which the terms of the lease are implemented.

Lease Expiration Exposure Schedule A chart of the total square footage of all current leases that expire in each of the next five years, without taking renewal options into account.

Lease Option A financing option that provides for homebuyers to lease a home with an option to buy, with part of the rental payments being applied toward the down payment.

Leasehold The limited right to inhabit a piece of real estate held by a tenant.

Leasehold State A way of holding a property title in which the mortgagor does not actually own the property but has a long-term lease on it.

Leasehold Interest The right to hold or use property for a specific period of time at a given price without transferring ownership.

Lease-Purchase A contract that defines the closing date and solutions for the seller in the event that the buyer defaults.

Legal Blemish A negative count against a piece of property such as a zoning violation or fraudulent title claim.

Legal Description A way of describing and locating a piece of real estate that is recognized by law.

Legal Owner The party who holds the title to the property, although the title may carry no actual rights to the property other than as a lien.

Lender A bank or other financial institution that offers home loans.

Letter of Credit A promise from a bank or other party that the issuer will honor drafts or other requests for payment upon complying with the requirements specified in the letter of credit.

Letter of Intent An initial agreement defining the proposed terms for the end contract.

Leverage The process of increasing the return on an investment by borrowing some of the funds at an interest rate less than the return on the project.

Liabilities A borrower's debts and financial obligations, whether long- or short-term.

Liability Insurance A type of policy that protects owners against negligence, personal injury, or property damage claims.

London InterBank Offered Rate (LIBOR) The interest rate offered on Eurodollar deposits traded between banks and used to determine changes in interest rate for ARMs.

Lien A claim put by one party on the property of another as collateral for money owed.

Lien Waiver A waiver of a mechanic's lien rights that is sometimes required before the general contractor can receive money under the payment provisions of a construction loan and contract.

Life Cap A limit on the amount an ARM's interest rate can increase during the mortgage term.

Lifecycle The stages of development for a property: pre-development, development, leasing, operating, and rehabilitation.

Lifetime Payment Cap A limit on the amount that payments can increase or decrease over the life of an ARM.

Lifetime Rate Cap The highest

possible interest rate that may be charged, under any circumstances, over the entire life of an ARM.

Like-Kind Property A term that refers to real estate that is held for productive use in a trade or business or for investment.

Limited Partnership A type of partnership in which some partners manage the business and are personally liable for partnership debts, but some partners contribute capital and share in profits without the responsibility of management.

Line of Credit An amount of credit granted by a financial institution up to a specified amount for a certain period of time to a borrower.

Liquid Asset A type of asset that can be easily converted into cash.

Liquidity The ease with which an individual's or company's assets can be converted to cash without losing their value.

Listing Agreement An agreement between a property owner and a real estate broker that authorizes the broker to attempt to sell or lease the property at a specified price and terms in return for a commission or other compensation.

Loan An amount of money that is borrowed and usually repaid with interest.

Loan Application A document that presents a borrower's income, debt, and other obligations to determine credit worthiness, as well as some basic information on the target property.

Loan Application Fee A fee lenders charge to cover expenses relating to reviewing a loan application.

Loan Commitment An agreement by a lender or other financial institution to make or ensure a loan for the specified amount and terms.

Loan Officer An official representative of a lending institution who is authorized to act on behalf of the lender within specified limits.

Loan Origination The process of obtaining and arranging new loans.

Loan Origination Fee A fee lenders charge to cover the costs related to arranging the loan.

Loan Servicing The process a lending institution goes through for all loans it manages. This involves processing payments, sending statements, managing the escrow/

impound account, providing collection services on delinquent loans, ensuring that insurance and property taxes are made on the property, handling pay-offs and assumptions, as well as various other services.

Loan Term The time, usually expressed in years, that a lender sets in which a buyer must pay a mortgage.

Loan-to-Value (LTV) The ratio of the amount of the loan compared to the appraised value or sales price.

Lock-Box Structure An arrangement in which the payments are sent directly from the tenant or borrower to the trustee.

Lock-In A commitment from a lender to a borrower to guarantee a given interest rate for a limited amount of time.

Lock-In Period The period of time during which the borrower is guaranteed a specified interest rate.

Lockout The period of time during which a loan may not be paid off early.

Long-Term Lease A rental agreement that will last at least three years from initial signing to the date of expiration or renewal.

Loss Severity The percentage of lost principal when a loan is foreclosed.

Lot One of several contiguous parcels of a larger piece of land.

Low-Documentation Loan A mortgage that requires only a basic verification of income and assets.

Low-Rise A building that involves fewer than four stories above the ground level.

Lump-Sum Contract A type of construction contract that requires the general contractor to complete a building project for a fixed cost that is usually established beforehand by competitive bidding.

Magic Page A story of projected growth that describes how a new REIT will achieve its future plans for funds from operations or funds available for distribution.

Maintenance Fee The charge to homeowners' association members each month for the repair and maintenance of common areas.

Maker One who issues a promissory note and commits to paying the note when it is due.

Margin A percentage that is added to the index and fixed for the mortgage term.

Mark to Market The act of changing the original investment cost or value of a property or portfolio to the level of the current estimated market value.

Market Capitalization A measurement of a company's value that is calculated by multiplying the current share price by the current number of shares outstanding.

Market Rental Rates The rental income that a landlord could most likely ask for a property in the open market, indicated by the current rents for comparable spaces.

Market Study A forecast of the demand for a certain type of real estate project in the future that includes an estimate of the square footage that could be absorbed and the rents that could be charged.

Market Value The price a property would sell for at a particular point in time in a competitive market.

Marketable Title A title that is free of encumbrances and can be marketed immediately to a willing purchaser.

Master Lease The primary lease that controls other subsequent leases and may cover more property than all subsequent leases combined.

Master Servicer An entity that acts on behalf of a trustee for security holders' benefit in collecting funds from a borrower, advancing funds in the event of delinquencies and, in the event of default, taking a property through foreclosure.

Maturity Date The date at which the total principal balance of a loan is due.

Mechanic's Lien A claim created for securing payment priority for the price and value of work performed and materials furnished in constructing, repairing, or improving a building or other structure.

Meeting Space The space in hotels that is made available to the public to rent for meetings, conferences, or banquets.

Merged Credit Report A report that combines information from the three primary credit-reporting agencies including: Equifax, Experian, and TransUnion.

Metes and Bounds The surveyed

boundary lines of a piece of land described by listing the compass directions (bounds) and distances (metes) of the boundaries.

Mezzanine Financing A financing position somewhere between equity and debt, meaning that there are higher-priority debts above and equity below.

Mid-Rise Usually, a building which shows four to eight stories above ground level. In a business district, buildings up to 25 stories may also be included.

Mixed-Use A term referring to space within a building or project which can be used for more than one activity.

Modern Portfolio Theory (MPT) An approach of quantifying risk and return in an asset portfolio which emphasizes the portfolio rather than the individual assets and how the assets perform in relation to each other.

Modification An adjustment in the terms of a loan agreement.

Modified Annual Percentage Rate (APR) An index of the cost of a loan based on the standard APR but adjusted for the amount of time the borrower expects to hold the loan.

Monthly Association Dues A payment due each month to a homeowners' association for expenses relating to maintenance and community operations.

Mortgage An amount of money that is borrowed to purchase a property using that property as collateral.

Mortgage Acceleration Clause A provision enabling a lender to require that the rest of the loan balance is paid in a lump sum under certain circumstances.

Mortgage Banker A financial institution that provides home loans using its own resources, often selling them to investors such as insurance companies or Fannie Mae.

Mortgage Broker An individual who matches prospective borrowers with lenders that the broker is approved to deal with.

Mortgage Broker Business A company that matches prospective borrowers with lenders that the broker is approved to deal with.

Mortgage Constant A figure comparing an amortizing mortgage payment to the outstanding mortgage balance.

Mortgage Insurance (MI) A policy, required by lenders on some loans, that covers the lender against certain losses that are incurred as a result of a default on a home loan.

Mortgage Insurance Premium (MIP) The amount charged for mortgage insurance, either to a government agency or to a private MI company.

Mortgage Interest Deduction The tax write-off that the IRS allows most homeowners to deduct for annual interest payments made on real estate loans.

Mortgage Life and Disability Insurance A type of term life insurance borrowers often purchase to cover debt that is left when the borrower dies or becomes too disabled to make the mortgage payments.

Mortgagee The financial institution that lends money to the borrower.

Mortgagor The person who requests to borrow money to purchase a property.

Multi-Dwelling Units A set of properties that provide separate housing areas for more than one family but only require a single mortgage.

Multiple Listing Service A service that lists real estate offered for sale by a particular real estate agent that can be shown or sold by other real estate agents within a certain area.

National Association of Real Estate Investment Trusts (NAREIT) The national, non-profit trade organization that represents the real estate investment trust industry.

National Council of Real Estate Investment Fiduciaries (NCREIF) A group of real estate professionals who serve on committees; sponsor research articles, seminars and symposiums; and produce the NCREIF Property Index.

NCREIF Property Index (NPI) A quarterly and yearly report presenting income and appreciation components.

Negative Amortization An event that occurs when the deferred interest on an ARM is added, and the balance increases instead of decreases.

Net Asset Value (NAV) The total value of an asset or property minus leveraging or joint venture interests.

Net Asset Value Per Share The total value of a REIT's current assets divided by outstanding shares.

Net Assets The total value of assets minus total liabilities based on market value.

Net Cash Flow The total income generated by an investment property after expenses have been subtracted.

Net Investment in Real Estate Gross investment in properties minus the outstanding balance of debt.

Net Investment Income The income or loss of a portfolio or business minus all expenses, including portfolio and asset management fees, but before gains and losses on investments are considered.

Net Operating Income (NOI) The pre-tax figure of gross revenue minus operating expenses and an allowance for expected vacancy.

Net Present Value (NPV) The sum of the total current value of incremental future cash flows plus the current value of estimated sales proceeds.

Net Purchase Price The gross purchase price minus any associated financed debt.

Net Real Estate Investment Value The total market value of all real estate minus property-level debt.

Net Returns The returns paid to investors minus fees to advisers or managers.

Net Sales Proceeds The income from the sale of an asset, or part of an asset, minus brokerage commissions, closing costs, and market expenses.

Net Square Footage The total space required for a task or staff position.

Net Worth The worth of an individual or company figured on the basis of a difference between all assets and liabilities.

No-Cash-Out Refinance Sometimes referred to as a Rate and Term Refinance. A refinancing transaction that is intended only to cover the balance due on the current loan and any costs associated with obtaining the new mortgage.

No-Cost Loan A loan for which there are no costs associated with the loan that are charged by the lender, but with a slightly higher interest rate.

No-Documentation Loan A type of loan application that requires no income or asset verification, usually granted based on strong credit with a large down payment.

Nominal Yield The yield investors receive before it is adjusted for fees, inflation, or risk.

Non-Assumption Clause A provision in a loan agreement that prohibits transferring a mortgage to another borrower without approval from the lender.

Non-Compete Clause A provision in a lease agreement that specifies that the tenant's business is the only one that may operate in the property in question, thereby preventing a competitor moving in next door.

Non-Conforming Loan Any loan that is too large or does not meet certain qualifications to be purchased by Fannie Mae or Freddie Mac.

Non-Discretionary Funds The funds that are allocated to an investment manager who must have approval from the investor for each transaction.

Non-Investment-Grade CMBS Also referred to as High-Yield CMBS. Commercial mortgage-backed securities that have ratings of BB or B.

Non-Liquid Asset A type of asset that is not turned into cash very easily.

Non-Performing Loan A loan agreement that cannot meet its contractual principal and interest payments.

Non-Recourse Debt A loan that limits the lender's options to collect on the value of the real estate in the event of a default by the borrower.

Nonrecurring Closing Costs Fees that are only paid one time in a given transaction.

Note A legal document requiring a borrower to repay a mortgage at a specified interest rate over a certain period of time.

Note Rate The interest rate that is defined in a mortgage note.

Notice of Default A formal written notification a borrower receives once the borrower is in default stating that legal action may be taken.

Offer A term that describes a specified price or spread to sell whole loans or securities.

One-Year Adjustable-Rate Mortgage An ARM for which the interest rate changes annually, generally based on movements of a published index plus a specified margin.

Open Space A section of land or water that has been dedicated for public or private use or enjoyment.

Open-End Fund A type of commingled fund with an infinite life, always accepting new investor capital and making new investments in property.

Operating Cost Escalation A clause that is intended to adjust rents to account for external standards such as published indexes, negotiated wage levels, or building-related expenses.

Operating Expense The regular costs associated with operating and managing a property.

Opportunistic A phrase that generally describes a strategy of holding investments in underperforming and/or under-managed assets with the expectation of increases in cash flow and/or value.

Option A condition in which the buyer pays for the right to purchase a property within a certain period of time without the obligation to buy.

Option ARM Loan A type of mortgage in which the borrower has a variety of payment options each month.

Original Principal Balance The total principal owed on a mortgage before a borrower has made a payment.

Origination Fee A fee that most lenders charge for the purpose of covering the costs associated with arranging the loan.

Originator A company that underwrites loans for commercial and/or multi-family properties.

Out-Parcel The individual retail sites located within a shopping center.

Overallotment A practice in which the underwriters offer and sell a higher number of shares than they had planned to purchase from the issuer.

Owner Financing A transaction in which the property seller agrees to finance all or part of the amount of the purchase.

Parking Ratio A figure, generally

expressed as square footage, that compares a building's total rentable square footage to its total number of parking spaces.

Partial Payment An amount paid that is not large enough to cover the normal monthly payment on a mortgage loan.

Partial Sales The act of selling a real estate interest that is smaller than the whole property.

Partial Taking The appropriating of a portion of an owner's property under the laws of Eminent Domain.

Participating Debt Financing that allows the lender to have participatory rights to equity through increased income and/or residual value over the balance of the loan or original value at the time the loan is funded.

Party in Interest Any party that may hold an interest, including employers, unions, and, sometimes, fiduciaries.

Pass-Through Certificate A document that allows the holder to receive payments of principal and interest from the underlying pool of mortgages.

Payment Cap The maximum

amount a monthly payment may increase on an ARM.

Payment Change Date The date on which a new payment amount takes effect on an ARM or GPM, usually in the month directly after the adjustment date.

Payout Ratio The percentage of the primary earnings per share, excluding unusual items, that are paid to common stockholders as cash dividends during the next 12 months.

Pension Liability The full amount of capital that is required to finance vested pension fund benefits.

Percentage Rent The amount of rent that is adjusted based on the percentage of gross sales or revenues the tenant receives.

Per-Diem Interest The interest that is charged or accrued daily.

Performance Bond A bond that a contractor posts to guarantee full performance of a contract in which the proceeds will be used for completing the contract or compensating the owner for loss in the event of nonperformance.

Performance Measurement The process of measuring how well an investor's real estate has performed regarding individual assets, advisers/managers, and portfolios.

Performance The changes each quarter in fund or account values that can be explained by investment income, realized or unrealized appreciation, and the total return to the investors before and after investment management fees.

Performance-Based Fees The fees that advisers or managers receive that are based on returns to investors.

Periodic Payment Cap The highest amount that payments can increase or decrease during a given adjustment period on an ARM.

Periodic Rate Cap The maximum amount that the interest rate can increase or decrease during a given adjustment period on an ARM.

Permanent Loan A long-term property mortgage.

Personal Property Any items belonging to a person that is not real estate.

PITI Principal, Interest, Taxes, Insurance. The items that are included in the monthly payment to the lender for an impounded loan,

as well as mortgage insurance.

PITI Reserves The amount in cash that a borrower must readily have after the down payment and all closing costs are paid when purchasing a home.

Plan Assets The assets included in a pension plan.

Plan Sponsor The party that is responsible for administering an employee benefit plan.

Planned Unit Development (PUD) A type of ownership where individuals actually own the building or unit they live in, but common areas are owned jointly with the other members of the development or association. Contrast with condominium, where an individual actually owns the airspace of his unit, but the buildings and common areas are owned jointly with the others in the development or association.

Plat A chart or map of a certain area showing the boundaries of individual lots, streets, and easements.

Pledged Account Mortgage (PAM) A loan tied to a pledged savings account for which the fund and earned interest are used to gradually reduce mortgage payments.

Point Also referred to as a Discount Point. A fee a lender charges to provide a lower interest rate, equal to 1 percent of the amount of the loan.

Portfolio Management A process that involves formulating, modifying, and implementing a real estate investment strategy according to an investor's investment objectives.

Portfolio Turnover The amount of time averaged from the time an investment is funded until it is repaid or sold.

Power of Attorney A legal document that gives someone the authority to act on behalf of another party.

Power of Sale The clause included in a mortgage or deed of trust that provides the mortgagee (or trustee) with the right and power to advertise and sell the property at public auction if the borrower is in default.

Pre-Approval The complete analysis a lender makes regarding a potential borrower's ability to pay for a home as well as a confirmation of the proposed amount to be borrowed.

Pre-Approval Letter The letter a lender presents that states the amount of money they are willing to lend a potential buyer.

Preferred Shares Certain stocks that have a prior distributions claim up to a defined amount before the common shareholders may receive anything.

Pre-Leased A certain amount of space in a proposed building that must be leased before construction may begin or a certificate of occupancy may be issued.

Prepaid Expenses The amount of money that is paid before it is due, including taxes, insurance, and/or assessments.

Prepaid Fees The charges that a borrower must pay in advance regarding certain recurring items, such as interest, property taxes, hazard insurance, and PMI, if applicable.

Prepaid Interest The amount of interest that is paid before its due date.

Prepayment The money that is paid to reduce the principal balance of a loan before the date it is due.

Prepayment Penalty A penalty that

may be charged to the borrower when he pays off a loan before the planned maturity date.

Prepayment Rights The right a borrower is given to pay the total principal balance before the maturity date free of penalty.

Prequalification The initial assessment by a lender of a potential borrower's ability to pay for a home as well as an estimate of how much the lender is willing to supply to the buyer.

Price-to-Earnings Ratio The comparison that is derived by dividing the current share price by the sum of the primary earnings per share from continuing operations over the past year.

Primary Issuance The preliminary financing of an issuer.

Prime Rate The best interest rate reserved for a bank's preferred customers.

Prime Space The first-generation space that is available for lease.

Prime Tenant The largest or highest-earning tenant in a building or shopping center.

Principal The amount of money originally borrowed in a mortgage, before interest is included and with any payments subtracted.

Principal Balance The total current balance of mortgage principal not including interest.

Principal Paid over Life of Loan The final total of scheduled payments to the principal that the lender calculates to equal the face amount of the loan.

Principal Payments The lender's return of invested capital.

Principle of Conformity The concept that a property will probably increase in value if its size, age, condition, and style are similar to other properties in the immediate area.

Private Debt Mortgages or other liabilities for which an individual is responsible.

Private Equity A real estate investment that has been acquired by a noncommercial entity.

Private Mortgage Insurance (PMI) A type of policy that a lender requires when the borrower's down payment or home equity percentage is under 20 percent of the value of the property.

Private Placement The sale of a security in a way that renders it exempt from the registration rules and requirements of the SEC.

Private REIT A real estate investment company that is structured as a real estate investment trust that places and holds shares privately rather than publicly.

Pro Rata The proportionate amount of expenses per tenant for the property's maintenance and operation.

Processing Fee A fee some lenders charge for gathering the information necessary to process the loan.

Production Acres The portion of land that can be used directly in agriculture or timber activities to generate income, but not areas used for such things as machinery storage or support.

Prohibited Transaction Certain transactions that may not be performed between a pension plan and a party in interest, such as the following: the sale, exchange or lease of any property; a loan or other grant of credit; and furnishing goods or services.

Promissory Note A written agreement to repay the specific amount over a certain period of time.

Property Tax The tax that must be paid on private property.

Prudent Man Rule The standard to which ERISA holds a fiduciary accountable.

Public Auction An announced public meeting held at a specified location for the purpose of selling property to repay a mortgage in default.

Public Debt Mortgages or other liabilities for which a commercial entity is responsible.

Public Equity A real estate investment that has been acquired by REITs and other publicly traded real estate operating companies.

Punch List An itemized list that documents incomplete or unsatisfactory items after the contractor has declared the space to be mostly complete.

Purchase Agreement The written contract the buyer and seller both sign defining the terms and conditions under which a property is sold.

Purchase Money Transaction A transaction in which property is acquired through the exchange of money or something of equivalent value.

Purchase-Money Mortgage (PMM) A mortgage obtained by a borrower that serves as partial payment for a property.

Qualified Plan Any employee benefit plan that the IRS has approved as a tax-exempt plan.

Qualifying Ratio The measurement a lender uses to determine how much they are willing to lend to a potential buyer.

Quitclaim Deed A written document that releases a party from any interest they may have in a property.

Rate Cap The highest interest rate allowed on a monthly payment during an adjustment period of an ARM.

Rate Lock The commitment of a lender to a borrower that guarantees a certain interest rate for a specific amount of time.

Rate-Improvement Mortgage A loan that includes a clause that entitles a borrower to a one-time-only cut in the interest rate without having to refinance.

Rating Agencies Independent firms that are engaged to rate securities' creditworthiness on behalf of investors.

Rating A figure that represents the credit quality or creditworthiness of securities.

Raw Land A piece of property that has not been developed and remains in its natural state.

Raw Space Shell space in a building that has not yet been developed.

Real Estate Agent An individual who is licensed to negotiate and transact the real estate sales.

Real Estate Fundamentals The factors that drive the value of property.

Real Estate Settlement Procedures Act (RESPA) A legislation for consumer protection that requires lenders to notify borrowers regarding closing costs in advance.

Real Property Land and anything else of a permanent nature that is affixed to the land.

Real Rate of Return The yield given to investors minus an inflationary factor.

Realtor A real estate agent or broker who is an active member of a local real estate board affiliated with the National Association of Realtors.

Recapture The act of the IRS recovering the tax benefit of a deduction or a credit that a taxpayer has previously taken in error.

Recorder A public official who records transactions that affect real estate in the area.

Recording The documentation that the registrar's office keeps of the details of properly executed legal documents.

Recording Fee A fee real estate agents charge for moving the sale of a piece of property into the public record.

Recourse The option a lender has for recovering losses against the personal assets of a secondary party who is also liable for a debt that is in default.

Red Herring An early prospectus that is distributed to prospective investors that includes a note in red ink on the cover stating that

the SEC-approved registration statement is not yet in effect.

Refinance Transaction The act of paying off an existing loan using the funding gained from a new loan that uses the same property as security.

Regional Diversification Boundaries that are defined based on geography or economic lines.

Registration Statement The set of forms that are filed with the SEC (or the appropriate state agency) regarding a proposed offering of new securities or the listing of outstanding securities on a national exchange.

Regulation Z A federal legislation under the Truth in Lending Act that requires lenders to advise the borrower in writing of all costs that are associated with the credit portion of a financial transaction.

Rehab Short for Rehabilitation. Refers to an extensive renovation intended to extend the life of a building or project.

Rehabilitation Mortgage A loan meant to fund the repairing and improving of a resale home or building.

Real Estate Investment Trust (REIT) A trust corporation that combines the capital of several investors for the purpose of acquiring or providing funding for real estate.

Remaining Balance The amount of the principal on a home loan that has not yet been paid.

Remaining Term The original term of the loan after the number of payments made has been subtracted.

Real Estate Mortgage Investment Conduit (REMIC) An investment vehicle that is designed to hold a pool of mortgages solely to issue multiple classes of mortgage-backed securities in a way that avoids doubled corporate tax.

Renewal Option A clause in a lease agreement that allows a tenant to extend the term of a lease.

Renewal Probability The average percentage of a building's tenants who are expected to renew terms at market rental rates upon the lease expiration.

Rent Commencement Date The date at which a tenant is to begin paying rent.

Rent Loss Insurance A policy that covers loss of rent or rental value for a landlord due to any condition that renders the leased premises inhabitable, thereby excusing the tenant from paying rent.

Rent The fee paid for the occupancy and/or use of any rental property or equipment.

Rentable/Usable Ratio A total rentable area in a building divided by the area available for use.

Rental Concession See: Concessions.

Rental Growth Rate The projected trend of market rental rates over a particular period of analysis.

Rent-Up Period The period of time following completion of a new building when tenants are actively being sought and the project is stabilizing.

Real Estate Owned (REO) The real estate that a savings institution owns as a result of foreclosure on borrowers in default.

Repayment Plan An agreement made to repay late installments or advances.

Replacement Cost The projected

cost by current standards of constructing a building that is equivalent to the building being appraised.

Replacement Reserve Fund
Money that is set aside for replacing of common property in a condominium, PUD, or cooperative project.

Request for Proposal (RFP)
A formal request that invites investment managers to submit information regarding investment strategies, historical investment performance, current investment opportunities, investment management fees, and other pension fund client relationships used by their firm.

Rescission The legal withdrawing of a contract or consent from the parties involved.

Reserve Account An account that must be funded by the borrower to protect the lender.

Resolution Trust Corp. (RTC)
The congressional corporation established for the purpose of containing, managing, and selling failed financial institutions, thereby recovering taxpayer funds.

Retail Investor An investor who

sells interests directly to consumers.

Retention Rate The percentage of trailing year's earnings that have been dispersed into the company again. It is calculated as 100 minus the trailing 12-month payout ratio.

Return on Assets The measurement of the ability to produce net profits efficiently by making use of assets.

Return on Equity The measurement of the return on the investment in a business or property.

Return on Investments The percentage of money that has been gained as a result of certain investments.

Reverse Mortgage See: Home Equity Conversion Mortgage.

Reversion Capitalization Rate The capitalization rate that is used to derive reversion value.

Reversion Value A benefit that an investor expects to receive as a lump sum at the end of an investment.

Revolving Debt A credit arrangement that enables a customer to borrow against a predetermined line of credit when purchasing goods and services.

Revenue per Available Room (RevPAR) The total room revenue for a particular period divided by the average number of rooms available in a hospitality facility.

Right of Ingress or Egress The option to enter or to leave the premises in question.

Right of Survivorship The option that survivors have to take on the interest of a deceased joint tenant.

Right to Rescission A legal provision that enables borrowers to cancel certain loan types within three days after they sign.

Risk Management A logical approach to analyzing and defining insurable and non-insurable risks while evaluating the availability and costs of purchasing third-party insurance.

Risk-Adjusted Rate of Return A percentage that is used to identify investment options that are expected to deliver a positive premium despite their volatility.

Road Show A tour of the executives of a company that is planning to go public, during which the executives travel to a variety of cities to make presentations to underwriters and analysts regarding their company and IPO.

Roll-Over Risk The possibility that tenants will not renew their lease.

Sale-Leaseback An arrangement in which a seller deeds a property, or part of it, to a buyer in exchange for money or the equivalent, then leases the property from the new owner.

Sales Comparison Value A value that is calculated by comparing the appraised property to similar properties in the area that have been recently sold.

Sales Contract An agreement that both the buyer and seller sign defining the terms of a property sale.

Second Mortgage A secondary loan obtained on a piece of property.

Secondary Market A market in which existing mortgages are bought and sold as part of a mortgages pool.

Secondary (Follow-On) Offering An offering of stock made by a company that is already public.

Second-Generation or Secondary Space Space that has been occupied before and becomes available for lease again, either by the landlord or as a sublease.

Secured Loan A loan that is secured by some sort of collateral.

Securities and Exchange Commission (SEC) The federal agency that oversees the issuing and exchanging of public securities.

Securitization The act of converting a non-liquid asset into a tradable form.

Security The property or other asset that will serve as a loan's collateral.

Security Deposit An amount of money a tenant gives to a landlord to secure the performance of terms in a lease agreement.

Seisen (Seizen) The ownership of real property under a claim of freehold estate.

Self-Administered REIT A REIT in which the management are employees of the REIT or similar entity.

Self-Managed REIT See: Self-Administered REIT.

Seller Carry-Back An arrangement in which the seller provides the financing to purchase a home.

Seller Financing A type of funding in which the borrower may use part of the equity in the property to finance the purchase.

Senior Classes The security classes who have the highest priority for receiving payments from the underlying mortgage loans.

Separate Account A relationship in which a single pension plan sponsor is used to retain an investment manager or adviser under a stated investment policy exclusively for that sponsor.

Servicer An organization that collects principal and interest payments from borrowers and manages borrowers' escrow accounts on behalf of a trustee.

Servicing The process of collecting mortgage payments from borrowers as well as related responsibilities.

Setback The distance required from a given reference point before a structure can be built.

Settlement or Closing Fees Fees that the escrow agent receives for carrying out the written instructions in the agreement between borrower and lender and/or buyer and seller.

Settlement Statement See: HUD-1 Settlement Statement.

Shared-Appreciation Mortgage A loan that enables a lender or other party to share in the profits of the borrower when the borrower sells the home.

Shared-Equity Transaction A transaction in which two people purchase a property, one as a residence and the other as an investment.

Shares Outstanding The number of shares of outstanding common stock minus the treasury shares.

Site Analysis A determination of how suitable a specific parcel of land is for a particular use.

Site Development The implementation of all improvements that are needed for a site before construction may begin.

Site Plan A detailed description and map of the location of improvements to a parcel.

Slab The flat, exposed surface that is laid over the structural support beams to form the building's floor(s).

Social Investing A strategy in which investments are driven in partially or completely by social or non-real estate objectives.

Soft Cost The part of an equity investment, aside from the literal cost of the improvements, that could be tax-deductible in the first year.

Space Plan A chart or map of space requirements for a tenant that includes wall/door locations, room sizes, and even furniture layouts.

Special Assessment Certain charges that are levied against real estates for public improvements to benefit the property in question.

Special Servicer A company that is hired to collect on mortgages that are either delinquent or in default.

Specified Investing A strategy of investment in individually specified properties, portfolios, or commingled funds are fully or partially detailed prior to the commitment of investor capital.

Speculative Space Any space in a rental property that has not been leased prior to construction on a new building begins.

Stabilized Net Operating Income

Expected income minus expenses that reflect relatively stable operations.

Stabilized Occupancy The best projected range of long-term occupancy that a piece of rental property will achieve after existing in the open market for a reasonable period of time with terms and conditions that are comparable to similar offerings.

Step-Rate Mortgage A loan that allows for a gradual interest rate increase during the first few years of the loan.

Step-Up Lease (Graded Lease) A lease agreement that specifies certain increases in rent at certain intervals during the complete term of the lease.

Straight Lease (Flat Lease) A lease agreement that specifies an amount of rent that should be paid regularly during the complete term of the lease.

Strip Center Any shopping area that is made up of a row of stores but is not large enough to be anchored by a grocery store.

Subcontractor A contractor who has been hired by the general contractor, often specializing in a certain required task for the construction project.

Subdivision The most common type of housing development created by dividing a larger tract of land into individual lots for sale or lease.

Sublessee A person or business that holds the rights of use and occupancy under a lease contract with the original lessee, who still retains primary responsibility for the lease obligations.

Subordinate Financing Any loan with a priority lower than loans that were obtained beforehand.

Subordinate Loan A second or third mortgage obtained with the same property being used as collateral.

Subordinated Classes Classes that have the lowest priority of receiving payments from underlying mortgage loans.

Subordination The act of sharing credit loss risk at varying rates among two or more classes of securities.

Subsequent Rate Adjustments The interest rate for ARMs that adjusts at regular intervals, sometimes differing from the duration period of the initial interest rate.

Subsequent Rate Cap The maximum amount the interest rate may increase at each regularly scheduled interest rate adjustment date on an ARM.

Super Jumbo Mortgage A loan that is over $650,000 for some lenders or $1,000,000 for others.

Surety A person who willingly binds himself to the debt or obligation of another party.

Surface Rights A right or easement that is usually granted with mineral rights that enables the holder to drill through the surface.

Survey A document or analysis containing the precise measurements of a piece of property as performed by a licensed surveyor.

Sweat Equity The non-cash improvements in value that an owner adds to a piece of property.

Synthetic Lease A transaction that is considered to be a lease by accounting standards but a loan by tax standards.

Taking Similar to condemning, or any other interference with rights

to private property, but a physical seizure or appropriation is not required.

Tax Base The determined value of all property that lies within the jurisdiction of the taxing authority.

Tax Lien A type of lien placed against a property if the owner has not paid property or personal taxes.

Tax Roll A record that contains the descriptions of all land parcels and their owners that is located within the county.

Tax Service Fee A fee that is charged for the purpose of setting up monitoring of the borrower's property tax payments by a third party.

Teaser Rate A small, short-term interest rate offered on a mortgage in order to convince the potential borrower to apply.

Tenancy by the Entirety A form of ownership held by spouses in which they both hold title to the entire property with right of survivorship.

Tenancy in Common A type of ownership held by two or more owners in an undivided interest in the property with no right of survivorship.

Tenant (Lessee) A party who rents a piece of real estate from another by way of a lease agreement.

Tenant at Will A person who possesses a piece of real estate with the owner's permission.

Tenant Improvement (TI) Allowance The specified amount of money that the landlord contributes toward tenant improvements.

Tenant Improvement (TI) The upgrades or repairs that are made to the leased premises by or for a tenant.

Tenant Mix The quality of the income stream for a property.

Term The length that a loan lasts or is expected to last before it is repaid.

Third-Party Origination A process in which another party is used by the lender to originate, process, underwrite, close, fund, or package the mortgages it expects to deliver to the secondary mortgage market.

Timeshare A form of ownership involving purchasing a specific period of time or percentage of interest in a vacation property.

Time-Weighted Average Annual Rate of Return The regular yearly return over several years that would have the same return value as combining the actual annual returns for each year in the series.

Title The legal written document that provides someone ownership in a piece of real estate.

Title Company A business that determines that a property title is clear and that provides title insurance.

Title Exam An analysis of the public records in order to confirm that the seller is the legal owner, and there are no encumbrances on the property.

Title Insurance A type of policy that is issued to both lenders and buyers to cover loss due to property ownership disputes that may arise at a later date.

Title Insurance Binder A written promise from the title insurance company to insure the title to the property, based on the conditions and exclusions shown in the binder.

Title Risk The potential impediments in transferring a title from one party to another.

Title Search The process of analyzing all transactions existing in the public record in order to determine whether any title defects could interfere with the clear transfer of property ownership.

Total Acres The complete amount of land area that is contained within a real estate investment.

Total Assets The final amount of all gross investments, cash and equivalents, receivables, and other assets as they are presented on the balance sheet.

Total Commitment The complete funding amount that is promised once all specified conditions have been met.

Total Expense Ratio The comparison of monthly debt obligations to gross monthly income.

Total Inventory The total amount of square footage commanded by property within a geographical area.

Total Lender Fees Charges that the lender requires for obtaining the loan, aside from other fees associated with the transfer of a property.

Total Loan Amount The basic

amount of the loan plus any additional financed closing costs.

Total Monthly Housing Costs The amount that must be paid each month to cover principal, interest, property taxes, PMI, and/or either hazard insurance or homeowners' association dues.

Total of All Payments The total cost of the loan after figuring the sum of all monthly interest payments.

Total Principal Balance The sum of all debt, including the original loan amount adjusted for subsequent payments and any unpaid items that may be included in the principal balance by the mortgage note or by law.

Total Retail Area The total floor area of a retail center that is currently leased or available for lease.

Total Return The final amount of income and appreciation returns per quarter.

Townhouse An attached home that is not considered to be a condominium.

Trade Fixtures Any personal property that is attached to a structure and used in the business but is removable once the lease is terminated.

Trading Down The act of purchasing a property that is less expensive than the one currently owned.

Trading Up The act of purchasing a property that is more expensive than the one currently owned.

Tranche A class of securities that may or may not be rated.

TransUnion Corporation One of the primary credit-reporting bureaus.

Transfer of Ownership Any process in which a property changes hands from one owner to another.

Transfer Tax An amount specified by state or local authorities when ownership in a piece of property changes hands.

Treasury Index A measurement that is used to derive interest rate changes for ARMs.

Triple Net Lease A lease that requires the tenant to pay all property expenses on top of the rental payments.

Trustee A fiduciary who oversees property or funds on behalf of another party.

Truth-in-Lending The federal legislation requiring lenders to fully disclose the terms and conditions of a mortgage in writing.

TurnKey Project A project in which all components are within a single supplier's responsibility.

Two- to Four-Family Property A structure that provides living space for two to four families while ownership is held in a single deed.

Two-Step Mortgage An ARM with two different interest rates: one for the loan's first five or seven years and another for the remainder of the loan term.

Under Construction The time period that exists after a building's construction has started but before a certificate of occupancy has been presented.

Under Contract The period of time during which a buyer's offer to purchase a property has been accepted, and the buyer is able to finalize financing arrangements without the concern of the seller making a deal with another buyer.

Underwriter A company, usually an investment banking firm, that is involved in a guarantee that an entire issue of stocks or bonds will be purchased.

Underwriters' Knot An approved knot according to code that may be tied at the end of an electrical cord to prevent the wires from being pulled away from their connection to each other or to electrical terminals.

Underwriting The process during which lenders analyze the risks a particular borrower presents and set appropriate conditions for the loan.

Underwriting Fee A fee that mortgage lenders charge for verifying the information on the loan application and making a final decision on approving the loan.

Unencumbered A term that refers to property free of liens or other encumbrances.

Unimproved Land See: Raw Land.

Unrated Classes Usually the lowest classes of securities.

Unrecorded Deed A deed that transfers right of ownership from one owner to another without being officially documented.

Umbrella Partnership Real Estate Investment Trust (UPREIT) An organizational structure in which a REIT's assets are owned by a holding company for tax reasons.

Usable Square Footage The total area that is included within the exterior walls of the tenant's space.

Use The particular purpose for which a property is intended to be employed.

VA Loan A mortgage through the VA program in which a down payment is not necessarily required.

Vacancy Factor The percentage of gross revenue that pro-forma income statements expect to be lost due to vacancies.

Vacancy Rate The percentage of space that is available to rent.

Vacant Space Existing rental space that is presently being marketed for lease minus space that is available for sublease.

Value-Added A phrase advisers and managers generally use to describe investments in underperforming and/or under-managed assets.

Variable Rate Mortgage (VRM)

A loan in which the interest rate changes according to fluctuations in particular indexes.

Variable Rate Also called adjustable rate. The interest rate on a loan that varies over the term of the loan according to a predetermined index.

Variance A permission that enables a property owner to work around a zoning ordinance's literal requirements which cause a unique hardship due to special circumstances.

Verification of Deposit (VOD) The confirmation statement a borrower's bank may be asked to sign in order to verify the borrower's account balances and history.

Verification of Employment (VOE) The confirmation statement a borrower's employer may be asked to sign in order to verify the borrower's position and salary.

Vested Having the right to draw on a portion or on all of a pension or other retirement fund.

Veterans Affairs (VA) A federal government agency that assists veterans in purchasing a home without a down payment.

Virtual Storefront A retail business presence on the Internet.

Waiting Period The period of time between initially filing a registration statement and the date it becomes effective.

Warehouse Fee A closing cost fee that represents the lender's expense of temporarily holding a borrower's loan before it is sold on the secondary mortgage market.

Weighted-Average Coupon The average, using the balance of each mortgage as the weighting factor, of the gross interest rates of the mortgages underlying a pool as of the date of issue.

Weighted-Average Equity The part of the equation that is used to calculate investment-level income, appreciation, and total returns on a quarter-by-quarter basis.

Weighted-Average Rental Rates The average ratio of unequal rental rates across two or more buildings in a market.

Working Drawings The detailed blueprints for a construction project that comprise the contractual documents which describe the exact manner in which a project is to be built.

Workout The strategy in which a borrower negotiates with a lender to attempt to restructure the borrower's debt rather than go through the foreclosure proceedings.

Wraparound Mortgage A loan obtained by a buyer to use for the remaining balance on the seller's first mortgage, as well as an additional amount requested by the seller.

Write-Down A procedure used in accounting when an asset's book value is adjusted downward to reflect current market value more accurately.

Write-Off A procedure used in accounting when an asset is determined to be uncollectible and is therefore considered to be a loss.

Yield Maintenance Premium A penalty the borrower must pay in order to make investors whole in the event of early repayment of principal.

Yield Spread The difference in income derived from a commercial mortgage and from a benchmark value.

Yield The actual return on an investment, usually paid in dividends or interest.

Zoning Ordinance The regulations and laws that control the use or improvement of land in a particular area or zone.

Zoning The act of dividing a city or town into particular areas and applying laws and regulations regarding the architectural design, structure, and intended uses of buildings within those areas.

INDEX

AUTHOR BIOGRAPHY

Frankie Orlando is a freelance writer living in Fairfax, Virginia. She lives there with her husband, two daughters, and three cats. Frankie has watched real estate prices double in the ten years that she has lived in the Northern Virginia area. Frankie and her family enjoy visiting the museums in Washington, D.C. and study Tae Kwon Do together (currently at the green belt level). In her free time, Frankie tries catching up with her photo albums.